Citizen Leadership

Published by
ACADEMIC FOUNDATION
in association with

Knowledge is Power
PRIA

Citizen Leadership

Deepening Democratic Accountability in India, Brazil and South Africa

Editors

VIKAS JHA
BHAVITA VAISHNAVA
KAUSTUV KANTI BANDYOPADHYAY

ACADEMIC FOUNDATION
NEW DELHI

www.academicfoundation.com

First published in 2011
by

ACADEMIC FOUNDATION
4772-73 / 23 Bharat Ram Road, (23 Ansari Road),
Darya Ganj, New Delhi - 110 002 (India).
Phones : 23245001 / 02 / 03 / 04.
Fax : +91-11-23245005.
E-mail : books@academicfoundation.com
www. academicfoundation.com

in association with

PRIA (Society for Participatory Research in Asia).

Cataloging in Publication Data--DK
Courtesy: D.K. Agencies (P) Ltd. <docinfo@dkagencies.com>

Citizen leadership:deepening democratic accountability in India, Brazil and South Africa / editors, Vikas Jha, Bhavita Vaishnava, Kaustuv Kanti Bandyopadhyay.
P. cm.
Contributed articles.
ISBN 13: 9788171888672
ISBN 10: 8171888674

1. Political participation--India. 2. Democracy--India. 3. Political participation--Brazil. 4. Democracy--Brazil. 5. Political participation--South Africa. 6. Democracy--South Africa. I. Jha, Vikas. II. Vaishnava, Bhavita. III. Bandyopadhyay, Kaustuv Kanti.

DDC 323.0420954 22

Typeset by Italics India, New Delhi.
Printed and bound in India.

Contents

About the Editors/ Contributors

Editors:

Kaustuv Kanti Bandyopadhyay is Director, PRIA Global Partnership in Society for Participatory Research in Asia (PRIA), New Delhi. He was a Senior Research Fellow in Anthropological Survey of India and has done his Ph.D. from Ranchi University, India. He has 18 years of professional work experience with universities, government research institutions and civil society organisations with respect to citizen participation and democratic governance in urban and rural contexts. His areas of expertise are urban governance, social accountability, capacity building, organisation development, strategic planning, participatory planning, monitoring and evaluation and project management. An internationally renowned professional in the development sector, he has worked with various countries as an expert in different capacities.

Vikas Jha is doctorate from Jawaharlal Nehru University, New Delhi specialising in the area of 'Democracy in Russia: A Study of Presidential Elections (1991-2000)'. He has 10 years of professional experience in the development sector mainly relating to participatory research, citizens' participation, social accountability, capacity building and community mobilisation. Jha has coordinated two national level surveys on 'Status of Implementation of Right to Information in India', in the year 2008-09 for Society for Participatory Research in Asia (PRIA). He has important publications namely *Tribal Domestic Workers in Delhi* (Indian Social Institute, New Delhi) and *Unknown Story of Exploitation* (Economic and Political Weekly, India).

Bhavita Vaishnava, Masters in Social Work from Lucknow University, India, has around five years of experience in the field of urban governance, citizen participation, capacity building of community based organisations and promoting microfinance among women self-help groups. She has also worked in the areas of reproductive and child health as well as youth leadership development. She is presently associated with Society for Participatory Research in Asia (PRIA) as a Programme Officer.

Contributors:

Patricia L.N. Cobra, Urbanist Architect, is a specialist in land market and policies (National University of Colombia and Lincoln Institute of Land Policy, 2008) and Masters student in urban territorial ordering at the Faculty of Arts at the National University of Colombia. She has worked in slum urbanisation projects, master plans, formal and informal estate market researches, research on urban instruments of asset recovery and on urban land in urban fringes. She is a researcher at the Urbanism Team at Polis Institute since 2006 and at the Laboratory of Urban and Regional Planning at Universidade de São Paulo and works as a consultant on housing plans for municipalities in the metropolitan region of São Paulo.

Ina Conradie is Coordinator in Development Research Division, South Africa—German Centre for Development Research and Criminal Justice at University of Western Cape, Cape Town, South Africa.

Alice Morris, Master of Philosophy from Jawaharlal Nehru University, New Delhi, has been working with UNNATI for Development Education for the past 16 years leading its activities on issues concerning impact of various economic policies and programmes and natural events affecting the poor and marginalised including those arising out of land acquisition, urbanisation, and structural adjustment of economic policies. She has also worked intensively on decentralised governance with focus on urban self-governance institutions, women in local governance, management of urban services especially water and sanitation and civic engagement to make governance more accountable. Her areas of expertise include participatory research and action and mobilising people to voice their interests. Having years of hands-on experience, she has published extensively and done research for national and international organisations.

Viviane Nebó Carlos Oliveira holds a degree in Public Relations and has been working at Polis Institute's School of Citizenship, São Paulo, Brazil for five years.

Lizandra Serafim, a Social Scientist, holds an MA in Political Science at the University of Campinas, where she is currently a PhD candidate in social sciences. She has been working as a researcher on citizen participation, participatory governance, public policies and democracy since 2005 at the Citizen Participation and LogoLink Latin American teams at Polis Institute and at the Democracy and Collective Action Nucleus at CEBRAP (Brazilian Center for Analysis and Planning). She is also a member of the Democratic Construction Research Group at Unicamp and of the Social Movements and 21st Century Cultural-Political Transformations Inter-University Consortium on the Americas.

Manish Sisodia is a founding member of Kabir and currently holds the position of chief executive responsible for general management of the organisation. He has a background in journalism and has worked as a producer and newsreader with Zee News, India. Sisodia has also served as an active volunteer with Parivartan, the citizens' initiative working on Right to Information in Delhi.

Chris Tapscott is Dean, School of Government, University of Western Cape, Cape Town, South Africa. He is closely associated with The African Centre for Citizenship and Democracy (ACCEDE), which conducts research in both the form and practice of democracy and in the factors which inhibit effective participation by the poor and marginalised in decision-making processes. On the theme of citizenship and democracy, he has important publications namely 'The Challenges of Building Participatory Local Government', in L. Thompson (ed.), *Participatory Governance? Citizens and the State in Southern Africa* (African Centre for Citizenship and Democracy, 2007); 'The Challenges of Deepening Democracy in Post-Apartheid South

Africa', in F. Saito (ed.), *Foundations for Local Governance: Decentralisation in Comparative Perspective* (New York: Springer. (forthcoming)).

Lisa Thompson is Director, African Centre for Citizenship and Democracy (ACCEDE) and Professor at the School of Government, University of the Western Cape. Her work focusses on issues of socioeconomic development in the context of the global political economy. She has published widely on research pertaining to regional development and democratisation processes in southern Africa, including her monograph, *Participatory Governance? Citizens and the State in South Africa* (ACCEDE, 2007). She serves as South African coordinator of the Development Research Centre on Citizenship, Participation and Accountability.

Acronyms

AC	Assistant Commissioner
ADB	Asian Development Bank
AEIS	*Áreas Especiais de Interesse Social*/Areas of Special Social Interest
ANC	African National Congress
APL	Above Poverty Line
BDC	Bhuj Development Council
BhADA	Bhachau Urban Development Authority
BRIC	Brazil, Russia, India and China
BOR	Basic Operating Rule
BPL	Below Poverty Line
CAA	Constitutional Amendment Act
CBO	Community Based Organisation
CDHU	Housing and Urban Development Company
CDP	City Development Plan
CEB	*Communidades Eclesiais Base*/Basic Ecclesial Communities
CEF	Caixa Economica Federal
COLACOCO	Coalition for Langa Community Concerns
COPE	Congress of the People
CMP	*Central de Movimentos Populares*/Central Popular Movement

CPL	Community Participation Law
CSC	Citizen Support Cell
CSO	Civil Society Organisation
DA	Democratic Alliance
DC	Deputy Commissioner
DDA	Delhi Development Authority
DEM	Democrats
DPR	Detailed Project Report
ER	Emergency Room
FIR	First Information Report
FSO	Food and Supplies Officer
FUMAPIS	Municipal Fund for Support of Social Interest Housing
GDP	Gross Domestic Product
GoG	Government of Gujarat
GPCA	Green Point Common Association
GSDMA	Gujarat State Disaster Management Authority
GUDC	Gujarat Urban Development Company Limited
HDI	Human Development Index
HSC	Himalayan Study Circle
IBSA	India, Brazil and South Africa
IEC	Information Education and Communication
IGP	Income Generation Project
IT	Information Technology
JJ	*Jhuggi-Jhopri* Clusters
JNNURM	Jawaharlal Nehru National Urban Renewal Mission
JPEVS	Junavada Punarvasan Evam Vikas Samiti
KDF	Khayelitsha Development Forum

LOS	*Leis Orgânicas*/Organic Law of Health
MCD	Municipal Corporation of Delhi
MKSS	Mazdoor Kisan Shakti Sangathan
MSS	Mohalla Swachata Samiti
NCPRI	National Campaign for People's Right to Information
NGO	Non-Governmental Organisation
NSK	Nagrik Sahyog Kendra
PAS	Plan of Health Attendance
PB/OP	Participatory Budget/*Orçamento Participativo*
PC	Public Council
PDS	Public Distribution System
PGC	Public Grievance Commission
PHP	Peoples Housing Project
PRIA	Society for Participatory Research in Asia
PPB	Brazilian Progressive Party
PSF	*Program Saúde da Família*/Family Health Program
PSDB	Brazilian Social Democracy Party
PT	*Partido dos Trabalhadores*/Workers' Party
RDP	Reconstruction and Development Programme
RTI	Right to Information Act
RWA	Resident Welfare Association
SANCO	South African National Civic Organisation
SAB	Societies of Neighbourhood's Friends
SC	Street committees
SHO	Station House Officer
STAC	Sulabh Thermophilic Aerobic Composting
SUS	*Sistema Únicode Saúde*/Unified Health System

SWM	Solid Waste Management
TRA	Temporary Relocation Area
TWO	Tibetan Welfare Office
UBS	*Unidades Básicas de Saúde*/Basic Healthcare Units
UMPS	Union of the Popular Health Movements of São Paulo/ *União dos Movimentos Populares de Saúde*
ULB	Urban Local Body
WDF	Ward Development Forums
ZUPI	*Zona de Uso Predominantemente Industrial*/ Predominantly Industrial Use Zone

Acknowledgements

A few years back during the tea break of a workshop organised by the Institute of Development Studies (IDS) in Brighton, UK, one of the authors of this book engaged in a conversation with Dr. John Gaventa from IDS, Prof. Bishnu N. Mohapatra from the Ford Foundation, New Delhi and Jose Carlos Vaz, from the Polis Institute, Brazil. The conversation focussed on how in varied contexts like India, Brazil and South Africa citizen leaders with the support from intermediary civil society organisations and social movements engage with state institutions to demand accountability. The discussion moved on to further explore the impacts of such organised civic engagement. We all agreed that it will be worth it. A few months later this conversation was translated into a concrete research proposal which the Ford Foundation, Delhi office agreed to support.

This book is a result of a research project on 'Promoting Learning on Citizen Leadership: Synthesizing Experiences of India, Brazil and South Africa (IBSA)' initiated to nurture learning between communities and civil societies of the three countries on issues of participation, citizen leadership and accountability. Society for Participatory Research in Asia (PRIA) (India) took the lead in the research with support from Polis Institute (Brazil) and University of Western Cape (South Africa). Therefore, it goes without saying that this initiative would have been incomplete without their cooperation especially that of Lizandra Serafim and Viviane Nebó Carlos Oliveira of Polis Institute, São Paulo, Brazil and Prof. Chris Tapscott and Prof. Lisa Thompson of the University of Western Cape, South Africa. At every stage of the research process, Prof. Bishnu N. Mohapatra, Programme Officer of the Ford Foundation took keen interest and provided valuable support.

We would like to acknowledge the contribution of partner organisations in India specially Alice Morris of UNNATI (Gujarat), Manish

Sisodia and Bibhav Kumar of Kabir (New Delhi) and Rajan Chaudhary of Shikshit Rojgar Kendra Prabandhak Samiti (SRKPS), Jhunjhunu (Rajasthan) in organising, undertaking and facilitating the research studies. We are also grateful to our collogues from PRIA, Kamleshwar Singh, Vikas Khanna, Dona Kurian, Pushpita Bandyopadhyay, Mandakini Pant, Sejuti Dasgupta and Zakir Hussain for their unconditional help and support. We would like to thank Dr. Ranjita Mohanty for her initial inputs, Sumitra Srinivasan for leading us through the publication process and Madhuri Lamba for copy editing the book.

We also owe our appreciation and gratitude to the Academic Foundation for publishing this book and helping in bringing out this knowledge source to a wider audience.

Last but most importantly, we take this opportunity to express our gratitude to Dr. Rajesh Tandon for his guidance in making this book more meaningful. His valuable comments and feedback helped in giving the right direction to the book.

We dedicate this book to the communities and citizen leaders of India, Brazil and South Africa, for their strenuous efforts and commitment towards raising accountability issues. We sincerely thank them for recounting their experiences, struggles and challenges in bringing about desired change.

Vikas Jha
Bhavita Vaishnava
Kaustuv Kanti Bandyopadhyay

Preface

In the winter of 2003, the global community began to suddenly notice a new axis of cooperation called IBSA—India, Brazil and South Africa. The trade negotiations under WTO found a common 'southern' voice—the IBSA voice. There had been various other conceptualisations around the emerging economies—BRIC—Brazil, Russia, India and China; these four economies had arrived on the global stage to define and redefine global economics.

At that time, BRIC formulation had captured the imagination of global leaders and academics. In November 2009, in Copenhagen, a new axis of cooperation was born—BASIC—Brazil, South Africa, India and China. During the past two years, G20 formation has begun to gradually replace the old G8 club. From economic, trade and global hegemony point of view, each of these coalitions, when viewed from the 'global top', have certain significance.

However, when viewed from the 'global bottom', it is the IBSA axis of cooperation which seems to be most important. IBSA represents the voice of democratic south; India, South Africa and Brazil are contemporary beacons of functioning democracies. In these countries, dissent, debate and participation of and by ordinary citizens is firmly rooted in the public sphere. These may not be the fastest growing economies; these three may not be most efficiently functioning societies; but they are certainly the most democratically governed societies.

Of course, failures of governments and institutions, corruption and resource wastage, continued poverty and exclusion are endemic in these three countries. Recent economic growth has resulted in extremes of inequality in income and wealth. Yet, in India, Brazil and South Africa today, citizens can ask questions of their rulers, protest on the streets and enjoy access to a reasonably open media.

It is this recognition that has prompted us in PRIA to undertake a systematic and in-depth exploration of the dynamics of citizen leadership and democratic accountability in India, South Africa and Brazil. It is our perspective that these three democracies can learn a great deal from each other. It is also our conviction that these three democracies can inspire similar processes of citizen leadership and democratic accountability in other southern countries of Africa, Asia and Latin America.

Perhaps they can also become a source of knowledge on these important aspects of deepening democracy in other G20 countries (specially since the democratic deficits in former G8 countries have also grown in the past decade).

Framing the Study

The empirical and conceptual materials of relevant discourses can be grouped around two major concepts—democracy and citizenship. Most of the traditional notions of democracy have limited themselves to institutions and representatives; in democracies, you build certain institutions and you have elected representatives. Likewise, most traditional notions of citizenship limited the definition to vertical relations of individual citizens to the state; states confer rights and duties on their citizens.

The vast experiences of social movements, citizen assertions and activists around the world have begun to point out the constraining effects of such narrow conceptions of democracy and citizenship. Experiences and discourses on participation and accountability have broadened these concepts. Participatory democracy practiced on a daily basis is shown to be in addition to, different from and sometimes complementary to representative and institutional democracy. Horizontal solidarities and obligations among citizens and their collectives have been recognised as organic forms of active and participatory citizenship, with or without the state conferring certain rights and duties on its subject-citizens.

It is in these new alignments of democracy and citizenship, mediated through active agency and participation of citizens, that many exciting advances in promoting accountability have been made in the last decade. Accountability of elected representatives (elected to govern) is not merely restricted to periodic elections; accountability of government officials is not merely assessed on the basis of welfare schemes planned and implemented. Direct forms of social accountability are now being demanded from elected representatives and appointed officials.

This demand is coming from citizens, who have refused to stick to the narrow identities of voters or beneficiaries of democratic governance. It is in this sense that democratic accountability is being sought and demanded by citizens, hitherto ignored or abandoned by institutions and representatives of democracies.

Three inter-related questions emerge from the above:

1. What catalytic conditions trigger citizens' assertions to demand accountability? How are these related to denial of new rights or violation of existing rights? How are existing conditions of deprivation and exclusion triggering these demands? What sensitivities and capabilities make some citizens demand these more than others?
2. What forms do these demands take? Who are the targets of these demands? Are they political representatives or appointed officials or both? In what sphere of governance are these demands being made (local, provincial, national)? What balance of struggle, protest and dialogue are woven together in these forms? How are these choices made?
3. What are the outcomes of these demands? Do these outcomes enable 'reclaiming' of citizens' rights? Are the outcomes in terms of concrete services and benefits? Are certain outcomes related to deepening the accountability regimes and mechanisms?

In examining these questions, it may be imperative to specially focus on two forces that mediate such demands. One force is the nature of distribution of power between the institution and the citizen; do constitutional and statutory provisions create some bases for citizen power?

Do political interests and institutional designs create a power-distance *vis-à-vis* citizens? How are these power relations negotiated?

The second force is leadership; how do citizens exercise leadership as a force for change? How is such leadership strengthened? How does citizen leadership strengthen its base constituencies? How does citizen leadership engage with institutions and power-holders? It is in the concrete interplay of these two sets of forces—leadership and power—that the nature of demands and outcomes for accountability get determined.

Locating the Study in IBSA

How do these study questions become relevant in the context of IBSA? Democracies in India, Brazil and South Africa have grown during different historical periods.

India's democracy is rooted in the struggle against colonial rule. Democracy in India was thus closely related to gaining independence (in 1947) from external European colonisers. It was also the period that had just witnessed the end of a bloody World War. A highly centralised form of political authority was considered necessary then for uniting different states and principalities in India. The European countries had already practiced the construct of 'nation-states'. It was almost natural that the British model of Westminster form of democracy will be installed in independent India. The constitution so framed and adopted in 1950 is essentially a state-centric document where the role of the citizens is rather passive as a voter or beneficiary.

In contrast, Brazil's new democracy grew out of decades of struggle against military dictatorship (during the 1960s to 1980s). Re-establishing democratic governance in Brazil in the early 1980s was very different from its earlier period of democracy. Brazil's new constitution is shaped by the growing demands for more accountable states in the world and more so in Latin America. Its new constitution redefined the relationship between citizen and the state in a far more balanced and mutually accountable manner. Brazil's constitution thus mandated several forms of participatory structures and mechanisms for citizens to access to deepen participatory democracy.

South Africa gained its independence from apartheid in 1994. Its struggle for liberation against its own minority rulers was a struggle for democracy. The new constitution of South Africa came into being in a period where cold war dynamics was over, where globalisation was gaining speed, where assertions of civil society (specially in Eastern Europe) were influencing the discourse on democracy. Thus, the new constitution of South Africa has given a place of respect and justice to all its citizens; it has also integrated various spheres of governance—local, provincial and national—in respect of responsibilities for delivering rights and mechanisms for participation of citizens in ensuring accountability.

These historical conditions in India, Brazil and South Africa have significantly shaped the democracies of these countries. The most interesting difference, from the vantage point of this study, is the nature of constitutionally defined relationship between citizens and the state (a new social contract) and statutory mechanisms and spaces for citizen participation and engagement. It is these differences that shape, initially, the design of democratic institutions and the aspirations of citizens. It is in the exercise of leadership—political and citizens—that the actual processes of engagement and accountability happen. The study makes an attempt to capture these nuances of democracies in IBSA at the beginning of the 21st century.

— Rajesh Tandon,
President,
Society for Participatory Research in Asia (PRIA),
New Delhi

Section - I

Conceptual Framework

1 Introduction

Kaustuv Kanti Bandyopadhyay

In the last half-century, more countries have embraced some form or the other of democracy. A report published by Freedom House (1999) reported that at the end of the 20th century out of the 192 countries existing all over the world there were 120 electoral democracies. The report declared the 20th century as the 'democracy century' and seeing the spread of democracy, this was certainly not an exaggeration. However, a host of other discourses on democracy, on the other hand, express deep anguish, agony and concern over the diminishing quality of such democracies. We are therefore confronted with a paradox. The triumphalists' view of democracy building is largely its spread and quantity and also creating a standardised recipe of institutional designs around the world. For those concerned with its deficits, it is also about deepening its quality and meaning especially in terms of how citizens engage within democratic spaces to create more just and equitable states and societies.[1]

The democracies of India, Brazil and South Africa are comparable in terms of the challenges and opportunities faced by the citizens of these countries. Historically, all these societies have witnessed numerous social and political movements challenging undemocratic rulers, either colonial (India), authoritarian (Brazil) or pro-apartheid (South Africa). All such movements provided democracy a strong foundation to flourish in. In the democratic regimes, the institutions and procedures in all the countries have achieved considerable maturity, which in turn provided stable regimes which pursued higher economic growth. Even in the face of the global financial meltdown, these economies showed considerable resilience. The progress with regard to democratic decentralisation and empowerment of local governance institutions in these countries has always been a source of

1. Gaventa (2006a): 8.

inspiration and emulation for other developing countries. Despite these remarkable achievements, poverty, marginalisation and inequality continue to be a daunting challenge. Many such exclusions and inequalities are rooted in the historicity; however, they are also the reflection of several democratic deficits.

Gaventa's analysis on the emerging practices in response to such democratic deficits is quite lucid in all these countries. Such responses include the neo-liberal market approach, which argues for an increasing role of the private market with a decreasing role played by the state. In this approach, citizens are equated with mere consumers. In the liberal representative model, emphasis is on getting the institutions and procedures of democracy right and focussing on competitive multiparty electoral processes. In this model, citizens participate through elections and in return, they enjoy certain rights. However, the liberal representative notion is extended by a third view, which is increasingly referred to as the 'deepening democracy' approach. This approach emphasises the democratic processes that enable citizens to exercise ever deepening control over decisions, which affect their lives and as such it is also constantly under construction.[2]

The experiences of citizens described in this book illustrate how citizens, social movements and civil society have acted as agents of social and political transformation to advance the 'deepening' views of 'democratisation' and to address some of these democratic deficits. A variety of approaches, from organised protest to collaboration with governance agencies, have been applied to utilise existing spaces or create new spaces for participation. Such participatory engagements have been used to bring transparency, address corruption, get responses and gain concessions from governance institutions.

A substantive and deepening democracy approach argues for inbuilt mechanisms of participation and citizen involvement in the functioning of a democratic state. However, the perspective and meanings of participation have undergone change through the years in various contexts. Gaventa tracing back the history of participation highlights four significant stages. The first stage, was 'participation from below' where terms like 'popular

2. Ibid: 11.

participation' or 'participatory development' emerged towards the end of the 1960s and early 1970s emphasising the participation of the excluded through organised groups and social movements to articulate or negotiate their demands; in a way 'challenging' the ones who exercise power or control. In the second stage, by the early 1980s participation began to be understood as the involvement of beneficiaries helping in the fulfillment of goals and the concept of 'beneficiaries' and 'users' of development projects was emphasised. In the 1990s however, terms like 'excluded' or 'beneficiaries' gave way to a more neutral term like 'stakeholders', which led to the third stage of participation. The World Bank (1994) defined participation as 'a process through which stakeholders influence and share control over development initiatives and the decision and resources which affect them.' The fourth perspective of participation emerged in the late 1990s where participation came to be seen as a 'right' of 'citizens rather than an opportunity' for the beneficiaries. As development changed from service delivery to means of empowerment and then to governance, so did participation; from effective and efficient ways of delivery of development to ownership of development through active engagement and paying for developmental benefits to finally rights to engage and demand accountability.[3] Participation depends upon the availability of 'spaces' for civic engagement either provided by the state or created by the citizens themselves. The 'new democratic spaces' have been classified by Gaventa[4] into three categories. The first is 'closed or provided spaces', where decisions are taken by a set of people behind closed doors in a non-participatory manner whereas within the state they are conceived as 'provided' spaces where the elite (bureaucrats, experts or elected representatives) take decisions and provide services to 'the people'. The second is 'invited' spaces, which result from widening the magnitude of participation and moving from 'closed' to 'open' spaces where people (citizens, beneficiaries etc.) are invited by the state to participate. The third category is that of 'claimed or created spaces' that are claimed by the marginalised and the less powerful actors from the powerful that hold authoritative positions in society. The concept of 'space' has also been

---

3. Cornwall (2000) as cited in Mohanty (2006): 69.
4. Gaventa (2006b) : 60-61.

explored by Ranjita Mohanty[5] in three somewhat different categories namely: (i) participation in state-created institutions, (ii) participation in the form of social movements, and (iii) participation enabled by intermediary civil society organisations for communities to articulate their rights from the state. It further emphasises that inclusion and participation are sought in a variety of ways where people mobilise on their own in the form of social movements or through the help of civil society organisations as compared to the state-created institutions where inclusion is often within the state given framework. It argues that state-created institutions do not completely change the landscape of discrimination, exclusion and marginalisation as they give little scope for participation whereas in the other two forms of participation, inclusion is attained through critiquing, partnering or demanding accountability and transparency from the state.

The concept of accountability is inextricably associated with the discourse on 'deepening democracy'. Accountability has been historically linked with how to restrain and check the abuse of power and to keep it in line with the established rules and procedures.[6] On this note, accountability is seen 'application of checks, oversight and institutional constraint on the exercise of power.'[7] The case studies in this book particularly look at the governance agencies' accountability towards citizens, as the fundamental principle of democracy is that citizens have the right to demand accountability and governance agencies have an obligation to account for and respond to it. Accountability implies both a measure of answerability (providing an account for actions undertaken) and enforceability (punishment or sanctions for poor or illegal performance).[8] Producing accountability is thus fundamentally changing the power relationship between citizens and governance institutions. The concept and practice of 'democratic accountability' discussed in this book goes far beyond the 'institutional designs of accountability' which are often referred to as 'horizontal accountability'.[9] A variety of approaches have been used by citizens to demand direct accountability from the governance agencies,

5. Mohanty (2006): 80-84.
6. Newell (2006): 39.
7. Ibid.
8. Pande (2008).
9. Newell *op.cit.*: 46.

which could be referred to as 'vertical or social accountability'.[10] One can also see that citizens have used an intelligent mix of social accountability approaches to make the established institutional accountability mechanisms more transparent and responsive.

The case studies analysed in this book illustrate the role of citizen leadership in promoting accountability from governance institutions. Citizen leadership is exercised when active citizens enable other citizens to act, when they promote citizen activism in society and polity. Active citizens are those citizens from the community who undertake activities individually or collectively that seek public solutions to a relative lack of access to the goods necessary for the enjoyment of citizenship rights.[11] The role of citizen leaders as discussed by Bandyopadhyay[12] could be categorised as: (1) society building which includes the role of social mobilisation of the community, overcoming social exclusion and managing intra and inter-community differences, divisions and conflicts; and (2) engaging governance institutions which includes amplifying the community members' voices, negotiating with different stakeholders and ensuring credibility of the community and collectives.

This book was the result of a research project on 'Promoting Learning on Citizen Leadership: Synthesising Experiences from India, Brazil and South Africa', which was supported by the Ford Foundation, India. The research is premised on the relevance of studying various developing democracies, as most of these democracies are new and searching for new ways of democratic governance. As there is no ideal democratic model, there is a need to rethink democracy, discuss the various democratic experiences which ensure people's participation and the constraints or limitations of democratic experiences so that one learns from the other.

The project's aim was to document and analyse successful cases where citizen leaders from local communities mobilised the communities to engage with governance agencies, which eventually resulted in greater accountability and improved service delivery. In its conceptualisation, it made three important assumptions, which are:

10. Ibid.

11. Houtzager *et al.* (2007): 18.

12. Bandyopadhyay (2007): 158-159.

1. Citizen participation is essential for accountable governance;
2. Increased accountability from governance agencies lead to improvement in service delivery to the marginalised;
3. Successful engagement with governance agencies enhances the feelings of inclusive citizenship among the marginalised.

Each case study specifically looked at: (a) the processes of collectivisation, development of citizen leadership and facilitation of mobilisation; (b) the nature of engagement with governance and governance agencies; and (c) outcomes.

The questions, which the case studies addressed under each section, were as follows:

1. Processes of collectivisation, development of citizen leadership and facilitation of mobilisation.
   - What are the processes of building collectives?
   - How does citizen leadership emerge from among the collectives?
   - What role do the citizen leaders play in the collective mobilisation process?
   - What role does the intermediary facilitating organisation play in the process of collectivisation, leadership development and mobilisation?
2. Engagement with governance agencies.
   - What kind of engagement (for example—negotiation/petition/campaign/working together through collaboration etc.) do the citizen leadership and the collectives have with various governance agencies responsible for service delivery?
   - How do the governance agencies respond to the needs/interests/demands of the collectives? What factors lead to positive response?
   - What do the collectives learn about the governance agencies during their engagement? And how does this learning affect their further engagement?
3. Outcome.

The outcome has two aspects:

(a) Accountability

- What patterns of accountability (for example—transparency in functioning/checks in corruption/adherence to legal/policy provisions etc.) emerge as a result of citizen participation?

(b) Improved service delivery

- What tangible outcomes (for example—improvement of existing facilities/new facilities/new policies) related to service delivery follow, when governance agencies are made accountable through citizen participation?

The research project was conceptualised and implemented in an innovative manner. One of the central purposes of the project was to document and analyse successful cases that illustrate how citizen leaders in urban locations, in India, Brazil and South Africa, make governance agencies accountable and promote improved service delivery. However, the process of conducting the research was distinctively different from the traditional case study method in several ways. First, the research teams comprised both external academic researchers as well as the principal actors in the chosen cases. It not only ensured the validation of the case analysis but also provided rich information and interpretation. Second, the documentation and preliminary analysis of cases was followed by exchange visits between all three countries by the research teams. This provided an opportunity for all the research teams to interact with the actors at all the case locations. These first hand interactions between various countries' research teams as well as between research teams and principal actors in the respective cases enabled them to arrive at a much richer analysis and cross-comparison of the contexts, actors, actions and results. Third, the preliminary findings and the research study's conclusions were presented at an International Conference on 'Democratic Accountability and Citizen Participation' to an audience of international academicians, civil society practitioners and policymakers, drawn not only from these three countries, but also participants from United States, Canada, Cambodia, Nepal, Bangladesh and Uganda. This interaction provided further inputs from a variety of other contexts to the final analysis of the research study. The study findings and conclusions were, therefore, revalidated and refined at different stages and levels of the project.

The book is organised into three sections. Section I is the introductory chapter, which discusses the conceptual elements dealt in subsequent analysis. Section II is the analytical synthesis of key lessons from the case studies and Section III comprises 7 case studies—3 from India, 2 from Brazil and 2 from South Africa.

Chapter 2 aims to analytically compare the seven case studies from India, Brazil and South Africa from the perspective of citizen participation in democratic spaces, the role of intermediary organisations and citizen leadership and the extent to which they are able to influence the accountability of governance agencies. It is further divided into four dimensions which have been discussed in the following paragraphs.

Dimension I on democratic spaces and citizen's voices elaborates on the different kinds of democratic spaces, which have been classified in the chapter as 'invented' and 'invited' spaces. It gives a description of how these spaces have been used by citizens and intermediary organisations differently on different occasions. The section also explores the association between the two spaces, where they have been found to be mutually supportive and complementary to each other in the different case studies. Through empirical evidence from the three countries it has been explained how invented spaces lead to the creation of invited spaces and how the former help in legitimising the latter once they come into existence. The challenges of democratic spaces have also been explained in the section in terms of the power relations that exist in society and thereby within these spaces as well.

Dimension II on intermediation talks about the meaning and types of intermediation. It explains how different intermediary organisations have an important role to play in mobilising communities to participate and influence the decision-making process. Through various examples in the case studies, it has been shown how intermediation by these groups and organisations also facilitates the state's accountability towards the citizens. The levels of intermediation are further discussed, which range from local groups and organisations like youth and women groups, resident welfare associations, India, Green Point Common Association (GPCA) and Coalition of Langa Community Concerns (COLACOCO), South Africa and various community based organisations (Brazil) that were primarily of grassroot origin to that of state or national level organisations and coalitions like PRIA, Parivartan and UNNATI (India), *União dos Movimentos Populares de Saúde*—Union of Popular Health Movements, UMPS (Brazil) and Joe Slovo Task Team (South Africa). The case studies reflect how these intermediaries whether at the local, state, national or international level helped citizens in translating their thoughts into action. In India, it was seen that grassroot community based organisations and groups were also as active as in other countries and civil society organisations played critical role in community mobilisation and collectivisation. The mode/ways in which these intermediary organisations interacted with the state is also analysed, for example, petitions/representations, dialogues/negotiations and also confrontations. The analysis shows that intermediaries have used all the three modes at different points of time in their interaction with the state, depending upon the situation.

Dimension III illustrates the different ways in which active citizens from the community emerged as leaders and also inspired other citizens to participate and be a part of the governance processes. It explains the different socioeconomic and political conditions under which citizens assume the characteristics of citizen leaders and the ways in which they are distinct from other political and religious leaders. In most cases, it was seen that active citizens took leadership roles as they were compelled to do so due to the dismal state of affairs, which they decided to improve/change. The role of citizen leaders is further discussed, which ranges from that of facilitators of mobilisation in the community to that of actors in engagement with the state along with intermediary organisations. The section further elaborates on the difficulties and conflicts of citizen leaders, which are mostly centred on their political affiliations and links. However, the issue of whether political inclination is better than having an apolitical approach could not be compared, as the case studies did not reflect the same or vice-versa. In South Africa and Brazil citizen leaders are associated with political parties as they are newer democracies and citizens have more hopes attached with their state as compared to India where citizens are already disappointed with the state's performance and attitude towards the citizens.

Dimension IV delves into the changes and outcomes that were brought about in the three democracies due to the efforts of the citizens and intermediaries and their participation in the democratic spaces. This is specially analysed in the context of enhanced accountability in three spheres i.e., changes in policies, practice and in the notions of citizenship and rights among the marginalised. All the areas of accountability are explained with the help of empirical evidence. There are instances where changes in policies can be witnessed in India (RTI in Delhi and rehabilitation plan in Bhachau, Gujarat) and Brazil (modification in master plan in Diadema and the decentralised health system in São Paulo). With regard to changes in practice, the GPCA in South Africa yielded certain concessions even though it could not completely stop the construction of the FIFA World Cup stadium. Similarly, cases from India (Delhi and Dharamshala), South Africa (Khayelitsha) and Brazil (east zone of São Paulo and Diadema) indicate improvements in service delivery on the part of the local authorities based on citizens' demand for the same. There were also changes in notions of citizenship and participation among the marginalised, which resulted in their enhanced participation in decision-making processes. Instances where the youth, women, marginalised and vulnerable groups have actively participated in the governance system could be seen in the case studies from these three countries.

The case studies from India, Brazil and South Africa presented in Section III of the book give a comprehensive picture of the participatory processes initiated and controlled by the citizens to influence a range of governance issues that surround recent as well as established democratic states. All the case studies represent the unique characteristics and dynamics of participatory spaces that exist in the three countries and also the role of citizen leaders and intermediary civil society organisations in exacting accountability from the state.

The case study from South Africa on 'Citizen Leadership in Cape Town—A Tale of Three Communities, South Africa' brings to light the struggle of three different communities distinguished by race, class and leadership in asserting their rights over land and housing.

The first community, largely comprised white and middle class citizens, was fighting for recreational space (Green Point Common) in their area, which had been proposed as the potential site for the construction of a stadium for the FIFA World Cup 2010. Concerned citizens formed the GPCA and tried to negotiate with the authorities to shift the stadium to some other location and also mobilised the community on the same. While the GPCA did not succeed in halting/diverting the construction of the stadium, it was successful in gaining some concessions from the state like a commitment to retain the common as a recreational area; a commitment that the stadium will not be surrounded by a village which might subsequently be sold off as housing; the allocation of alternative land for the Metropolitan Golf Course to compensate for land lost in the construction of the stadium; and a commitment by the city to compensate or employ the club for a loss of earnings and to cover staff costs until such time as it is again fully operational.

The case of the Langa community illustrates the efforts made by the backyard dwellers to raise issues of housing and alter the 70:30 allocation of houses for Joe Slovo informal settlements and backyard dwellers respectively under the Gateway Housing Scheme. As regular interfaces with the authorities did not yield any results, they formed the COLACOCO to raise their concerns through public meetings, participation in ward committees, petitioning the authorities and organising protest marches. However, the coalition failed to adopt new measures to confront the state and COLACOCO members learnt the efficacy of formal democratic channels for engagement with the state.

As far as the Joe Slovo informal settlement was concerned, it was faced with the problem of relocation to Langa instead of the pre-decided area as a result of the fire that broke out in 2005. They were faced with a double crisis as they had no home and the Langa community was not happy with the 70:30 split in the Gateway Project. However, with the same insecurity as the backyard dwellers, the Joe Slovo Task Team proved to be more responsive and rapidly changed its tactics when confronted with the state. Through their regular demands and protests, they were successful in reserving 70 per cent houses for their settlement.

The case study on 'Using Participatory Spaces for Improving Housing and Urban Services: Diadema, São Paulo, Brazil' highlights how social movements and their leadership interfaced with state agencies to draw attention to the problem of inadequate housing and service infrastructure and later how the state agencies responded positively to the citizens' demand for accountability.

Rapid industrialisation of the great ABC region led to severe pressure on infrastructure and urban services like houses, water, sanitation and health in Diadema. This resulted in irregular occupation of plots of land, emergence of *favelas* (slums) and other types of informal settlements. Initially, the housing movement evolved under such circumstances and was led by popular and trade union organisations. It later saw the participation of CEBs (*Communidades Eclesiais Base*; basic ecclesial communities), the Church, women and neighbourhood organisations, which demanded accountability from the state for improved housing services. Both open and invited spaces like door-to-door campaigns, demonstrations, involvement in participatory budget, meetings and conferences, participation in city development plan were used by the housing movement at different points of time to voice their concerns.

A unique feature of the case study was the crucial role played by the state in mobilising and facilitating the participation of citizens in the planning of the town. The state collaborated with the housing movement and community organisations to organise them into inhabitant commissions and encouraged them to scale up their issues from demanding basic services to *favela* urbanisation and land regularisation.

The case study on 'Citizens' Improving Urban Services through Citizens' Actions, Dharamshala, Himachal Pradesh, India' highlights how citizen leaders and community based organisations through engagement and participation accessed sanitation services from the municipality especially related to garbage collection. Dharamshala is one of the major tourist destinations of Himachal Pradesh in India and attracts more than 100,000 domestic and foreign tourists every year. This has resulted in an increased number of commercial and business establishments contributing to substantial solid waste generation in the town. About 10-12 tonnes of solid waste is generated every day in the town and the municipality is able to collect only 70 per cent of it.

An intermediary civil society organisation, PRIA acted as a catalyst in mobilising and strengthening *mohalla samitis* (neighbourhood committees) at the ward level. The citizen leaders were provided with training, orientation and exposure visits in the best practices on solid waste management. Along with the *mohalla samitis,* a number of *mahila mandals* (women's groups) were also catalysed and provided with capacity building support. The *mohalla samitis* and *mahila mandals* with support from PRIA undertook the monitoring of the performance of key municipal services especially in water, sanitation and solid waste management. Using media and the provisions of Right to Information (RTI) for mobilisation drives, the citizen leaders engaged with the municipal authorities are not only to share their monitoring results but also demand better services and provide feasible solutions.

These endeavours led to the creation of an active citizenry and enhanced awareness among the community regarding their potential role in the governance of their town. Citizen leaders and community based organisations like Gamru Youth Brigade Club; women's groups etc., used participatory spaces to raise their concerns. Open spaces like ward committees, rallies, citizen monitoring exercises, media etc. and invited spaces like the Right to Information Act (RTI Act) were used to demand better services from the municipal authorities.

These processes at the grassroot level not only resulted in effective service delivery but also created an enabling environment for ensuring accountability and transparency by the government. Compliance with the provisions of Proactive Disclosure of information under the RTI Act and the preparation of a Detailed Project Report (DPR) on solid waste management by the Dharamshala municipality are prominent examples of how citizen and state interface and the active engagement of citizens can mould the course of development.

The case study on 'Women Leaders and Intermediary Organisations in Khayelitsha, South Africa' unravels the understanding of citizenship, rights, civic action and activism among the women of Khayelitsha *vis-à-vis* their individual and communitarian political identities. It also examines the role of women leaders at the grassroot level in attaining their rights to service delivery through a variety of participatory mobilisation strategies, through street committees to direct dialogue with local government through representatives such as ward councillors, NGOs and community based organisations like the South African National Civic Organisation (SANCO).

The role of organisations like SANCO, Khayelitsha Development Forum (KDF) and street committees in providing a platform for citizens to participate and articulate their demands is very evident in the case study but is also marked by the politicised nature of these organisations.

The case study on 'Engaging Community in Rehabilitation and Reconstruction Planning, Bhachau Town, Gujarat, India' highlights how citizen leaders after the massive disaster in Bhachau town rose up to the challenge of defending the rights of the excluded citizens. On 26 January 2001, Gujarat was struck by a massive earthquake ranging 7.7 on the Richter scale. Bhachau, a small town in the district of Kutch was one of the worst affected areas. More than 10,000 buildings collapsed in the town killing approximately 2,000 people. The estimated loss in the town was approximately Rs. 29.4 billion. Immediately after the devastation, the Government of Gujarat (GoG) announced a rehabilitation package within 20 days for four towns and came up with a development plan scheme. The development plan was to be prepared by the Bhachau Area Development Authority (BhADA) and the Urban Development Department of GoG. As the rehabilitation package stated that the plans would be prepared in a participatory manner, priority was given to soliciting people's opinion on the plan. However, it was soon realised that the plan benefited only a small proportion of the population and there was a need to protect the interest of the other citizens, particularly the vulnerable groups.

At this point of time, an intermediary civil society organisation, UNNATI facilitated a process of participatory planning for Bhachau to incorporate the views and suggestions of the marginalised and the excluded groups of the town. A series of mobilisation drives were undertaken like multistakeholder dialogues, exposure visits etc., along with the formation of Nagrik Sahyog Kendra, NSK (Citizen Support Cell), promotion of community based rehabilitation and assessment of the reconstruction process. Apart from UNNATI, community based organisations like Junavada Punarvasan Evam Vikas Samiti (JPEVS) and Navagam Vikas Samiti (NVS) actively shouldered the task of rehabilitation and planning in their respective areas.

A distinctive feature of the reconstruction of Bhachau was the prominent role played by local citizens in the entire process. Citizens formed *falia* (cluster) level committees to regularly monitor the rehabilitation process and also identify vulnerable families. These *falia* committees also organised rallies and marches to raise their concerns on the draft plan. The community-driven approach as compared to planner-driven development resulted in a participatory, community-owned plan for the town. Infact, the major achievements of the participatory planning process were the modifications that citizens could negotiate in the draft rehabilitation plan for the town in favour of the marginalised and neglected like demarcation of a residential zone for Junavada settlements, Vadinar being brought back to its original location, reduction in the size of institutional area and accommodation of Rabarivas at its existing location.

The participatory rehabilitation process not only led to a more informed and engaged citizenry but also enhanced the accountability of the state towards its citizens. The setting up of the NSK at the BhADA office (with the support of UNNATI) to help generate awareness among citizens regarding different rehabilitation schemes/policies is an example of the state's increased sense of responsibility and commitment towards the citizens.

The case study on 'Reclaiming Participatory Spaces in Health: A Study of East Zone, São Paulo, Brazil' highlights the dynamics of the relationship between the health movement and the state in order to show the roadblocks created by the latter to subvert participatory spaces. It also illustrates the evolution of the health movement from the perspective of citizen leaders who played a critical role in reclaiming these spaces from the state.

The east zone of São Paulo at the end of the 1970s was inhabited by nearly one-third of the city's population and characterised by poor sanitation conditions. As a result, epidemics of meningitis, typhoid and high infant mortality rates were quite common. The issue was taken up by the Popular Health Movement, a loose coalition of social and political groups, which included health professionals and occupational groups (sanitary doctors), intellectuals, trade unions, CEBs, clubs of mothers, Societies of Neighbourhood's Friends (SABs), the workers' movement and

Pastoral da Saúde (health pastorals or social movements related to the Catholic church). Apart from these actors, women and the Church also played a crucial role in the mobilisation process for demanding better health services. Between the 1970s and 1990s, other health movements were started in various other regions of São Paulo, which were unified in 1997 with the formation of the UMPS.

The leaders of the health movement were successful in asserting certain rights and privileges like the construction of a hospital, creation of *Sistema Únicode Saúde* (SUS or Unified Health System), municipal councils etc., through the use of participatory spaces. These processes were characterised by myriad vicissitudes in terms of their relation with the government in power.

The case study on 'Using Right to Information for Improving the Public Distribution System and Basic Infrastructure in Delhi, India' highlights how common citizens in Delhi used the RTI Act to access the public distribution system (PDS) and improve basic infrastructure with the support of Parivartan, an intermediary civil society organisation.

The PDS in India is extremely inefficient and food supplies are usually siphoned off. People face tremendous difficulties in getting food grains from the PDS shops due to large-scale corruption. Hence, Parivartan initiated a movement demanding transparency and accountability in the system with citizens' support. Various methods were used to mobilise citizens for using the RTI Act such as media engagement, house-to-house meetings, campaigns etc. As a result, a number of citizens filed RTI applications, which disclosed the authorities' malpractices. Social audits, surveys, sit-ins and public hearings were also conducted to exert pressure on the authorities and throw light on the PDS's dynamics.

The RTI Act was also used to improve the infrastructure facilities especially roads in Delhi. Huge discrepancies were revealed in the construction of roads in certain areas in terms of the quantity and quality of material used against the figures quoted in government records. Here resident welfare associations and citizens' collectives were instrumental in raising transparency issues and holding the Municipal Corporation of Delhi (MCD) into account through the use of both invited and open spaces.

These seven case studies probed with the assumptions and research questions outlined in the beginning of the chapter would possibly give new insights into intermixing of different kinds of 'spaces', criticality of the role of citizen leaders and intermediaries' organisations in mobilising citizens and ensuring accountability from the governance agencies, inclusive citizenship and deepening democracy.

References

Bandyopadhyay, K. (2007). "Strengthening Citizen Leadership", in M. Kak and R. Tandon (ed.), *Citizen Participation and Democratic Governance: In Our Hands*. New Delhi: PRIA.

Cornwall, A. (2000). as cited in Mohanty, R. (2006). "Citizen Participation in Development: Issues of Identity, Inclusion and Voice", in R. Mohanty and R. Tandon (ed.), *Participatory Citizenship: Identity, Exclusion, Inclusion*. New Delhi: Sage.

Freedom House (1999). *Democracy's Century: A Survey of Global Political Change in the 20th Century*. Washington D.C.: Freedom House.

Gaventa, J. (2006a). "Triumph, deficit or Contestation? Deepening the 'Deepening Democracy' Debate", *Working Paper 264*, Brighton: Institute of Development Studies.

———. (2006b). "Perspectives on Participation and Citizenship", in R. Mohanty and R. Tandon (ed.), *Participatory Citizenship: Identity, Exclusion, Inclusion*, New Delhi: Sage.

Houtzager, P., A. Acharya and A. Lavalle (2007). "Associations and the Exercise of Citizenship in New Democracies Evidence from São Paulo and Mexico City", *Working Paper* 285, Brighton: Institute of Development Studies.

Mohanty, R. (2006). "Citizen Participation in Development: Issues of Identity, Inclusion and Voice", in R. Mohanty and R. Tandon (ed.), *Participatory Citizenship: Identity, Exclusion, Inclusion*. New Delhi: Sage.

Pande, Suchi (2008). "The Right to Information and Societal Accountability: The Case of the Delhi PDS Campaign", in P. Houtzager, Anuradha Joshi and Adrian Gurza La (ed.), *State Reform and Social Accountability: Brazil, India and Mexico*, IDS Bulletin 38(6), January.

Newell, Peter (2006). "Taking Accountability into Account: The Debate so far", in Peter Newell and Rajesh Tandon (ed.), *Rights, Resources and the Politics of Accountability*. London and New York: Zed Books.

World Bank (1994). *The World Bank and Participation*. Washington: World Bank Operations Policy Department.

Section - II

Comparative Analysis

2 Citizen Leadership: Deepening Democratic Accountability in India, Brazil and South Africa

Vikas Jha and Bhavita Vaishnava

Introduction

About 64 countries in different parts of the world have adopted some form of democratic political system since mid-1970s.[1] Citizens around the world are rethinking about democratic models and want to explore new democratic experiences, which show new ways of relating to state institutions. New democratic experiments have the objectives of making the governance not only inclusive but also accountable. It assumes significance in view of the fact that the 'new democracies'[2] have largely not been able to deliver rights and entitlements of the citizens. Moreover, these political systems have been marked by huge mismanagement of public money by the selected few, leading to the voice of robust accountability system where citizens also exercise some control. Citizens in the 'new democracies' have tried and showed tremendous ingenuity in using the democratic processes to demand accountability of the state. Participatory budgeting, public councils (Brazil), social audit (India), citizen monitoring, citizen report card and other social accountability mechanisms are some of the examples of such endeavours in different parts of the world. So, new contours of citizenship and its relations with the state are emerging from grassroot experiences into the world.

The dynamics of changing citizen—state relationship can be seen in the seven case studies from India, Brazil and South Africa (IBSA) where citizens have tried out different democratic experiments for making the

---

1. Polity IV data, Freedom House scores, *www.freedomhouse.org* as quoted in Haerpfer *et al.* (2009): 58.
2. Countries progressing significantly towards democracy since 1972, have been referred to as new democracies in the paper.

political system inclusive and accountable. So the discourses on democratic spaces and accountability are becoming linked, leading to knowledge generation and sharing of the experiences of developing democratic countries. The cooperation between the three developing democracies has already taken the shape of a new axis, IBSA that is trying to lead south-south cooperation and give voice to the developing and underdeveloped countries on the global stage.

In order to highlight different facets of democratic experiences, we have tried to do a comparative analysis of seven case studies from the three countries. We are not trying to select, assess or showcase the best democratic experiences/model from the three countries but are trying to share how citizens in different contexts in the three continents have been able to ensure the state's accountability to get their rights and entitlements. It might motivate people of new democracies to develop their own democratic experiences or to adapt experiences from other countries and make the states accountable.

In the Synthesis Chapter, we shall compare and contrast the seven cases from the three countries and explore various facets of democratic spaces, citizen leadership and accountability. These themes have been investigated from four dimensions namely: (i) 'democratic spaces and citizens' voices', (ii) 'intermediation in accountability', (iii) 'citizen leadership', and (iv) 'enhancing accountability'.

The first dimension, democratic spaces and citizens' voices, discusses and questions, what kind of spaces for citizen participation are enabling their voices that demand accountability from governance institutions, how do various spaces interact with the democratic system to raise voices and what are the challenges faced by democratic spaces?

The second dimension, intermediation in accountability, deals with the questions, what forms do intermediations take? What functions does intermediation perform in enabling citizens to secure democratic accountability? What are the dynamics of intermediaries—state interface that affect citizens' rights and entitlements?

The third dimension, citizen leadership, takes up the questions, how does citizen leadership emerge? What is the role of a citizen leader? What are the dilemmas and conflicts encountered in exercising citizen leadership?

The fourth dimension, enhancing accountability discusses the questions, what are the changes in policies and practices brought about by citizen efforts (struggle, movements, representations etc.)? How inclusive are the processes of participation? What are the constraints in exercising citizenship? We begin the exploration of the democratic experiences with the first dimension.

I

Democratic Spaces and Citizens' Voices

Before engaging in discussion on democratic spaces and citizens' voices in three different political context, it is necessary to demystify the characteristics and complexities of 'democratic spaces' and examine how and whether they have been able to enhance citizens' voices effectively at different levels of the governance system. Before going into these details, it is important to understand what 'space' means in the context of participation and how it can assume a 'democratic' nature. Citizen participation and engagement have been recognised the world over as a means to foster tenets of democratic governance. Different arenas of participation are increasingly being created and utilised by governments and citizens in various democracies, specially the developing ones. It is these arenas for citizen participation that can be understood as a 'space' where citizens get an opportunity to 'act' and 'engage' with their governments either individually or through collectives. As explained by Andrea Cornwall, 'a space can be emptied or filled, permeable or sealed; it can be an opening, an invitation to speak or act. Spaces can also be clamped shut, voided of meaning, or depopulated as people turn their attention elsewhere.'[3]

Thus spaces for participation can assume different forms, they not necessarily be physical structures or formal institutions/systems for citizens to participate but also take the shape of informal, indigeneous and traditional means of participation like community based groups, street committees, neighbourhood groups and also individual or collective action like protests, rallies, sit-ins etc. Citizens can choose to participate in these

3. Cornwall (2004).

spaces through a variety of ways as per the demand of the situation. However, it is only when these spaces are inclusive and participatory in nature that they can be truly called democratic.

As spaces for participation provide an opportunity for interface between the state and the citizens, Cornwall and Coelho (2007: 1) mention that 'new democratic spaces', are a link between the state and society and conduits for negotiation, information and exchange, which they also refer to as the 'participatory sphere'.

The use of democratic spaces is often viewed from the perspective of demand and supply i.e., from the perspective of citizens and the state respectively. Active participation and engagement by citizens in the governance system is extremely essential for exercising citizenship and demanding accountability, whereas nurturing such participation by creating a favourable environment for them to grow in is also crucial from the lens of the state. It can be said that only when both the demand and the supply side work in unison that the democratic spaces are fully utilised and democracy is deepened.

Engaging citizens in governance and encouraging them to participate in decision-making on issues that affect their lives have become popular measures of enhancing state's accountability across the world. There are myriad examples of participatory mechanisms being institutionalised by states in different countries, specially the developing ones. What is important here is to reflect on and analyse the magnitude of participation and how effectively all the sections of society, irrespective of their vulnerabilities, are able to utilise it.

Though, democratic spaces have been successful in initiating and promoting processes of change at the local level, they cannot be considered free from societal prejudices and completely transform the landscape of participation in any given country. The following sections shall discuss in detail the emerging democratic spaces in India, Brazil and South Africa that have helped citizens raise their voices and demand accountability from the state. However, the extent to which these 'spaces for participation' have translated into 'spaces for change' needs to be understood from a wider perspective of the dynamics that exists in and around these spaces as well as the nature of relationship between citizens and the state. In other words, a mere creation of 'space' for participation does not ensure a desired 'change' to happen unless that space is productively utilised. Factors like 'who' actually participates in that space, 'till what extent' and 'for what purpose' determine the degree and quality of participation, which ultimately creates a platform for change. Thus, it can be said that 'spaces for participation' can be graduated into 'spaces for change' if they are complemented by a favourable support system from the outside and an active and engaged citizenry from within.

In light of thc abovc, these democratic spaces have been analysed through the following perspectives on the basis of the seven empirical studies.

Types of Democratic Spaces

Multitudes of such democratic spaces, which facilitate the process of citizen participation, are surfacing in democracies all across the world. Different scholars and social researchers have named these participatory arenas differently, based on their evolution and characteristics. In this book , they have been termed as 'invited' and 'invented' spaces, which have been explained in the following paragraph.

'Invited' spaces can be understood as spaces that are given by the state to citizens to participate in the governance system. Gaventa (2006: 60) defines them as 'those into which people (as users, as citizens, as beneficiaries) are invited to participate by various kinds of authorities, be they government, supranational agencies or non-governmental organisations.' He further elaborates on another set of spaces called 'closed or provided spaces' where decisions are made by certain people behind closed doors, in a non-inclusive manner, which are conceived by the state as provided spaces where elites make decisions and provide services to the people. Invited spaces have also been termed as 'state created spaces' by Mohanty (2006: 80).

'Invented' spaces on the other hand are those arenas where citizens articulate their demands outside the institutionalised spaces, as they are not able to raise their voices effectively through the 'invited' ones. Therefore, it can be said that 'invented' spaces came into existence due to the limitations of 'invited' spaces. They have also been referred to as 'popular' spaces by Cornwall (2004) and 'claimed/created' spaces by Gaventa (2006: 61). Invented spaces are also referred to as 'open' spaces as they open up new avenues for citizen engagement. These are the spaces that have greater room for innovations and can be used by citizens either in a collective or individual manner.

Empirical evidences from the three countries reveal the use of both 'invited' and 'invented' spaces in various forms, which can be demonstrated with the help of Table 2.1. The table depicts the different ways in which citizens have created space for participation and decision-making.

Table 2.1

Types of Democratic Spaces

No.	*Case Studies*	*Invented Spaces*	*Invited Spaces*
1.	Citizen Leadership in Cape Town: A Tale of Three Communities (Langa and Green Point, Cape Town, South Africa)	• Protest marches and hostel invasions by the coalition • Green Point Common Association (GPCA) Coalition for Langa Community Concerns COLACOCO • Use of Internet, creating website of the GPCA • Engagement in ward committees • Petitions by the COLACOCO • Project Steering Committee under the Gateway Housing Scheme	• Engagement in ward committees • Petitions by the COLACOCO • Project Steering Committee under the Gateway Housing Scheme
2.	Using Participatory Spaces for Improving Housing and Urban Services: Diadema, São Paulo, Brazil	• Door to door mobilisation, dissemination of pamphlets and demonstrations by trade union leaders • Demonstration by associations in Sanko in front of Housing and Urban Development Company's headquarters • Neighbourhood groups, basic ecclesial communities • Associations like 'Our Fight, Our Land', Freedom Pro-Housing Association and Association of Slum Inhabitants etc.	• Municipal Housing Councils • Promotion of associations and commissions during *favela* urbanisation • Concession of Rights of Actual Use • Territorialisation of associations into North, South, East and West • City Master Plan • Social interest special areas • Municipal Fund to support Social Interest Housing (FUMAPIS Council) • Participatory budgeting

contd...

...contd...

No.	*Case Studies*	*Invented Spaces*	*Invited Spaces*
3.	Improving Urban Services through Citizens' Action (Dharamshala, Himachal Pradesh, India)	• Rally on cleanliness • Individual efforts by citizen leaders like Mr. Prem David, Col. M.G. Sharma etc. • Mobilisation for the formation of ward committees, *mahila mandals* • RTI mobilisation drives • Mobilisation by PRIA (exposure visit) • Gamru Youth Brigade Club • Ward meetings and formation of ward committees • Resident Welfare Associations • Media engagement	• Consultation on DPR preparation • RTI Act
4.	Women Leaders and Intermediary Organisations in Khayelitsha, South Africa	• Street committees • Income Generation Projects (IGPs) • South African National Civic Organisation (SANCO) • Khayelitsha Development Forum (KDF)	• Ward forums under the Cape City Council
5.	Engaging Community in Rehabilitation and Reconstruction Planning (Bhachau Town, Gujarat, India)	• Individual efforts by citizen leaders like Ismail bhai • *Falia* (cluster) level committees • Junavada Punarvasan Evam Vikas Samiti (Committee for the rehabilitation and development of Junavada) • Navagam Vikas Samiti (Navagam Development Committee) • Multi-stakeholder consultations to discuss the draft development plan • Citizen Support Cell • Nagarvani (Voice of the town) monthly bulletin • Citizen monitoring as part of the social watch initiative	• Development plan under the rehabilitation package • Public consultation on draft plan
6.	Reclaiming Participatory Spaces in Health: A Study of Health Movement (São Paulo, Brazil)	• Popular Health Movement (a loose coalition of health professionals and occupational groups, intellectuals, trade unions, basic ecclesial communities, clubs of mothers, societies of neighbourhood friends, etc.)	• Unified Health System (SUS) • Popular councils (demanding services) and manager councils (monitor services) • Participatory budgeting

contd...

...contd...

No.	Case Studies	Invented Spaces	Invited Spaces
		• Closure of Anhanguera highway by citizens. • Mobilisation/awareness generation by civil society organisations • Individual efforts by citizen leaders like Geralda Marfisa • Union of Health Popular Movements (legal entity: citizenship and health)	• Basic Operating Rules (BOR) to access funds from National Health Funds • Law of the manager councils
7.	Using Right to Information for Improving Public Distribution System and Basic Infrastructure in Delhi, India	• March by 400 people to the Food Commissioner's Office • Signature campaign by 4,000 citizens • Public meetings • Survey by Parivartan (CSO) • Social audit • Media campaign on RTI Act • Public hearing on development works in Sundarnagari	• Use of Right to Information Act by individuals • Public Interest Litigation by Parivartan • Filing of cases by Parivartan and individual citizens with the police

Thus the table details out a variety of invented spaces used by citizens in the three countries for demanding accountability, apart from the conventional spaces provided by the state through legislations, policies and institutional frameworks. It is important to discuss how these democratic spaces were used by citizens to demand their rights and entitlements.

One can also notice that citizens have adopted different methods of participation and interface with the governance system while making use of invented spaces. Therefore it can be said that invented spaces take varied forms and characteristics. Some of which, that have emerged from the case studies are 'social or public action' like citizens' participation in rallies, marches, sit-ins, mobilisation and awareness generation campaigns etc., where citizens have voiced their demands, exhibited their feelings and discontentment towards government policies and reforms. Second is the 'formation of groups/associations' where citizens have collectivised and joined hands to form networks, coalitions, groups and associations for example the GPCA (Green Point Common Association) and COLACOCO (Coalition of Langa Community Concerns) in Cape Town South Africa, neighbourhood groups and associations like 'Our Fight Our Land' in

Diadema (Brazil) as well as community based groups like Junavada Punarvasan Evam Vikas Samiti (JPEVS), Navagam Vikas Samiti (NVS) and Gamru Youth Brigade Club in Bhachau and Dharamshala (India) respectively. Apart from the above, citizens and intermediaries have also used certain 'tools and mechanisms' to enhance their participation like social audits, public hearings, citizen monitoring through citizen report cards, internet, media etc., that have played a crucial role in amplifying their voices. Similarly, the formation of Citizen Support Cell in Bhachau (India) is a unique example of how UNNATI created a space for interaction between the authorities and the community. Invented spaces and their use can further be explained through the following examples.

The case study of Khayelitsha, South Africa shows how 'invented spaces' in the form of income generation groups of women were used as platforms to identify and address local issues. In the two income generation groups namely, sewing and catering, women mentioned their involvement and association with street committees[4] that acted as crucial platforms for their participation. Similarly, in Diadema, the leaders of the housing movement and the trade unions were involved in massive mass mobilisation initiatives like door-to-door campaigns, disseminating pamphlets etc., to promote people's participation and make them aware of their rights. In fact, the housing and health movements in Brazil are examples of the potential role that 'invented spaces' can play in influencing or pressurising the government about various issues.

Empirical evidence from the three countries also demonstrates that 'invented spaces' were used by citizens and civil society organisations to not only 'demand better services' but also to 'monitor the same'. The case study of Dharamshala reveals how the community with the help of civil society organisations developed tools for assessing basic services. The citizens' report cards and field surveys were used as instruments for highlighting the present status and 'demanding better services' by pressurising local government authorities. Monitoring groups were formed to track basic services on a regular basis. The health movement in Brazil

4. A Street Committee may consist of anything between 15 or more members who all live in the same area, mostly a street but sometimes the area may also be divided in a different way.

also reflects on how the popular and manager councils raised the communities' demands and monitored health services at the health centres.

The use of the media as an 'invented space' for participation as well as a means of stimulating participation is witnessed in the case studies from India and South Africa. Be it the citizens' struggle for basic services in Dharamshala or the joint efforts of Parivartan and the Indian Express in Delhi for the promotion of the Right to Information (RTI) Act, the media has been effectively used to foster people's greater participation and exert pressure on the government for better service delivery. In South Africa, the GPCA used Information Technology (IT) specifically the internet as a means to popularise their struggles. The Association campaigned for its case through an online blog to elicit public debate, issuing press releases, etc. Thus, it can be seen how virtual platforms were used to mobilise communities on issues affecting their lives.

However, it can also be seen through the case studies that though media and IT are increasingly gaining acceptance as popular spaces for participation, the importance of conventional spaces at the grassroot level has not yet been diminished, as they are widely being used by communities to assert their demands. This can be attributed to the fact that media (print as well as electronic) and IT (Internet, mobiles etc.) cater to a limited audience i.e., only those who have access to them, which is highly subjected to the socioeconomic conditions of the individual/community. The case of GPCA (South Africa), which created its own website for popular support was possible as it comprised elite and educated members from the society. Therefore, it can be said that traditional means of participation like community meetings, neighbourhood groups and street committees etc., are still widely being used by citizens as they are relatively more inclusive in nature as compared to media and IT. Another aspect related to the use of media and IT is the dominant role played by intermediary organisations in popularising the same among the citizens. In all the case studies where media and IT have been tapped as a space for participation, one can witness the facilitation of intermediaries in some way or the other. For instance in India, Parivartan (Delhi) and PRIA (Dharamshala) played a significant role in bridging the gap between the media and local communities.

As far as 'invited' spaces are concerned, instances of their being provided by the state and used by citizens can be gleaned from case studies of all the three countries. In India, the application of the RTI Act by citizens in Delhi and the participatory development plan in Bhachau highlight the fact that spaces are provided by the state to promote people's participation at the grassroot level. Similar spaces are found in Brazil in the form of health and housing councils that are based on the premise of participation by all sections of society and their equal share in decision-making. The participatory budget in Diadema in the case of the housing movement is an example of acknowledging people's participation through invited spaces. In South Africa, petitions by COLACOCO and the formation of project steering committees under the Gateway Housing Scheme reveal how citizens brought state institutionalised participatory spaces into play. The Khayelitsha case study reflects how community based organisations, NGOs, churches and groups of people were invited by the ward councillor to participate in the ward forum to discuss and advise her on social needs, health issues, education, early childhood, disability, religious issues, etc.

Empirical evidence from the three countries shows that in terms of experimentation and innovation, 'invented spaces' provide a wide scope for interested actors/citizens as compared to the 'invited spaces'. This can be seen through the use of media, citizen monitoring initiatives and other such local forms of participation like neighbourhood groups/*mohalla samitis*, street committees etc., that give ample space for citizens to practice their citizenship rights even in unstructured and informal ways. In the case of 'invited spaces' however, participation gets restricted as citizens rarely get the freedom to experiment different forms of participation and have to do so in a given formal pattern designed by the state.

Interaction of Invented and Invited Spaces

Democratic spaces by nature of their being deeply associated with the communities and different stakeholders that exist within its purview are closely related to each other. Both 'invited' and 'invented spaces' have their own specific characteristics that make them distinct; however they are in the process of continuous interaction with each other, as they co-exist within the same realm of the 'participatory sphere'. The interface between 'invited' and 'invented' spaces can be analysed from the perspective of the myriad ways in which they relate to and the extent to which they influence and legitimise each other.

As mentioned earlier, democratic spaces cannot be viewed in isolation as they are mutually dependent on and complement each other. Citizens, groups and intermediary organisations used both these spaces at different times in the course of their struggle for raising their voices. The case studies from Brazil show that both the housing and the health movements used 'invented' and 'invited' spaces at different times like demonstrations, door-to-door campaigns and participatory budgeting respectively to put forward their concerns. The same interaction between the spaces can also be seen in South Africa, where the COLACOCO conducted protest marches and hostel invasions in the migrant workers hostel on the one hand and petitioned as well as participated in ward committees on the other. Thus it can be understood that invented and invited spaces synergyse and support each other. It also leads us to the conclusion that the key for effective articulation of demands and accountability from governance institutions lies in the appropriate use of both the spaces at the right time, where they can produce optimum results.

Another aspect in which invented and invited spaces interact is the manner in which they keep a check on each other. It is widely understood that even after 'invited spaces' are provided by the state for citizen participation, they have to be constantly monitored from the outside through the use of 'invented spaces' by citizens and civil society organisations. This is because 'invited spaces' though provided by the state are often not patronised by them as they pose a threat to the state's ownership of resources and power. Empirical evidences show that invented spaces were used to legitimise the existence of invited ones, which can be explained with the help of the following examples.

In India, the case study of the public distribution system (PDS) and development works in Delhi reflect how ordinary citizens used 'invited spaces' i.e., the RTI Act, as a tool to keep a check on the schemes and services that they are entitled to. Further, the case study reveals how apart from 'invited spaces', 'invented spaces' in the form of collective marches/

walks by a group of citizens to the Food Commissioner's office, public hearings, etc., were also used to exert pressure on government departments to hold them accountable.

Similarly in Brazil, citizens used health councils and participatory budgeting along with demonstrations/blockades etc., to demand their rights to quality health services. Such dynamics was witnessed in Diadema as well, when housing associations involved in construction in Sanko (which was a 96,000 square metre private estate negotiated by the housing movement under the government's Social Interest Housing Scheme) camped in front of the Housing and Urban Development Company (CDHU) headquarters, because it was not releasing resources for construction. In this case, the interaction between the two spaces led to better articulation of demands and ensured accountability of the state.

The third mode of interaction between the two spaces is with regard to the influence that one has on the other i.e., 'invented spaces' lead to the creation of 'invited spaces' as can be seen in the examples of Brazil and India. In Brazil, the efforts and struggle of the housing and health movements facilitated by the re-democratisation process in the 1980s resulted in the adoption of 'invited spaces' in the form of municipal housing and health councils. The struggles of the housing movement compelled the municipal authorities to establish FUMAPIS Council and start consultative process for preparation of city master plan. In India, the RTI movement, public hearings and social audit in Delhi led to creation of disclosure laws which facilitated in regular monitoring of official records by citizens.

Thus, it can be said that invented and invited spaces exist in a dynamic relationship to each other, which adopts different forms based on the need and demand of the situation. The dynamics of interaction between the democratic spaces also determines to a great extent the fulfilment of citizens' demands for state's accountability.

Challenges of Democratic Spaces

The above sections give a glimpse of the ways in which democratic spaces were utilised by citizens across the three countries. It reflects that democracies all round the world are taking initiatives to incorporate mechanisms of people's participation through the provisioning of participatory spaces. However, participation of communities in these democratic spaces is to a very great extent influenced by their sociocultural and economic background, the notion of which is deeply imbibed in our societies since ages. Specially when it comes to inclusive participation the questions of representation like 'who participates in these spaces?', 'what is the level of their participation even if they get to do so?' and 'to what extent their voices are being heard?' etc., need to be critically analysed. Therefore the discussion on democratic spaces cannot be considered as complete without mentioning the dynamics that envelopes these spaces, some of which have been elaborated in this section. The dynamics of democratic spaces acts as a biggest challenge in their effective functioning as it hinders inclusive participation and restricts citizenship rights of the marginalised and vulnerable sections of the society. In light of the above, a close look at the use of democratic spaces from the case studies in terms of 'inclusive participation' and 'citizenship' reveals the extent to which they are affected by societal stereotypes and prejudices.

As far as 'invited spaces' are concerned, it has been increasingly understood that they reproduce power dynamics in society.[5] This can also be witnessed in the case studies from India and South Africa, where instances of 'invited spaces' being taken over by the middle class or the elite are seen.

The development plan in Bhachau reflects these dynamics where the participation of important stakeholders like slum dwellers, the informal sector and women was not sought in making the draft plan for the town. Surprisingly, the plan did not acknowledge the existence of many small slums because of which they were excluded from the rehabilitation plans. It was only after several rounds of dialogue between the cluster committees and the state, that inclusion of poor was ensured in the development plan of the city.

The case of COLACOCO in South Africa also brings to light the discrimination in 'invited spaces', which can be seen in the composition of the project steering committee formed under the Gateway Housing

5. Cornwall (2008): 44.

Scheme, launched to eradicate shack dwellings in the major cities of South Africa. This committee was set up by the ward councillor to bring together all interested parties of the Gateway Housing Scheme and amongst those invited to participate were local government councillors, city officials, representatives of housing and construction companies, representatives of NGOs and members from the Joe Slovo settlement. In its final composition, however, the steering committee comprised 30 members out of which only 2 were from COLACOCO. It meant that real stakeholders were not represented in steering committee because of which the coalition could not present its concerns effectively.

The excluded group in Diadema also felt that the consultative mechanisms at the higher tiers of governance were not accessible to them, while such bodies namely participatory budgeting and Municipal Fund for the Support of Social Interest Housing (FUMAPIS) council being closer to them provided appropriate avenues of participation.

Thus it can be concluded from the above examples that though 'invited spaces' are created with the intention of inviting all the sections of the society to participate, they are often hijacked by the more powerful and influential ones. Due to the limited scope of participation in the invited spaces the poor mostly have been found expressing themselves through 'invented spaces' with the support of civil society organisations. However there have been instances where some form of discrimination and biasness has also been witnessed in the case of invented spaces.

For example in India, social constructs like caste, ethnic groups, class and gender remained hindering factors in citizen participation. This was reflected in Dharamshala, where communities could not galvanise themselves around the larger community interests as it was a heterogeneous group, with people from varied backgrounds (immigrants from different states, different ethnic and caste groups—Gaddi, Rajputs and Brahmins) and classes. Therefore it became difficult for them to come together on a common platform and discuss issues of concern as they already had their own biases and perspectives.

Similarly, when women groups in Dharamshala decided to identify and seek solutions for certain crucial issues, they faced a number of challenges. For instance, they tried to take up the issue of excessive alcohol consumption by men in their communities but they were not successful in bringing about any substantial change. In fact, they were discouraged from taking up this issue by their male counterparts, which reflects the degree of patriarchal influence and control in determining the extent of participation by women. Thus, ensuring the participation of the entire community was a challenge for active citizens and intermediaries in this case. This reflects the fact that issues of caste, class and gender deeply control the behaviour of communities, especially when it comes to their active participation in the development processes. However, in Delhi and Bhachau, the enormity of the problem faced by citizens helped in overcoming these social constraints and they demanded their rights and entitlements.

Looking through the prism of a larger framework, the democratic practice in Indian democracy has been deeply compromised by a number of social limitations and challenges inherited from the past in the form of nepotism and the criminalisation of politics in the free and fair electoral system, control of 'local governance' by the local elite and the virtual collapse of the Indian legal system with a backlog of pending cases.[6] These factors together create a system which stifles the participation of citizens in development and governance.

The cases of the GPCA and COLACOCO in Cape Town, South Africa underline the fact that social caste and class structures play a crucial role in determining the strength of citizens' voice and thereby challenge the tenets of inclusive participation. Both the associations show similar signs in terms of their struggle for claiming their right but are different with regards to their socioeconomic status. While the community involved in the GPCA comprised the white middle class, COLACOCO was formed of citizens from the poor and marginalised classes. However, the GPCA did not succeed in halting or diverting the construction of the FIFA 2010 stadium, they were successful in extracting concessions from both the metropolitan and provincial governments at the end of their struggle as compared to their counterparts in COLACOCO who could not claim their housing rights. This was due to the fact that the GPCA manifested a far greater degree of homogeneity in terms of socioeconomic standing (predominantly

6. Dreze and Sen (2002): 350-352, 378.

white and middle class), level of education and political affiliation than their counterparts mobilising in Langa.

The above examples reflect that power relations within the society adversely affect the participation of the marginalised and weaker sections even in invented spaces. As mentioned by Cornwall, these spaces for participation are neutral but are themselves shaped by power relations, which both surround and enter them.[7] Thus it can be inferred that both the 'invented and invited spaces' have their own peculiar limitations in terms of the inclusion of the poor and marginalised, which implies that participatory spaces in general are affected by 'power dynamics' whether related to caste, class or gender. However, within the invited spaces this discrimination becomes more prominent and takes a structured form as 'power holders' i.e., the state and the rich/elites ally against the marginalised, who are left with limited space for participation. Therefore, as compared to invited spaces, invented ones provide far greater opportunity for the poor and vulnerable to participate and express themselves. The challenge of democratic spaces therefore lies, in not only making the invited spaces more inclusive and meaningful but also enhancing the quality of participation in the invented spaces. It is here that intermediary organisations and citizen leaders have a crucial role to play i.e., mobilising the citizens to participate and engage more effectively with their governments on one hand and sensitising the authorities to be more responsive and accountable towards their citizens on the other. As the notions of power, class, caste, hierarchy and gender are deeply entrenched in our societies and mindsets, the challenge lies in influencing the citizens and state to detach themselves from these prejudices and further adopt more inclusive, egalitarian and democratic approach. Thus, making democratic spaces function efficiently to bring about desired change needs to be understood from a two-pronged perspective of demand and supply.

One of the other challenges of 'invented spaces' is the question of their sustainability in terms of the continued participation of citizens. This can be seen in the case of the housing movement in Diadema,

7. Cornwall (2002) as cited by Gaventa (2006).

Brazil. The case reveals that though the movement was successful in organising different housing nuclei for demanding better services, it became difficult to sustain all of them once their demands were met. For example, the *Jardim Maria Tereza* housing nucleus that was prominent in the 1970s, completely removed itself from the housing movement when the municipal authorities fulfilled their demands. This was due to the loss of effective citizen leaders in the nucleus who were instrumental in mobilising the inhabitants' participation. On the other hand, in some of the housing nuclei, such as the *Jardim das Praias*, the inhabitants association still stimulates the participation of the community, encouraging struggles in other areas like health, education, sports etc. Thus, it can be said that continued participation in 'invented spaces' cannot be ensured, it is a phenomenon that is subject to the availability of effective enabling mechanisms like active local leadership and a supportive external environment.

Thus, the case studies from the three countries bring to light the myriad ways in which citizens have been participating in 'democratic spaces' and raising their voices for improved service delivery. They no doubt faced numerous challenges in utilising these spaces which certainly hindered the collectivisation efforts but citizens found a way out to put up their demands. However, these challenges would remain an issue of concern in future as well. On the brighter side, the case studies illustrate that citizenship is being realised as an important element in the development scenario not only as mere 'recipients' of services but also as crucial 'actors' in the designing and provisioning of these services. Evidence reveals that they have been able to raise their voices effectively through a multitude of 'invented' and 'invited' spaces available to them. These democratic spaces therefore have been instrumental in amplifying citizens' voices and have given them a platform to not only flag issues but to pursue them with regard to the state's accountability. These spaces have played a two-pronged role of creating a cadre of citizen leaders by allowing them to practice citizenship on one hand and compelling the state to realise its accountability towards the citizens on the other.

II

Intermediation in Accountability

Numerous examples of 'invented' and 'invited spaces' from India, Brazil and South Africa demonstrate that these spaces have provided opportunities for the people to present their demands and negotiate with the state. However, the participation of people, as can be seen from the case studies, depends upon the intermediaries. Not only do they play a critical role in mobilising and organising the communities, helping in media and internet coverage but also engage in intense negotiation with the state.

Coming to the functions performed by the intermediaries in the three countries, it is seen that they have actively taken up initiatives for ensuring the state's accountability. Such initiatives are appropriate and timely as people in developing countries are becoming disenchanted by the failure of the state to protect democratic rights, promote equality, deliver services and promote public good. This disenchantment may be slightly low in South Africa and Brazil as they are 'new democracies'[8] where people still believe that the state will deliver. However, disenchantment with the state is quite high in India. This has made it necessary for intermediaries to devise mechanisms/methods to ensure the accountability of elected representatives, public officials and state institutions. Citizen's report cards, RTI, Community health monitoring, social audits, frequent representation to the state, participatory budgeting, protests, web-based advocacy, media campaigns, etc., are methods used by the intermediaries in India, South Africa and Brazil.

Before unpacking several issues related to the role of intermediaries in linking citizens with the state, functions performed by intermediaries in enabling citizens to secure democratic accountability, forms which intermediation takes in different context and the dynamics of interaction between intermediary organisations and the state, it is necessary to define the meaning of intermediaries.

By the term intermediaries, we mean organisations and associations who mediate on behalf of people. Intermediaries position themselves as the

8. Democracy was established in Brazil in 1988 and South Africa became democracy in 1994.

interface between communities and the state and take on the role of preventing or curbing the state's excesses and 'help in linking individuals to the state as active members of the citizenry'.[9] Intermediaries, we come across in these case studies are community groups like *mohalla* (residential) committees, street committees, neighbourhood committees, trade unions, groups of activists, NGOs, clubs of mothers, slum committees and community organisations created by the state. Most of these intermediaries had come into existence to fight for the demands of the people as seen in the case studies from the three countries. The birth of these organisations was spontaneous and occasioned by the environment prevailing in the locations. Some intermediaries like trade unions and NGOs were registered organisations, which were formed for taking up the rights of workers and people respectively and their growth cannot be exclusively linked to the demands of the people in the case studies. It is important to point out here that some of the intermediaries, especially in Brazil, were created by the government actively engaged in building capacity of citizens in understanding the health and housing issues in order to enable them to effectively present their demands. Thus, intermediation of various kinds and nature could be seen in the three countries.

Role of Intermediaries

The problems faced by urban citizens in the three countries were mainly related to inadequate housing, poor infrastructure, poor sanitation and hygiene in the neighbourhood, poor access to safe drinking water and electricity, service delivery problems in health care, education and the food distribution system. Hence, all the struggles for ensuring accountability were mainly focussed on solving these problems.

Intermediaries were at the forefront or at the backdrop of these struggles depending upon the capacity and preparedness of the community to carry on a sustained struggle. As observed in the case studies, people in most of the locations were poor, illiterate and un-informed and largely preoccupied with earning their livelihood, which made it difficult for them to carry on a sustained struggle. So, any initiative for ensuring accountability has to begin with mobilisation and empowerment of the

9. Gupta (2003): 222.

poor and marginalised. Intermediaries like trade unions and neighbourhood associations in the town of Diadema, Brazil conducted a door-to-door campaign disseminating pamphlets before regularly summoned assemblies to make people aware of the problems and chalked out an action plan for taking up their demands with the state for housing and delivery problems related to water supply and health care. Similarly in the east zone of São Paulo, Brazil several intermediaries, namely, women's communities, health pastorals, clubs of mothers, Societies of Neighbourhood's Friends (SABs), basic ecclesial communities (CEBs), the workers movement, sanitarian physicians, the Catholic church and NGOs got together to solve the problems related to poor health conditions, poor sanitation, scarcity of clean water and lack of medical facilities. They organised regular meetings and distributed newsletters in order to make the community aware of the poor health conditions and mobilised them to fight for their rights. These intermediaries got together under one umbrella and formed the Union of the Popular Health Movements of São Paulo (UMPS) in 1997, which led to the intermediaries being better organised. It also resulted in planned educational activities among the people and intensive dialogue with the state.

Civil society organisations in India adopted a slightly different strategy for mobilising people. PRIA and UNNATI (NGOs) engaged the community in conducting a first-hand survey of basic services provided in the town. It not only made the community aware of the poor state of their living conditions, e.g., shortage of water, poor solid waste management, non-involvement of people in urban planning but also helped in collecting the data with which they could confront the bureaucracy. Further, the establishing of a Citizen Support Cell, capacity building of citizen leaders and grassroots community organisations, publication of pamphlets and newsletters in Bhachau (Gujarat) and Dharamshala (Himachal Pradesh) helped in mobilisation, enabled peoples' participation in the planning process and improved delivery of basic services. In Delhi, activists of Parivartan (a community based organisation) helped people in filing applications to seek information by using the RTI Act, which helped them in getting timely delivery of subsidised food grains and improving infrastructure facilities.

In Khayelitsha, South Africa, which faced problems of housing, water, sanitation, health, etc., mobilisation of the community was done by street committees[10] through weekly meetings. These demands were taken up to the South African National Civic Organisation (SANCO)[11] general council, which took it up with city councillors. Another organisation, Khayelitsha Development Forum (KDF),[12] a civic body took up issues related to governance with the local government and city councils. So, SANCO and KDF were the two intermediaries active in the area. The struggle for open spaces and violations of environment regulations for building a FIFA stadium for World Cup 2010 were the issues before the GPCA in Cape Town. This association, mostly comprising the literate and rich people of Cape Town, adopted innovative media techniques for generating public opinion. They wrote press releases, drafted sound bytes for media and launched a website for online public debate to fight for public spaces in Cape Town.

We can observe that the intermediaries in these three countries, depending upon the specific context, undertook a variety of roles to mobilise and educate the community. The methods varied from participatory research and facilitating the filing of RTI applications in India, to door-to-door campaigns, assemblies/meetings, distribution of pamphlets, newsletters and web-based campaigning in Brazil and South Africa. The educational activities and mobilisation drives of the intermediaries build the capacity of the citizens to put up demands to the state. Though these demands were mainly related to solving service delivery problems but were ultimately seeking to establish durable accountability mechanisms. The scale and depth of intermediation was also determined by socio-economic-political context of the countries.

---

10. Street committees meet once a week. Similarly, representatives of SCs meet as block committees and then representatives of these committees.

11. Report to SANCO, a civic organisation front of the African National Congress which fought for citizens' right. SANCO was formed in the 1980s and is still functional.

12. KDF is a civic body created by the people in 1994 to control tensions in the area. KDF and ward development forums took up the issues related to governance.

Levels of Intermediation

It brings us to the question of levels of intermediation in these countries. The intermediaries collaborated with actors sharing similar objectives at local, state, national and international level to create pressure on the State (Table 2.2). It would be pertinent to analyse the processes of collaboration at various levels by which the rights and entitlements of citizens were advocated.

In the east zone of Sao Paulo, the main actors of the health and housing movements organised themselves under the umbrella of the UMPS which facilitated better coordination between intermediaries, utilisation of institutional spaces of participation (like public councils) and intensive dialogue with the state. It did not omit open spaces of participation like protests, marches and demonstrations from its strategies. UMPS also tried to manage resources for better organisation and education by the creation of a non-profit entity, Citizenship and Health.

Similarly, in Diadema, a number of neighbourhood associations got together under one platform—Association of Slum Inhabitants. This association took up the demands of the urban populace for improvement of urban services and revitalisation of public councils through demonstrations and dialogue with bureaucracy and councils. Pressured by the council, the government promoted partnerships and agreements between neighbourhood associations, CDHU[13] and Caixa Economica Federal (CEF)[14] for finding solutions to the demands for housing. Thus, the coming together of grassroots organisations into a larger platform or association was the common feature in both the east zone of São Paulo and Diadema, which helped in putting up a united voice and pressuring the public councils, municipalities and provincial governments to integrate peoples' demands into their programmes and policies.

In South Africa, GPCA and COLACOCO local level coalitions of social forces (these were also registered as community based organisations) were formed to take up the demands of the community. They, however, could not build or become aligned with national or international level

13. CDHU (State-owned housing and urban development company) managed resources for housing projects.

14. CEF is a state-owned Federal Bank in Brazil.

coalitions. Joe Slovo settlers, on the other hand, aligned with the Western Cape chapter of the anti-evictions campaign, Abahlali baseMjondolo (a shack-dweller's movement) and the Slum Dwellers International (SDI). Joe Slovo's leadership demonstrated more vision in pursuing national and international level collaborations, which not only highlighted the issues at the national and international forums but also increased the organisational skills and resources of the organisation. In Khayelitsha, the linkages of SANCO and KDF with national or international level organisations were quite limited.

In nearly all the case studies in India, poverty, poor awareness, non-existence and non-functional grassroots organisations and political apathy led to the pre-dominance of civil society organisations and activist groups in mobilisation and engagement with the state. This is not to suggest that citizens were not at the centre of the struggle, it indicates that leadership role was in the hands of intermediaries. For example Parivartan linked with National Campaign for People's Right to Information (NCPRI) to broad-base the movement and generate countrywide discussion and action on RTI. It created public opinion for transparency and accountability of the state, pressurising Central government to take steps. Similarly, PRIA and UNNATI generated public opinion at the provincial level which brought the government to the negotiating table. It would be a generalisation to say that this is true of the whole of India but the predominance of a few intermediaries in the specific case study locations does raise questions about the growing institutionalisation of open spaces in India. It would be a good question to research whether 'open spaces' are increasingly getting reduced or dominated by a specific set of intermediaries like institutional organisations, civil society organisations, community groups/networks supported by international donors and groups of activists, especially in urban India. These questions can be looked at in future research.

Intermediaries, thus in all three countries intervened at provincial, national and international levels to articulate the interests of citizens. These efforts certainly created noise at appropriate level, which either led to corrective measures by the state or created congenial environment for negotiation with the government.

Table 2.2

Levels of Intermediation

No.	*Case Studies*	*Local Level*	*State and National Level*	*International Level*
1.	Citizen Leadership in Cape Town: A Tale of Three Communities (Langa and Green Point, Cape Town, South Africa)	Formation of GPCA to fight for open spaces; Joe Slovo Task Team and COLACOCO for housing (registered organisations leading the movement). These bodies were local coalitions of social forces.	Joe Slovo struggle was included in the Western Cape Chapter of the Anti-Evictions Campaign and collaboration with Abahlali base-Mjondolo (a national NGO) Joe Slovo Task Team also formed alliances with community organisations in Khayelitsha	Joe Slovo Task Team formed an alliance with Slum Dwellers International (SDI)
2.	Using Participatory Spaces for Improving Housing and Urban Services: Diadema, São Paulo, Brazil	Associations like 'Our Fight Our Land', Freedom Pro-Housing Association, East Association etc., came together in the form of the Association of Slum Inhabitants (registered organisations leading the movement)	Demands were also taken up by national movements like Housing Movements Union and Popular Movements Central	
3.	Improving Urban Services through Citizens' Action (Dharamshala, Himachal Pradesh, India)	Local community based organisations came together to launch the campaign for sanitation like the Gamru Youth Brigade Club	Local community based organisations formed coalitions with Participatory Research in Asia (PRIA) to put up their demands	
4.	Women Leaders and Intermediary Organisations in Khayelitsha, South Africa	No local level coalitions. Citizens demands mainly discussed in 'invited spaces' like street committees, ward development forums, city councils, etc.		
5.	Engaging Community in Rehabilitation and Reconstruction Planning (Bhachau Town, Gujarat, India)	Junavada Punarvasan Evam Vikas Samiti, Navagam Vikas Samiti and Bhuj Development Council were the community organisations (social coalition representing the demands of the community)	UNNATI (NGO) brought all the community organisations on a common platform	

contd...

...contd...

No.	Case Studies	Local Level	State and National Level	International Level
6.	Reclaiming Participatory Spaces in Health: A Study of Health Movement (São Paulo, Brazil)	Number of community based organisations like women's community, health pastorals, clubs of mothers, Societies of Neighbourhood's Friends/Neighbourhood Associations, CEBs, Association of Slum Inhabitants took up health related demands of the people	These community organisations organised themselves under the umbrella of the Union of the Popular Health Movements of São Paulo (UMPS) in 1997 for better coordination between intermediaries, utilisation of institutional spaces of participation (like public councils) and intensive dialogue with the Executive	
7.	Using Right to Information for Improving Public Distribution System and Basic Infrastructure in Delhi, India	Resident Welfare Associations and community based organisations filed RTI applications and litigation. Parivaratan played a leading role in the mobilisation of RWAs and citizens in the area and brought them on a common platform	Linkages were established with National Campaign for Promotion of Right to Information (NCPRI), a national body spearheading the RTI campaign in India	

The question of the nature of intermediation can be analysed in the context of national and international donor agencies influencing the agenda of intermediaries' and the co-option of intermediaries by the state. With regard to the issue of national and international donor agencies influencing the agenda of intermediaries, we find that the Joe Slovo movement (South Africa), UMPS (Brazil), PRIA, UNNATI (India) were funded by national and international donors. Yet, there were no instances of national and international donors influencing the agenda of these agencies or the citizens' struggle in these locations. However, this is an important issue in the developing and underdeveloped countries where huge amounts of money flow in through international donors. The issue of co-option has been taken up in the following section.

Intermediaries' Interface with the State

Intermediaries have a complex and intricate relationship with the State which can be examined along the dimensions of petitions/ representations, dialogues/negotiations and confrontation (Table 2.3). An examination of this aspect in the case studies also tells us that this relationship cannot always be compartmentalised into fixed categories as intermediaries may use all these dimensions in one struggle in order to exact accountability from the state. These dimensions are more a matter of strategy rather than choice for intermediaries, which are primarily determined by the social-political context. Let us now see how the intermediaries' interfaced with the state.

Table 2.3

Intermediaries' Interface with the State

No.	*Case Studies*	*Petitions/ Representations*	*Dialogues/ Negotiations*	*Confrontations*
1.	Citizen Leadership in Cape Town: A Tale of Three Communities (Langa and Green Point, Cape Town, South Africa)	GPCA made representations to the Government of the City of Cape Town COLACOCO petitioned to senior administrators and political leaders	GPCA, COLACOCO and Joe Slovo Task Team used dialogues, meetings to negotiate with the city government and provincial government about their demands	Joe Slovo Task Team led a march to parliament and handed over a memorandum to the National Minister for Housing. They even blockaded the highway GPCA and Joe Slovo Task Team filed law suits
2.	Using Participatory Spaces for Improving Housing and Urban Services: Diadema, São Paulo, Brazil	Some community based organisations like 'Our Fight Our Land', East Association and West Association made representations to the municipal government for improvement in services.	Citizens participated in the designing of the Master Plan Meetings and conferences were organised by the Ministry of Cities for deliberating on these issues Municipal government convened workshops to explain areas of social interest housing Deliberations in Participatory Budget prioritised housing which led to an increase in allocations for housing	Associations camped in front of CDHU headquarters for release of resources for construction

contd...

...contd...

No.	*Case Studies*	*Petitions/ Representations*	*Dialogues/ Negotiations*	*Confrontations*
3.	Improving Urban Services through Citizens' Action (Dharamshala, Himachal Pradesh, India)	Community organisations made representations to the district administration	PRIA with participation from citizens, local CSOs in collaboration with municipal councils (Dharamshala and Kangra) prepares the voluntary disclosure document and district project report of solid waste management	
4.	Women Leaders and Intermediary Organisations in Khayelitsha, South Africa	Women made their demands through street committees, which took it up with SANCO. KDF also acted on behalf of the community.	Concerns of citizens are taken up in ward development forums and City Councils with councillors.	Women resorted to protests and marches when their demands were not addressed
5.	Engaging Community in Rehabilitation and Reconstruction Planning (Bhachau Town, Gujarat, India)	*Falia* (cluster) committees represented the demands of the community. Community organisations (Junavada Punarvasan Evam Vikas Samiti, Navagam Vikas Samiti) and citizen leaders made representations to the government	Multistakeholder consultations were organised by UNNATI. Citizen Support Cell provided a platform for collaboration between the government and citizens	
6.	Reclaiming Participatory Spaces in Health: A Study of Health Movement (São Paulo, Brazil)		Organic Law of Health created a decentralised health system in São Paulo which provided institutional spaces for citizens' participation	UMPS adopted the methods of campaigns and protests for the protection of participatory spaces
7.	Using Right to Information for Improving Public Distribution System and Basic Infrastructure in Delhi, India	Citizens demanded all the official records of food distribution system from the government Citizens made representations to Chief Minister of Delhi	Public hearing on development works especially sewer lines, roads, toilets was organised by Parivartan	Community led by Parivartan held a protest march to the Food Commissioner's office demanding disclosure of food records held by the Food Department. Parivartan filed public interest litigations in Delhi High Court for disclosure of all records related to development works in Sundarnagari

As can be seen from Table 2.3, the COLACOCO in Langa, South Africa used petitions and consultative meetings to put forward the demands for housing to senior government officers and political leaders. When these measures failed to elicit any positive outcomes, they resorted to protest marches and, in one case, some militant youths also attacked the resettlement houses. Similarly, the Joe Slovo Task Team, which was resisting eviction from the Joe Slovo informal settlement to Delft, which was 15 kilometres away, sent memorandums to the government, organised protest marches to the National Parliament and even blocked the arterial highway (N2) to the airport. The blockade turned violent, resulting in several people getting injured. The government rejected all their demands and acquired a court order to evict them from Joe Slovo. This court order was further challenged in the Constitutional court by the Joe Slovo Task Team with the help of the Legal Resource Centre, University of Western Cape and the court stayed the eviction. So we see that in both the locations, dialogue, negotiation, informal meetings between intermediaries and the state failed to yield results, which led the community to take direct action and the state to resort to coercive action. The issue, however, could not be resolved.

In Khayelitsha, intermediaries like SANCO and KDF held regular dialogues and consultations with elected representatives and the local government, which however did not seem to satisfy the community as they resorted to violent protests from time to time. Intermediaries in the Green Point struggle used media and web-based debates to put pressure on the government, which resulted in substantial victories in negotiations. It is difficult to say whether intermediaries deliberately engage in violent protests or the movement just slips out of their control when dialogue fails to yield results.

Intermediaries in India, especially in Bhachau and Dharamshala, engaged with the state through dialogue, representations, petitions, etc. Multistakeholder dialogues, which were organised in Bhachau and Dharamshala, for urban planning provided the community face-to-face interaction with officials. It was a forum where ideas were exchanged in a non-threatening environment, resulting in greater sensitivity among officials towards people's demands. Another forum, which proved to be effective, was the Citizen Support Cell[15] in Bhachau, Gujarat, where people could interact with officials on issues concerning them.

However, the methods of representations, face-to-face meetings etc., failed to yield results in Delhi. The officers in Government of Delhi refused to accept RTI applications for allowing access to government information. Finding all the formal channels closed, Parivartan with support of 300 people, blocked the offices of the Department of Food, closing all entry and exit points, virtually locking up officers inside the building. This direct action forced the officers to accept the applications, which was an indication to other government departments that it was their duty to accept RTI applications. In another location in Delhi, Parivartan held public hearings where a large number of officers, journalists, activists, elected representatives and people gathered to discuss the huge diversion of funds from infrastructure development projects in a locality. It helped in directly exposing corruption among government officers, which forced the state to take action. So the nature of engagement with the state in India was largely through petition and negotiation and confrontation was adopted when the state simply refused to follow the law.

In Diadema, intermediaries tried to use public councils and participatory budgeting to put forward the concerns of the people and to get more resources from the state. All their efforts were directed at revitalising democratic spaces where the dialogue between the government, community and intermediaries could take place. Apart from these instances of the effective participation by citizens, there were also incidences of confrontation with the state. In 1997, when the demands of people related to housing were not being heard by the state, they forcibly occupied estates and empty houses. The state showing its might reduced the powers of the FUMAPIS council and other consultative bodies. It took a long time to give back the powers to these bodies and reactivate them. So confrontation with the state often led to the suspension of democratic spaces, thereby showing unequal relations between the state and citizens and it proved to be a constraint in the participation of citizens.

15. The Citizen Support Cell was established in Bhachau in collaboration with the municipality. It acted as a knowledge centre which provided information on various government programmes, legislations, rules and procedures. It advised the poor and marginalised about the procedures of approaching the government.

Similarly, in the east zone of São Paulo, intermediaries made tremendous efforts to protect these participatory spaces. These participatory spaces like public councils (PCs)[16] had been created by the Workers' Party (*Partido dos Trabalhadores*) and became dysfunctional when the opposition party came to power. The opposition party never trusted the intermediaries, as they were seen to be close to the Workers' Party. Hence, when the opposition parties formed the local government they tried to neglect or even deny all the demands of the intermediaries. As a result, all the intermediaries' efforts were directed towards reinstating the Workers' Party in power. It eventually led to the politicisation of the 'third realm'.[17] In Brazil, close relationships between intermediaries and the Workers' Party had pushed the intermediaries into political conflicts thereby raising questions about their autonomy. The intermediaries, however, faced a difficult choice as their struggles for participatory spaces were identified with the Workers' Party.

Association of intermediaries with political parties or erstwhile movements was an important issue, which most intermediaries' in South Africa and Brazil continuously grappled with. In the new democracy of South Africa, the linkages between intermediaries and the main political party, the African National Congress (ANC), which was in the forefront of the anti-apartheid struggle, are quite strong. For example, mobilisation in Khayelitsha was done by street committees who were part of the organising structure of SANCO, an erstwhile civic organisation of the ANC. Though SANCO claims to be independent of ANC, it has several members who are also members of the ANC. Thus, the strong presence of the ANC still permeates 'open and invited spaces' in South Africa and intermediaries completely independent of political parties are few in number.

In contrast to COLACOCO, whose agenda was influenced by the senior leaders of ANC, the then ruling party in South Africa, the Joe Slovo Task Team kept its distance from ANC, which helped them in bargaining hard with the state. In India, the intermediaries had no association with

16. PCs are elected bodies from civil society. PCs are organised sectorally which means there is one PC for each sector for example education, health, housing etc. PCs are established by the municipality under the Central Law. They play an advisory role in planning and monitoring of the Executive.
17. Neera Chandhoke defines civil society as the third realm to be differentiated from economy and the State. See Chandhoke (2004): 239.

the political parties; in fact they maintained complete political neutrality during the course of the movement. The leaders of intermediaries believed that closeness to any political party would get them into unnecessary political battles and the demands of the citizens could be interpreted as 'nuisance' or 'tactics' of the opposition parties by the ruling parties. Not only the intermediaries maintained distance from the political parties but also the citizens who participated in the struggle kept distance from them, which was quite different from South Africa and Brazil where members of political parties participated in the movement.

The implication of close association of intermediaries with the political parties was both positive and negative. In Langa, the ANC influenced the agenda of the movement thereby completely deviating the demands of the people. In health movement of Brazil, citizens felt that close association of movement with Worker's Party closed all the doors of interaction with the parties in power. The movement often moved away from its objectives and got increasingly trapped in the battle between two political parties. However, it is worth noting that the demands of citizens regarding health services, activation of participatory spaces and hospitals were fulfilled only when Worker's Party came to power.

Similarly, in Khayelitsha, SANCO was able to solve problems of unemployment, inadequate housing, sanitation, water and lack of care of HIV/AIDs orphans to some extent due to close association with the ruling political party, ANC. While, the Green Point struggle in Cape Town was able to gain substantial concessions from the government as it maintained distance from the political parties. Two major political parties of South Africa, Democratic Alliance (ruling party in Cape Town) and ANC (ruling party at national level) tried hard to persuade GPCA to withdraw its demand as construction of FIFA 2010 stadium in the city was getting delayed but leaders refused to give in. Close association of GPCA with any of the political parties would have certainly compromised the demands as all the political parties were in consensus for making the stadium at any cost as they believed that 'nation's prestige' was at stake. The distance with the political parties in this case helped in maintaining the autonomy of the movement.

Thus, we find that in South Africa and Brazil, the allegiance of intermediaries with the political parties is still quite strong. In South

Africa, street committees have not been able to shake off their linkages with the ANC, while grassroots organisations in Brazil are still organically linked to the Left parties. In contrast to Brazil and South Africa, the relationship between the intermediaries and the political parties in India has ruptured and they do not trust each other. We can thus say that the nature of intermediation varied across the three countries and it is quite difficult for the intermediaries to completely break off from the past and take politically neutral position in new democracies. However, the intermediaries have to guard against erosion of their autonomy by the political parties.

Another important issue is the co-option of intermediaries by the state. Evidence of co-option could not be found in any of the seven case studies but this is an issue, which definitely affects some intermediaries in the three countries.

The case studies show that the 'might' of the state is difficult to be challenged unless the intermediaries build partnerships or coalitions, not only inside the country but also outside. The engagement of intermediaries with the state in Brazil, India and South Africa witnessed tremendous complexities as the strategies oscillated between petition and negotiation to confrontation. The permeation of boundaries between political parties and intermediaries, especially in South Africa and Brazil, further entangled this engagement. Despite these challenges, the intermediaries' struggle led to the provision of basic rights like housing, health and food for the people and the strengthening of participatory spaces, thereby ensuring the accountability of the state.

III

Citizen Leadership

Leadership in the movement, in citizens' initiatives and in intermediaries' organisations has been a crucial issue as they play an important role in educating and mobilising the citizens in the struggle for entitlements and rights. In the case studies, we find a variety of leaders who differ in terms of education, resources, their affiliation to political parties, class, gender and ethnicity etc. These differences proved to be quite critical in mobilisation drives, media coverage, internet campaigns, collaboration with national and international networks and negotiation with the government. Leadership also determined nature and direction of struggle. In this section, we would be going beyond the conventional leadership issues like political and elected and take up the issue of citizen leadership. It would be probed with the questions like, how do citizen leaders emerge. How are they nurtured? What is the role played by citizen leaders in ensuring democratic accountability? What is the dynamics of citizen-governance interface that empowers (or otherwise) citizen leadership? What kind of ambiguities, constraints and conflicts are encountered in exercising citizen leadership?

Making of Citizen Leaders

Before discussing these questions, it would be pertinent to understand the meaning of citizen leaders. Citizen leaders also referred to as active citizens, are those citizens from the community, who undertake activities individually or collectively to seek public solutions to lack of citizenship rights and legal entitlements.[18] For seeking solutions to public problems, they actively engage the community by motivating and influencing them to bring in positive social change in society. Citizen leaders help in fulfilling the needs of their communities through their cooperation and credibility. Citizen leadership is also exercised when active citizens enable other citizens to act, when they promote civic activism in society and polity. Thus, citizen leadership is about people being able to speak out and shape services for individual benefit and for public good. The citizen rights and basic services are demanded from the state, which makes citizen leaders act as bridges between citizens and the state. The endeavour of citizen leaders is to build a 'good society' and promote 'public good'.

One question which requires discussion here is, how citizen leaders are distinct from the political leaders, religious leaders, caste/kinship leaders and spiritual leaders. Political leaders seek political power, so their mobilisation strategies have objective of nurturing political constituency for the purpose. While the religious leaders and caste/kinship leaders mobilise

---

18. See Houtzager *et al.* (2007): 18.

people around a certain identity and try to protect the interests of particular religious and caste/kinship groups. These leaders might operate in completely exclusive sphere avoiding any interface with other religious, caste/kinship groups. The spiritual leaders might have religious overtones but are primarily guided by the objective of taking their followers to emancipation. In contrast to these leaders, citizen leaders are engaged with citizenship and development issues (efficient delivery of government programmes, conflict resolution, peace building etc.). For promoting public good, citizen leaders mobilise poor and marginalised for collective action for demanding equity and justice in the society; they amplify the voice of the community at the appropriate level and facilitate engagements with the government institutions for making development processes inclusive. The role of citizen leaders would be further probed in the case studies of the three countries.

What makes citizen leaders so critical in the three countries?, is the question which should be taken first for discussion. The citizens in India, Brazil and South Africa perceive the political leaders to be self-serving and the concerns of citizens are not always their topmost priority. This makes representation of peoples' concerns to the state extremely difficult. Even though institutional spaces for participation like local bodies (India), public councils, participatory budgeting (Brazil), street committees, ward development forum (South Africa) have been established in these three countries; social, cultural, racial and economic inequalities, extreme poverty, illiteracy and poor awareness restrict people from participating in these institutions. Further, the government institutions have become inaccessible to the common man as they find it extremely difficult to get information about government welfare schemes and there is indefinite delay in the provision of basic services and the quality of services continues to be very poor. These conditions necessitate the emergence of citizen leaders, who can mobilise, educate and organise the community and seek solutions to the problems through individual or collective action. Citizen leaders, thus, act as a bridge between the people and the state, pressuring the government to take action.

Another question, which is linked to the issue, is how do citizen leaders emerge? The case studies of the health and housing movement in Brazil, RTI in India and housing movement in South Africa demonstrate that the emergence of citizen leaders is occasioned by specific socio-economic conditions. In Langa, South Africa, a retired school principal was elected as leader of COLACOCO, an organisation of backyard dwellers by the people out of respect for the position of the teacher. Office bearers were also elected as per the procedures of the organisations. In COLACOCO, respect for the position influenced the election of leaders, while the leaders of the Joe Slovo Task Team were elected due to their anti-apartheid background and experience of many struggles. They were elected by the community as they could actively take up the demands for housing. The GPCA, South Africa had educated and professional people as its leaders. For example, a retired lawyer was elected as their leader. This struggle witnessed a slightly different pattern of leadership emergence as a highly educated group of people came together for a cause and they decided to work together and they gained knowledge through mutual learning. Lawyers, software professionals and media persons came together and developed web pages, press briefs etc., which helped the leaders in effectively presenting the demands.

The leaders of the housing and health movement in Brazil and the RTI movement in Delhi were from the community, which had been facing problems of housing, health and urban services for a long time. In the case studies from Brazil, the leaders were mostly women as their husbands went out to work and they had to bear the brunt of the water, health and housing issues. These women leaders were provided support and guidance by the trade unions and Left political parties, as Diadema and São Paulo were a hotbed of labour and Left movements. So the experiences of trade union and Left leaders in interface, negotiations and confrontation with the state were quite useful for the women leaders. Even the state agencies played the role of mobilisers and educators in the housing movement. In *favela* urbanisation, they helped in organising inhabitant commissions and educated them on the importance of land regularisation. They also explained the implications of the Areas of Special Social Interest (AEIS) urban policy through workshops and community meetings, which helped in focussing the community's demand for housing. In contrast, the state did not take an interest in the mobilisation and education of RTI in Delhi, this role was taken up by the people based organisation—Parivartan.

In all the above examples, we find that citizen leaders 'learnt by practice', which means that they gained knowledge by participation in the movement, support from intermediary organisations like trade unions and NGOs, collaborations with national and international actors and interface with the state. It is important to point out here that the learning of citizen leaders in all the above instances was a gradual process and they acquired knowledge as the movement progressed.

The pattern of leadership emergence and learning in Bhachau and Dharamshala (India) was different. In these locations, citizen leaders learnt through the structured training programmes, exposure visits and continuous support. The structured training programmes mainly focussed on the role of leaders, motivational stories, leaders as the change agents and local issues, which required action. The citizen leaders of Bhachau, which had been devastated by the earthquake, were trained in the monitoring of rehabilitation programmes and identification of gaps in development plans. The exposure visits to locations of good practices motivated them to replicate them in their areas. For example, citizen leaders of Dharamshala were taken to Pithoragarh, a nearby town where community groups had taken excellent initiatives for managing solid waste.

Citizen leaders thus built their capacity through various means. Agencies, which built their capacity also varied; they were trade unions, NGOs, community based organisations, political parties and even the state. The pace of learning through structured short duration capacity building programmes was faster, while learning processes taking place through interactions and mutual sharing moved at a slightly slower pace. Despite these variations in context, the citizen leaders tried to solve the problems faced by the community and ensure their rights and entitlements. They actively engaged with the community, motivating them to demand accountability from the state.

Role of Citizen Leaders

Citizen leaders in the case studies primarily took up the role of mobilising citizens for collective action. Citizens belonging to mainly disadvantaged classes and communities did not have the wherewithal to question the state, hence collective action for raising the voice was necessary. The purpose of collective action ranged from formation of citizens' collectives and articulation of the voice of the communities. In addition, they also assumed important role in engagement with government institutions, which involved encouraging, educating and capacity building of the citizens to monitor the government departments, to pressurise for making their programmes inclusive and negotiate for getting access to entitlements and public resources.[19] So the role of citizen leaders can be categorised along two dimensions, firstly as facilitators of mobilisation and secondly as actors in engagement with the state.

Facilitators of Mobilisation

In Dharamshala, citizen leaders mobilised the community around the issues of sanitation and urban services and facilitated them in the formation of ward committees (citizen groups at sub-city level). In Delhi, the leaders went house to house to mobilise citizens for transparency in functioning of Food & Supplies Department in Delhi and provided handholding support to the citizens in filing RTI applications.

In Brazil, the majority of citizen leaders in the housing and health movement were women. In Diadema, for example, the leaders were the wives of industrial workers who had settled in the public spaces in the city. Forced by the poor living conditions and quality of water, informal houses mostly shanties with no sanitation facilities and no sewage, the women came forward to demand an improvement in urban services and housing from the government. Their husbands being too busy earning their livelihood did not have time to be part of the struggle, which however, provided women the space to take on the leadership role. The women of Diadema took up the challenge and carried out excellent mobilisation drives. They went from house to house, contacted people on telephones, convened community meetings and distributed pamphlets to make people aware of the issue. Emphasising the role of the women in the housing movement, Vera, President of the association called 'Our Fight, Our Land', said that, 'women were natural leaders'. Adverse conditions like poor quality of water, lack of electricity and surviving in informal settlements or

19. Bandyopadhyay (2002): 20-24.

shanties had compelled women to raise and address these issues. Other leaders of the association said, 'Women have a determined and strong personality, which contributed to their becoming good leaders.' In their interviews, they never reflected that gender was a hindering factor in leading the communities.

The citizen leaders of the east zone of São Paulo were mostly women and they also belonged to the poor class who had been denied access to health services for years. The citizen leaders were mostly invisible but played a very crucial role in the mobilisation and organisation of people for marches and protests when the institutional spaces of participation like health councils and PB were stalled by the Paulo Maluf and Celso Pitta regime. The reforms in health administration had taken a long time to be implemented despite the launch of the Unified Health System (*Sistema Únicode Saúde,* SUS), which recognised health as the right of all citizens and decentralised the health system in Brazil in 1988. The relentless struggle by the citizen leaders backed by huge public support not only led to the reclaiming of participatory spaces provided by SUS but also the sanction of hospital construction in the PB in 2007. Citizen leaders, thus educated, build capacity and motivate citizens for collective action, which put pressure on the state to listen and act on the demands of the citizens.

Actors in Engagement with the State

As discussed earlier, citizen leaders engaged with the state through different methods *viz*., representations, pressurising by raising issues in media, monitoring the government programmes and negotiating with the government. In Dharamshala, a citizen leader, Colonel (retired) M.G. Sharma highlighted the poor condition of streetlights and water quality in the media, which led to a substantial improvement in both the services. Another leader acting individually filed about 50 RTI applications and tried to expose the corruption in the government departments and the misuse of forest land by urban departments in the Dharamshala city. The youth leaders instead of asking the government agencies to clear garbage from their locality formed the 'Green Team', which cleaned garbage from the streets on a daily basis. Similarly, in Delhi especially in middle class and rich colonies, the leaders sometimes acted in unison with RWAs (sometimes individually), used RTI to expose corruption in infrastructure projects. However, the leaders in the poorer colonies of Delhi acted with the community and organisations to file RTI applications to expose corruption in the PDS.

The leaders of cluster committees in the Bhachau city took up a monitoring role in the government's relief and rehabilitation programme and facilitated citizens' feedback on the city's development plan. These inputs in the government's programme were shared in consultative meetings or through representation with the government, which made the plans inclusive and led to better implementation of government programmes. The citizen leader, Ismail bhai from Bhachau, despite being a very poor tea stall owner acted as a disseminator of information about earthquake relief and rehabilitation offered by the government which improved accessibility of citizens to entitlements. In housing movement (Brazil), the citizen leaders also engaged with members of public councils, made representations to government departments and created pressure to prioritise housing in the PB.

Ronaldo Lacerda, a leader of the housing movement in Diadema said that initially the motivation was to fight for better living conditions but later it was realised that the problems of water, electricity, houses, urban services etc., need to be looked at holistically and should be taken up jointly with other regions. This perspective helped him in working closely with leaders of other regions and negotiating with the government for improvement in government services.

Thus, citizen leaders not only educated and motivated the citizens but also encouraged them to come to the forefront and engage with the state. Adopting different methods of engagement, they were able to voice the concerns of citizens at the appropriate level in the government thereby pressurising it to respond. They faced numerous dilemmas and conflicts in engaging with the state, which has been taken up for discussion in the next section.

Dilemma and Conflicts Encountered by Citizen Leaders

Citizen leaders in the three countries encountered various dilemmas and conflicts while taking up the cause of the people. They faced the dilemma of whether to be associated with the political parties or not, while the conflicts were related to social constructs, threats and poverty. It would be interesting to discuss, how the citizen leaders tackled the dilemmas and conflicts in the three countries.

In Delhi, the role as citizen leaders was quite risky as it entailed threats, physical attacks and even false police complaints. Poverty also weakened them at times as making several rounds of government offices for information meant the loss of daily wages and they also became tired of the daily struggle and protests. The prolonged struggle led to their abandoning the social audit process mid-way in Delhi just on the assurance of the PDS shopkeepers. It shows the constraints faced by citizen leaders in the RTI movement in Delhi.

The case studies from India also demonstrated that some of the leaders were very poor but undeterred by the threats, they came forward, mobilised and guided the community in their struggle for entitlements. The citizen leaders of Diadema, as seen in case study of Delhi were poor but they overcame this constraint to put up their demands collectively.

The citizen leaders in Brazil also faced slightly different challenge as they differed with the high profile leaders of UMPS, which was leading the movement for reforms in the health system in São Paulo. The leaders of UMPS were oriented to the Left and believed that confrontation and the removal of the existing municipal government were the only solutions to the stalling of all health reform in the east zone. The citizen leaders felt that sticking to a particular ideology closed all the spaces of negotiation with the government and led to a deadlock. Instead of focussing on continuous confrontation, they advocated dialogue and negotiations with the government. In South Africa especially at Langa, the citizen leaders had political affiliations with the ANC, which proved to be a constraint in negotiations with the government. The leader of COLACOCO, a retired school teacher, adopted the strategy of limited protest and trusted the assurances of the ANC's senior leaders. In the process, he compromised the independence of the housing movement and the housing rights of the people of Langa remained a distant dream. The ideological orientation hindered taking forward the agenda of the citizens.

In Joe Slovo, another site for the housing movement, the leaders maintained a distance from political parties, which helped in devising strategies according to the demands of the situation. The leaders who had the experience of the anti-apartheid struggle abandoned consultative mechanisms with the government as it failed to yield results and resorted to protests to press for their demands. The citizen leaders of Green Point being professionals had no affiliation with any of the political parties; in fact, they did not want to align themselves with any of the political parties and put up their demands independently. They used litigation in court and media and Internet campaigns to negotiate with the government, which helped them in getting substantial concessions from the government.

In all the cases mentioned above, the citizen leaders either maintained a distance from political parties or associated with them intensely. The complexity of the issue of political affiliation is revealed in the case study of Khayelitsha, where citizen leaders were trying to maintain a balance between their political affiliation and their responsibilities as citizen leaders. The leaders of SANCO had close associations with the ANC with one citizen leader saying that, 'SANCO is 100 percent ANC'. SANCO's close affiliation with ANC compromised their independence and may be the reason for their lack of tolerance for other political parties. Despite SANCO's overt political agenda, people in Khayelitsha felt that the leaders of the organisation were able to resolve the issues of criminality, unemployment, houses and care for HIV/AIDS orphans etc. Citizen leaders also negotiated with the government departments for getting entitlements for the people. On the other hand, citizen leaders of another civic organisation KDF tried to remain apolitical while continuing civic work among the community. The leaders of KDF, however, said that they were not politically neutral, which they believed was quite impossible in the area. In spite of political affiliations, they looked upon themselves as 'the agents of the people' and their work was appreciated by the people. In this township, citizen leaders found it quite difficult to completely detach themselves from the political parties, yet they continued to fight for the rights and entitlements of the people.

The constraints and conflicts faced by citizen leaders in India, South Africa and Brazil had some commonalities and some stark differences. Poverty and physical threats were the main commonalities. Endemic poverty hindered mobilisation and politicisation of the communities; also threats by vested interests was always looming large over the heads of citizen leaders in all the three countries. However, the citizen leaders undeterred by the physical attacks and threats overcame the constraints of poverty to amplify the voice of the community. Their role as mobilisers, educators and organisers of the communities, as the nodal point for information dissemination and being the key person in negotiations with the state was very critical in the struggle and it helped in protecting the rights of the people.

The differences were mainly seen in gender composition and political affiliations of the leadership in the three countries. The predominance of women citizen leaders in Khayelitsha (South Africa), Diadema and east zone of São Paulo (Brazil) was an important point of difference from the other struggles in South Africa and India. The emergence of women leaders in these locations was occasioned by poor living conditions, unavailability of their husbands who were industrial workers (not having enough time) and the support provided by intermediary organisations like trade unions, NGOs and community based organisations. They were the backbone of the movement in Khayelitsha, Diadema and east zone of São Paulo.

Another important point of difference was the degree of political affiliation of citizen leaders in the three countries. In most of the examples of Brazil and South Africa, we find that citizen leaders were affiliated to erstwhile movements and political parties. In the new democracies of South Africa and Brazil, it was quite difficult for them to completely detach themselves from the political parties, as they had been closely associated with these political parties in independent struggles before these countries declared themselves democracies. While in India, the detachment of citizen leaders from political parties was to the extent that citizen leaders did not trust them. We really do not know whether the affiliation of citizen leaders to political parties is desirable or not but from the examples in the case studies, it can be said that in some instances it helped in advancing the rights of the people and in other instances, it compromised the cause of the people. The dilemma of affiliation with the political streams or parties by the citizen leaders in new democracies would continue to be a challenge in the future. Despite these differences in approaches, the citizen leaders were able to protect the rights of the people and advance accountability in the governance systems in the three countries.

IV

Enhancing Accountability

The endeavour of all the actors was to ensure accountability of the state through petitions, representations, negotiations and protests. Before we delve into the issue of the success or failure of these citizens' initiatives, it would be useful to unpack the dimensions by which we are going to assess accountability. The dimensions[20] are:

1. Changes in policies—it includes the formulation of new policies, regulatory mechanisms, making the policies inclusive and reform in implementation of policies.
2. Changes in practices—it includes improved transparency, increased and equitable access to services, new mechanisms of accountability and actions on citizens' voices.
3. Changing notion of citizenship and rights among the marginalised—it includes inclusive processes of participation especially of the poor, women and ethnic groups, 'role of citizens in monitoring the enforcement of rights and demanding public scrutiny and transparency'[21], redressal of unequal power relations between the state and lesser citizens (marginalised), greater consciousness of citizenship and rights among the marginalised.

These dimensions would however depend upon the political context of the locations. Research has shown that it is more difficult to undertake changes in policies in the autocratic political system than in the democratic political system. Autocratic political system is closed and does not offer opportunities for representation, aggregation of interests in society, participatory spaces for the citizens, communication and accessibility to policymaking processes. Political volatility and violent conflicts (ethnic, political etc.) are some of the other variables which constrain the efforts of policy change. Democratic system on the other hand does provide freedom

---

20. The two dimensions—changes in policies and changes in practices—have been used in Foresti *et al.* (2007): 19.
21. Gaventa *et al.* (2002): 9.

for participation in the policymaking process. It also offers academic freedom, media freedom, spaces for participation for weaker sections of society and freedom to get organised for collective action etc., which makes policymaking processes accessible to citizens.[22]

The link between 'changes in policies' and 'changes in practices' is very crucial as translation of policies into practice determines whether citizens have access to rights and entitlements. 'Changes in practices' depend on the capacity and resources of institutions, which are given the responsibility of implementing policies. Often, policies cannot be implemented, as bureaucrats manning the institutions have not been adequately trained or given sufficient time and information to implement policies.[23] Threat of losing the privileges of the existing system also acts as a constraint for implementing policies. Removal of these inadequacies and pressure from people for accountability can go a long way in making the institutions effective. It is important to point out here that sometimes 'changes in practices' like demonstration projects, pilot projects etc., can build a strong case for 'changes in policies'; thus practices can also precede 'changes in policies' in the context where policymaking is complex and difficult exercise.

The last dimension of accountability changing notion of citizenship and rights among the marginalised might be the output of first two dimensions as citizens engage with the state for policies and programmes for access to the entitlements and rights. It might also be the result of legacy of struggle for rights in a context where citizens have historically resisted the imposition of policies by the state. It provides impetus to them to continuously engage with state, which not only challenges its power but also becomes the empowering process.

The choices of strategies of intermediaries and citizen leaders for bringing about changes in any of the three dimensions, thus, depended upon the political and institutional context and legacy of struggle for rights. Success in any of the dimensions should be considered significant as it consolidates the processes of accountability in the political system.

---

22. Julius and Cotterrell (2006): 13-20.
23. Ibid.

Changes in Policies

At first, the success of the citizens' initiatives in ensuring accountability of the state would be analysed through the prism of the first dimension i.e., changes in policies. The RTI movement in Delhi, India brought about significant changes in policies related to the disclosure of information on the PDS. The Government of Delhi yielding to citizens' pressure on transparency and accountability issued orders to the Food and Civil Supplies Department to make all the PDS records public. Under the new disclosure system, every citizen got the right to inspect official records pertaining to him/her on every Saturday at the District Food and Supply office. A system for the quick disbursal of complaints regarding the PDS was also established, which mandated that the licences of PDS shopkeepers should be cancelled with immediate effect if they were found to be diverting food grains. These policy measures brought transparency in the functioning of the PDS thereby facilitating the monitoring of PDS records by the citizens on a regular basis. It not only exposed corruption in the PDS but also deterred PDS shopkeepers and government officials from engaging in corrupt practices. Thus, the implication of the policy measure, 'official records in public domain' was tremendous for the food security of the poor.

Another important policy level change was witnessed in Bhachau, Gujarat, India where an earthquake had struck in 2001 completely destroying the city. The state government asked the Urban Department to prepare the reconstruction plan of the city, which was prepared without consultations with all stakeholders especially the poor. The result was a fragmented plan, which completely neglected the concerns of the poor and marginalised sections of society and also lacked environmental sensitivity. The plan caused considerable discontentment among the marginalised sections as dominant sections of society especially businessmen and dominant castes were able to influence the plan to protect their interests. Citizens represented their concerns through petitions, elected representatives and consultations convened by NGOs and government. These efforts resulted in modifications in the rehabilitation plan of the city, which addressed the concerns of the poor and marginalised. This policy level change was a long drawn out struggle for the people of Bhachau.

Similarly, the modification of the Master Plan of the city of Diadema, Brazil was the result of a prolonged struggle by the people of the city. The plan did not have any space for poor industrial workers who had been living in the city for nearly two decades. Living in unauthorised spaces meant that citizens did not have any facilities for water, sewage and sanitation. The city government through urban policies designated AEIS I and II and tried to construct housing units for the poor. These urban policies were to be integrated with the Master Plan, so that the dwelling units of the poor would develop holistically with other parts of the city. However, this integration was opposed by landowners and business segments who believed that it would make the city economically unsustainable. Citizens opposed these vested interests and created pressure for the integration of urban policies and the Master Plan, which ultimately paved the way for integration as well as the construction of houses for the poor in Diadema. The strong mobilisation of communities in Diadema led to the prioritisation of housing in the PB, which resulted in more resources for housing in the municipal budget. These resources helped in the completion of infrastructure projects and houses in Diadema.

The implementation of a decentralised health system under the Unified Health System in the east zone of São Paulo, Brazil was a significant milestone for the people as it aimed to provide universal and equitable health care for all. However, this reform was stalled by Paulo Maluf and Celso Pitta's regime (1993–2000) and Serra and Kassab's regime (2005-2008), who wanted to stop peoples' participation in health administration and privatised health services. These policies framed in contravention of the SUS, generated huge protests by the people who were led by the UMPS. The issue was resolved only in 2007 when a number of UMPS supported councillors were elected to the municipal councils and pushed for reforms in health administration. These reforms led to a substantial improvement in health services, the establishing of more health clinics and a big hospital in the east zone of São Paulo.

Changes in Practice

Mentioned above are some successful examples of changes in policies in the two countries. However, there were some instances where citizens were unable to bring about changes in policies but they definitely pushed some processes, which not only ensured equitable access to the services but also created new ways of ensuring accountability in governance. These are the issues, which will be discussed, in the second dimension of accountability i.e., changes in practices. In the Green Point struggle, South Africa, community mobilisation failed to stop the construction of the soccer stadium but was able to extract some concessions like recreational areas as compensation. The leaders of the movement belonging to the rich and middle class relied less on protests and demonstrations and more on litigation, internet campaigns, petitions and media briefings especially newspapers and radios to put forward their demands. They quite effectively demonstrated that there could be new ways of carrying out the campaign and influencing the state.

In the RTI movement in Delhi, citizens could not create a durable accountability mechanism for the PDS but it showed that seeking information under the RTI Act can deter PDS shopkeepers and government officials from engaging in corrupt practices. It also showed that the use of RTI by the activists with regular press briefs and media coverage can pressurise the government to take corrective measures. The examples of the use of RTI in Delhi in the PDS and infrastructure projects etc., demonstrate that the innovative use of existing legal instruments can ensure accountability of the state especially in the political context where the creation of durable accountability mechanisms takes a long time due to legislative and executive procedural complexities.

Other aspects of the second dimension of accountability *viz*., equitable access to services and actions on citizens' voices are reflected in the case studies from Delhi, Dharamshala (India), Khayelitsha (South Africa) and Diadema and the east zone of São Paulo (Brazil). With regard to equitable access to services, it was found that the RTI movement in Delhi ensured subsidised food grains to the poor, which provided food security to them. In Dharamshala, the demands related to poor quality of roads, sanitation, health services, water and sanitation were improved due to the citizens' persistent representation to the state. While the housing movement in Diadema provided houses at low prices and a clean liveable environment to the poor families, the health movement in São Paulo made health services accessible to people by establishing health clinics and a large hospital. In

Khayelitsha, citizens were able to solve the problems of care and housing for HIV/AIDS orphans, water and toilets with the active cooperation of intermediaries like SANCO and KDF. However, the change has been quite slow in this poor locality where the supply has not kept pace with the rising demand. Equitable access to all these services in the three countries was made possible after a long struggle, petitions, representations and even protests by the people in the specific contexts.

One important example of better implementation of disclosure laws could be seen in Dharamshala, India. The municipalities of Dharamshala and Kangra made an attempt to implement Section 4 of the RTI Act, thereby setting an example of best practices for improving transparency in the state. It is important to mention here that Section 4 of the RTI Act mandates every state agency to voluntarily disclose all their activities in a manual, so that citizens can get information about important functions of public institutions without asking for it. It is believed that disclosure of all information by the state agencies would check malpractices and corruption. However, the state agencies have refused to fall in line with Section 4 of RTI Act. The citizens and NGOs made several representations in order to demand and convince the municipalities of Dharamshala and Kangra for voluntary disclosure. The NGOs not only built the capacity of government departments for preparing the format for voluntary disclosure but also worked with them in preparing the voluntary disclosure document of the two municipalities. The implementation of Section 4 proved to be a model project for government departments in the state of Himachal Pradesh and removed the government departments' mental block that voluntary disclosure was a difficult task to implement. It had a cascading affect as citizens started demanding voluntary disclosures in all the governments of the province. This has the potential of making the governance system in India transparent.

Changes in Notion of Citizenship and Rights among the Marginalised

This brings us to the third dimension of accountability i.e., changing the notion of citizenship and rights among the marginalised. Citizenship has been defined by Marshall as a status bestowed by the state on the people through granting of rights.[24] Distinguishing the rights into three categories: (i) civil rights, (ii) political rights, and (iii) social rights, Marshall termed these rights positive rights, which means the right to live the life of a civilised being according to the standards provided in society.[25] In the contemporary world, the meaning of citizenship is not merely restricted to the grant of certain privileges to the citizens but, 'it entails the rights which are important to actualise citizenship'.[26] It means the use of rights to demand accountability from the state, demand justice for themselves and for fellow human beings, tolerate people who are ethically and religiously different and feel solidarity with human beings.[27] It underlines the need for participation of the citizen in the political sphere and civil society for the good of the larger community.[28] The idea of participation moves beyond 'beneficiaries' and 'users' framework to the more political idea of participation as citizens who bear both rights and responsibilities, which is also termed as participatory citizenship. It is seen as the mechanism to include the excluded in the process of development and governance.[29] We shall now analyse the case studies from the framework of participatory citizenship trying to probe the questions of the inclusion of the excluded especially poor, ethnic groups and women in the development processes and empowered communities demanding their rights from the state.

Empowered Communities Demand their Rights

The case studies from the three countries demonstrate that collectives of citizens once aware, mobilised and politicised, actively participated in the development processes. For example in Bhachau, they presented their concerns about the city development plan prepared by the government agency in multi-stakeholders dialogue and *falia* committees' meetings. They were also involved in designing houses and preparing cost estimates through regular community meetings, which were attended by technical persons from different government and non-government agencies. It helped

24. T.H. Marshall as quoted in Mohanty and Tandon (2006): 17.
25. T.H. Marshall as quoted in Heyhood (1997): 415.
26. Gaventa *et al.* (2002): 2-14.
27. World Bank (2007): 161.
28. Gaventa *et al.* (2002). *op.cit.*
29. Ibid: 2-14.

in the construction of affordable and seismically safe houses for every one in the town. The active involvement of the communities at all the stages of the project cycle made the government's city and housing plan citizen centric.

The *falia* committees were also instrumental in identifying families especially the poor who had been left out of the relief and rehabilitation programmes in earthquake hit Bhachau. The close collaboration of the *falia* committees with the government made these programmes inclusive as the distribution and monitoring of relief materials became transparent and community centric. Citizens became aware of what was being distributed and by whom and who the beneficiaries were. It helped in checking corruption in the relief and rehabilitation operations in Bhachau.

In urban India, institutional spaces for participation hardly exist, so citizens use open spaces and personal representations to demand their rights and entitlements.[30] It was seen in the case of Bhachau that a number of community based organisations were created to use the 'open' spaces. Similarly in Dharamshala and Delhi, community based organisations came into being in order to represent the interests of the poor and marginalised in development and governance. In Dharamshala, citizens especially the youth and women groups were mobilised to solve the problems related to poor sanitation and shoddy urban services. Citizens organised themselves into ward committees as per the territorial jurisdiction of their wards in order to collectively put up the demands for better urban services. The ward committees also took up the role of monitoring the urban services in order to put up their case strongly before the municipal government. Ward committees also acted as information disseminators for the urban services, the action taken by the government etc., which generated the interest of their fellow citizens towards their rights and entitlements.

The whole process engaged more and more people thereby making people conscious of citizenship rights. However, the creation of the citizens' forum at the ward level seemed to be a threat to the elected representatives

30. 73rd Amendment which set the laws of decentralised governance provides for the constitution of *gram sabhas* (village assembly) in rural India, while for urban India, no such assemblies of citizens exists. There is no institutional channel for representation of citizens' interests except through elected representatives.

of the wards and the government who questioned its legitimacy and took every effort to subvert it. Despite these constraints, ward committees have continued to operate as citizens' forums in urban locations in India.

Similarly, the youth club of a village in Dharamshala, when it failed to get the municipal government to fulfill its demand for sanitation, formed its own 'Green Team' and started collecting garbage themselves from every house. They had a 'detached relation' with the state but they soon realised that such a position could not take them very far, as they would find it difficult to construct water tanks, solve electricity problems and construct toilets for the people using their own resources. They soon abandoned this pattern of relationship with the state and started representing and negotiating their demands with the district administration. The realisation by the youth of their citizenship rights was a great achievement of the town.

In Khayelitsha, street committees represented the demands of the people to the councillors, ward forums, SANCO and KDF. Most of the time, their demands related to urban services were dealt by the government departments. In cases of delay or poor response, the street committees resorted to protests and sit-ins. In Diadema, the municipal government facilitated the formation of the inhabitant commission for resolving the problem of *favela* urbanisation and housing which also served as an intermediary between the community and municipal government. Being closer to the people, the commission enabled citizens' participation in the development process and pressurised the municipal government to approve the law, the concession of the real right to use, which provided occupancy rights to people living in the *favelas*. Further, citizens also worked closely with the government in deciding the criteria for the inclusion of families in the allotment of houses in the AEIS. Their representation in FUMAPIS council (a body consisting of officials and citizens for deciding upon and monitoring the resources for housing policies) ensured timely availability of land for the construction of houses. The council provided the space for the inclusion of excluded groups in the discussions and deliberations. Similarly in east zone of São Paulo, several citizens' collectives demanded the health rights from the municipal government and they were able to get the finances released for the construction of hospital through participatory budgeting.

The citizens' collectives like *falia* committees, inhabitant commission being closer to the people brought the excluded groups into the development process, which satisfied and empowered them as they felt that their voices were being heard and acted upon. Actives participation of citizens in these collectives not only solved the problems of urban service delivery but also established the processes through which these services could be monitored ultimately ensuring accountability of the state.

Inclusion of the Excluded especially Poor and Women

In the case studies of India, the participatory processes made the citizens especially excluded aware of their rights and entitlements but also included them in development and governance. They became members of monitoring committees, suggested modifications in city development plans and confronted and negotiated with the state in Bhachau, Delhi and Dharamshala.

In Delhi, the example of Nannu demonstrates that how poor people used RTI to get their entitlements from the government. Nannu, an uneducated and poor daily wage earner from the slum of Delhi had applied for the public distribution system card from the Food and Civil Supplies department. Being poor, he did not have the money to pay the bribe to the government officials. So he filed RTI to the department asking the reasons of delay in issuing the card. The application worked and he was given the card in two days. Nannu and several other people in Delhi saw a hope in the RTI Act as other methods of grievance redressal simply failed to solve their problems.

Similarly, several women from Delhi overcame all the constraints of patriarchal society to demand their rights. Triveni, a women living in the slums of Sundarnagari filed a RTI application to the Food and Civil Supplies Department to find out the details of food grains issued in her name. The information revealed that the food grains were being picked up in her name, while she was told by the PDS shopkeeper that he was not getting a supply of food grains from the government. When she confronted the shopkeeper with these details, she was immediately provided the food grains. This is not an isolated case study of one woman; several women filed RTI applications related to the delivery of food grains, sewage, scholarships for their children and the construction of public utilities like toilets. Santosh, a young woman citizen leader encouraged the poor especially women to file RTI applications to expose corruption in government development programmes in order to pressurise the government departments to take corrective measures. Women of this locality in Delhi, perhaps forced by the scarcity of resources and poor living conditions overcame the hurdle of patriarchy and participated in social audits, public hearings, marches and protests.

In addition, innovative participative processes like social audits and public hearings involved citizens in the exercise of demanding accountability from the state. These participatory processes gave confidence to the citizens to ask questions from the government authorities about their rights and entitlements. The state, hitherto, regarded as sacrosanct by the people began to be questioned. The participatory processes had redefined the relationship between the state and citizens where citizens became conscious of not only their rights and entitlements but also started demanding it through various public forums. They were in the forefront of protests organised at government departments. It is important to point out here that the poor people of this locality did not understand citizenship, rights, transparency and accountability in the beginning; what they understood was that the provision of food grains and urban services were the responsibilities of the state, so they put up these demands to the state. The demand for transparency and accountability in governance started with the provision of food supply and urban services but gradually the poor started looking beyond their interests to community interests and participated in the movement of transparency and accountability in India.

In Diadema also, the citizens especially poor were included at each stage of *favela* urbanisation and housing construction. The citizens' participation in *favela* organisations and housing policies had resulted in occupancy rights and a clean living environment. Manuel, a citizen of *Jardim das Praais*, said that an official address helped him to get better employment, credit from financial institutions and a guarantee against eviction. It meant that poor inhabitants would have the same rights and entitlements as other citizens. Poor citizens quite happy about the recognition of their rights and entitlements started believing that participation could improve their condition. Moreover, the participation of the poor especially women in the housing movement and the role they played in the decision-making process brought a sense of ownership among the citizens about the housing policies resulting in better and timely construction of houses.

In contrast to Diadema, the citizens in Joe Slovo, South Africa were not allowed to participate in the planning of housing policies. They were ordered by the government to shift to a new area, Delft, another temporary settlement. When all their demands for representation failed to yield results, citizens blockaded the highway to the airport, resulting in a violent confrontation with the state. This protest was followed by several consultations with various agencies of the government but the matter could not be resolved. The government thereafter acquired a government order to evict the citizens. So the participation of citizens was hardly seen at any stage of the housing project, they were treated as 'beneficiaries'. As a result there was no inclusiveness of the citizens in the housing scheme. The engagement of the state with the citizens' in the GPCA struggle was also of a similar nature, as the state granted some concessions under pressure but never encouraged the inclusion of neighbourhood groups in the process of the stadium's construction. The relationship between the state and citizens was quite adversarial and forums/spaces of interaction between the two were quite limited in Langa and Green Point, South Africa. In another case study in Brazil, "Reclaiming Participatory Spaces in Health: East Zone of São Paulo", open confrontation between the state and citizens was witnessed. The municipal government led by the mayors, Paulo Maluf and Celso Pitta (1993-2000) and Serra/Kassab (2005-2008) did not take steps to implement SUS, blocked all the spaces of participation like public health councils, PB and conferences and presented a programme, Plan of Health Attendance (PAS) which sought to privatise the health services. Citizens refused to allow the elected representatives to act against their interests, they organised huge protests in municipios, blocked the Anhanguera highway (the main highway that connects the countryside to the capital) and they continued holding civil society conferences demanding SUS and the reactivation of participatory spaces. In the forefront of these protests were large numbers of women who suffered the most as they had to take family members and children to distant hospitals, when they fell ill. So citizens fought hard for the implementation of law, which provided citizens the rights to monitor and manage health services in their locality.

In Khayelitsha, however, there were spaces of participation mainly in the form of street committees, where the concerns of the community were discussed. The citizens were informed prior to the meetings of the street committees and attendance in the meetings was quite high. The councillor of the ward, Theresa Bottoman said that the decisions were mostly taken in consensus with the community; however, she added that she took a few decisions on her own. The opportunity provided to women in the street committee meetings was a substantial departure from the past. Women in the locality pointed out that, 'women nowadays speak equally with men and young people patiently waited for their turn'. A substantial step in the direction of participation was that common issues were being discussed publicly and in a transparent manner and women were overcoming gender stereotypes and were participating in far greater numbers than before. Another positive development in the locality was the growing engagement of community leaders in local government development initiatives. They were appointed as project managers in place of private contractors. So a slow beginning was being made for the inclusion for citizens in the government's development programmes.

However, the consensus decision-making should not be taken at face value as they were likely to be influenced by vested interests and political identities of the citizens. How effective these participative processes were was difficult to assess as protests and road blocks are still quite common in Khayelitsha. Participation, thus, in the political context of South Africa has made a good beginning but political society still does not show the inclination to accommodate citizens in development processes, which results in frequent street protests and demonstrations.

Despite the variation in the scope and level of participation in the three countries, we find that citizens especially the poor have asserted their rights and entitlements. They have overcome the constraints of class, caste, ethnicity, gender etc., to make demands from the state. They have been able to revive existing mechanisms of accountability and construct new mechanisms of accountability. Though, they were not always successful in terms of results but they became aware of their rights and participatory processes which would enable them to fight further.

Conclusions

Citizens in India, Brazil and South Africa showed tremendous ingenuity in using 'invented spaces' in articulating their demands related to entitlements and rights. In fact, 'invented spaces' were used to resuscitate and expand the 'invited spaces'. Though there are several examples of both these spaces operating autonomously and being successful in improving service delivery and establishment of accountability mechanisms but the evidences also show that whenever these spaces interacted or were used complementarily, the results were achieved in short time. The importance of open spaces in democracies is underlined by the fact that 'invented spaces' lead to the creation of 'invited spaces' as not all invited spaces can be envisaged and created at a particular time. Hence, there is need to protect the invented spaces in order to strengthen democracy. The experience of use of invented spaces is especially relevant for new democracies as the institutions, which could fulfil the aspirations of citizens have still not been established in the political system. In such conditions, invented spaces are the avenues through which the demands of citizens can be articulated. That is why the experiences of invented spaces need to be shared extensively especially in new democracies.

These spaces were made vibrant and effective by intermediaries, which were primarily engaged in educating and mobilising the community. They enabled the participation of citizens in the development processes and build their capacity for engaging with the state. Though there are evidences of domination of the democratic spaces especially invited ones by the intermediaries but they stepped in when the movement started fledging or reached a deadlock in interface with the state. They also sustained the movement by taking up the cause through media campaigns, citizen report card and surveys etc., and motivated the citizens to continue the struggle. The role of intermediaries was quite critical in all the three countries in strengthening the processes of accountability of the state.

Close allegiance of intermediaries with the political parties especially in Brazil and South Africa was a cause of concern as the issues of citizens were increasingly getting caught into the web of conflicts between the political parties. On some occasions, intermediaries under the influence of political parties compromised the agenda of citizens. These kinds of threats will always loom large in new democracies where the democratic movements have been led by the political parties having close associations with the civil society organisations. The close linkages between civic organisations and political parties are difficult to sever in a short time. However, autonomous civic organisations would certainly serve the cause of citizens better as they are less likely to be compromised by the political parties and citizens' demand remains of paramount importance to them.

Citizen leaders like intermediaries played critical role in educating and mobilising the citizens. Their role has been often invisible especially in comparison to intermediaries who get highlighted in various media stories but they were the building blocks of the movement for accountability in all the three countries. Belonging mostly to poor communities, they learnt leadership skills through practice, experience sharing by trade union leaders and structured training programmes by the intermediaries. The emergence of citizen leaders had the correlation with socioeconomic and political conditions of the countries. The profile of citizen leaders had some similarities and differences across the three countries. Highly educated citizen leaders coexisted with the leaders belonging to economically poor background in most of the case studies but predominance of women citizen leaders in Brazil in comparison to India and South Africa was the significant feature of the citizens' struggle. Political affiliation of citizen leaders might be a cause of concern for the external eyes but the citizen leaders seemed to be quite comfortable with it and they never tried to hide their political affiliation especially in South Africa. Similarly, citizen leaders in Brazil had close allegiance with trade unions and left parties, while those in India steered clear of political parties. On some instances, the political affiliation benefited the citizen's struggle and in other instances, it deviated the struggle of its objectives. It is very difficult to say that political neutrality of the leaders would serve the cause of citizens especially in the political context of new democracies where linkages between citizen leaders and political parties are still very strong. We do not want to sound prescriptive by suggesting that citizen leaders should be politically neutral but they should avoid being agents of political parties and engage in building constituencies of the political parties. That would be negation of the cause of rest of the citizens who have entrusted them with leadership.

The critical role of intermediaries and citizen leadership for entitlements and rights should not undermine the role played by citizens in the struggle. They were always in the forefront whether it was invented and invited spaces. Their active participation could be seen in protest marches, sit-ins as well as in participatory budgeting, public councils and consultative meetings convened by the state. These actions resulted in inclusion of concerns of poor in the development processes and provided them significant role in monitoring and decision-making in governance. The inclusion of communities at different level of governance helped in actualising citizenship among the people in the three countries. It also redefined state-citizen relationship as the realisation gradually started setting in among the government agencies that citizens could no longer be treated as beneficiaries but as important stakeholders in the processes of governance. New democracies coming out of the authoritarian political systems where people were always treated as end-users with no role in decision-making would have a lot to learn for these experiences in the developing democracies. It also shows the actions and events that could unfold in new democracies propelled by growing realisation of rights among the citizens.

References

Bhargava, Rajeev and Helmut Reifeld (2005). *Civil Society, Public Sphere and Citizenship: Dialogue and Perceptions*. New Delhi: Sage Publication.

Bandyopadhyay, Kaustuv Kanti (2002). *Module on Role of Citizen Leadership*, New Delhi: PRIA (Unpublished).

Chandhoke, N. (2004). "The Civil and the Political in Civil Society: The Case of India", in Peter J. Burnell and Peter Lalvert (ed.), *Civil Society in Democratisation*. London: Taylor and Francis.

———. (2003). "Governance and Pluralisation of the State: Implications of Democratic Citizenship", *Economic and Political Weekly* 38(28), July 12, India.

Cornwall, Andrea and Coelho, Vera Schattan (ed.) (2007). *Spaces for Change? The Politics of Citizen Participation in New Democratic Arenas*. London: Zed Books.

Cornwall, Andrea, Jorge Romano and Alex Shankland (2008). "Brazilian Experiences of Participation and Citizenship: A Critical Look", *IDS Working Paper* 389. UK: University of Sussex.

Cornwall, Andrea (2008). *Democratising Engagement: What the UK Can Learn from International Experience*. UK: Demos.

———. (2007). "Deliberating Democracy: Scenes from a Brazilian Municipal Health Council", *IDS Working Paper* 292. UK: University of Sussex.

———. (2004). "Introduction: New Democratic Spaces? The Politics and Dynamics of Institutionalised Participation, New Democratic Spaces", *IDS Bulletin* 35(2): 1, April.

———. (2002) as cited by Gaventa, J. (2006). "Finding the Space for Change: A Power Analysis", *IDS Bulletin* 37(6).

Court, Julius and Lin Cotterrell (2006). "What Political and Institutional Context Issues Matter for Bridging Research and Policy? A Literature Review and Discussion of Data Collection Approaches", *Working Paper* 269, June. UK: Overseas Development Institute.

DRC (2006). *Building Effective States: Taking a Citizen's Perspective*. UK: Sussex, *http://www.drc-citizenship.org/docs/publications/reports/drccitizensperspective.pdf*

Dreze, J. and Amartya Sen (2002). *India: Development and Participation—The Practice of Democracy*. New Delhi and New York: Oxford University Press.

Elliott, M. Carolyn (2003). *Civil Society and Democracy—A Reader*. New Delhi: Oxford University Press, .

Foresti, Marta, Bhavna Sharma, Tammi O' Neil and Alison Evans (2007). *Evaluation of Citizens' Voice and Accountability Evaluation Framework*. London: Overseas Development Institute.

Gaventa, John (2007). "Triumph, Deficit or Contestation? Deepening the Deepening Democracy Debate", *IDS Working Paper* 264, UK: University of Sussex.

———. (2006). "Participatory Citizenship: Identity, Exclusion, Inclusion; Perspectives on Participation and Citizenship": 60.

———. (2003). *Education for Citizenship: Lessons from Paulo Freire and Myles Horton*. India: Akshar Bihar.

Gaventa, John, Alex Shankland and Joanna Howard (2002). "Making Rights Real: Exploring Citizenship, Participation and Accountability", *IDS Bulletin* 33. UK: IDS,

Gaventa, John and Camilo Valderrama (1999). "Participation, Citizenship and Local Governance", Background note prepared for workshop on *Strengthening Participation in Local Governance*, UK: Institute of Development Studies.

Gupta, Dipankar (2003). "Civil Society or The State: What Happed to Citizenship", in M. Carolyn Elliott, *Civil Society and Democracy—A Reader*, New Delhi: Oxford University Press, p.222.

Haerpfer, Christian W., Patrick Bernhagen, Ronald F. Inglehart and Christian Welzel (2009). *Democratisation*. New York: Oxford University Press.

Heyhood, Andrew (1997). *Politics*. New York: Palgrave.

Houtzager, Peter P., Arnab Acharya and Adrian Gurza Lavalle (2007). "Associations and the Exercise of Citizenship in New Democracies: Evidence from Sao Paulo and Mexico City", *IDS Working Paper* 285. UK: University of Sussex.

Kabeer, Naila (2005). *Inclusive Citizenship: Meanings and Expressions*. London & New York: Zed Books.

Knight, Barry, Hope Chigudu and Rajesh Tandon (2002). *Reviving Democracy: Citizens at the Heart of Governance*. London: Earthscan Publications Limited.

Leach, Melissa and Ian Scoones (2007). "Mobilising Citizens: Social Movements and the Politics of Knowledge", *IDS working Paper* 276, UK: University of Sussex.

Merrifeild, Juliet (1999). "Learning Citizenship", *IDS Working Paper* 158, UK: IDS; University of Sussex.

Mehta, Lyla (2007). "Somewhere Over the Rainbow? The Politics and Dilemmas of Researching Citizenship and Marginality", *IDS Working Paper* 288. UK: University of Sussex.

Mohanty, Ranjita and Rajesh Tandon (2006). *Participatory Citizenship: Identity, Exclusion and Inclusion*. New Delhi: Sage Publication.

Newell, P. and J. Wheeler (2006). "Making Accountability Count", *IDS Policy Briefing* 33. UK: University of Sussex.

Newell, Peter (ed.) (2005). *Rights, Resources and Politics of Accountability*. London & New York: Zed Books.

PRIA (2007). *Citizen Participation: Future of Governance*. India.

Tandon, Rajesh (2001). "Citizenship Participation and Accountability: A Perspective", *Innovations in Civil Society* 1(1). PRIA Publications.

Teixeira, Ana Claudia (2008). "The Challenges of the Democratic Management in Brazil", *Participation*. Brazil: Instituto Polis.

Thapan, Meenakshi (2006). "Docile Bodies, Good Citizens or Agential Subjects?: Pedagogy and Citizenship in Contemporary Society", *Economic and Political Weekly* 41(39). India, September.

World Bank (2007). "Development and Next Generation", *World Development Report*.

Section - III

Empirical Investigations

3 Citizen Leadership in Cape Town, South Africa

A Tale of Three Communities

Chris Tapscott

Background Issues

In highly differentiated societies such as South Africa, the channels for expression open to different communities to exert voice and influence decision-making are extremely varied and unequal. This chapter looks at attempts by citizens in three Cape Town communities, distinguished by race and class and leadership, to exercise their democratic rights and to redefine administrative decisions, which they perceive to adversely affect their interests. Faced with the reality that the state is generally unresponsive to demands raised through formal institutional channels (ward committees, local councillors etc.,) disaffected citizens and the organisations, which represent them have increasingly sought alternative means to express their grievances. The channels chosen have varied from among the communities, according to their social, economic and political contexts and they have differed in their effectiveness in extracting concessions from the state.

The discussion, which follows reflects on the fact that communities are able to mobilise and influence state policies (in this instance those of the local state) in the extent to which their leaders are able to capitalise on the opportunities which present themselves. As Meyer observes, 'the organisation of the polity and the positioning of various actors within it makes some strategies of influence more attractive and potentially efficacious than others. The wisdom, creativity and outcomes of activists choices—their agency—can only be understood and evaluated by looking at the political context and the rules of the game in which those choices are made—that is structure' (Meyer, 2004: 129). Before proceeding to an examination of the case studies and the different manifestations of their leadership and strategies, it is necessary to provide a brief backdrop to the contemporary space economy of metropolitan Cape Town, which forms the background to the citizen struggles under consideration.

Cape Town is the oldest urban settlement in South Africa, having been established in 1652 as a refreshment station for ships of the Dutch East India Company sailing from Europe to the East. As a sea port, Cape Town has always exhibited a more metropolitan character than other cities in the country, with a heterogeneous mix of people of European, African, Asian and people of mixed race. It has, nevertheless, always been geographically divided by race and, to a less obvious extent, by class distinctions. As a legacy of Apartheid, categories of race and class still tend to coincide. As a consequence of the rigid policies of racial segregation that were in place less than 15 years ago and notwithstanding the emergence of a black middle class, the majority of Cape Town's citizens still live in racially homogeneous suburbs. As Young observes in that regard, 'Processes that produce and reproduce residential segregation are obvious forms of social, economic and political exclusion... Residential segregation enacts or enlarges many material privileges of economic opportunity, quality of life, power to influence actions and events, and convenience.' (Young, 2002: 196) However, unlike their counterparts in many economically advanced countries such as the United States (Mott, 2004), the poor in South Africa do not form part of a racial minority and constitute both the largest class and the bed rock of the ruling African National Congress (ANC) party.

The case studies discussed below describe the responses of citizens to adverse administrative and political decisions and points to the ways in which the existing system of participatory democracy is failing the marginalised urban poor and the extent to which they have managed to extract concessions from the state. They are of particular interest in that the events took place simultaneously.

Resistance to the Location of the FIFA 2010 Soccer Stadium in Green Point

The first case study relates to the aggregated communities that are situated around Green Point Common, some five kilometres from the central business district of Cape Town. Although the area has become more racially integrated in the past two decades, its dominant demographic profile remains white and middle class.[1] Issue for the community at large was the proposal to construct a major new stadium for the 2010 Soccer World Cup on the Green Point Common, which is currently zoned as public recreational space. The development would not only turn the spotlight of the world on Cape Town but it was estimated that it would bring some R10 billion into the city in terms of infrastructure grants from the Central government and revenue from tourism and other multipliers associated with the 2010 World Cup.

Responsibility for the construction of the stadium fell to all three levels of the government: (i) the national government, which would cover major infrastructural costs, (ii) the provincial government, which was responsible for granting planning permission; and (iii) the municipal government for overseeing the construction process. The decision to locate the stadium on Green Point Common as opposed to on one of the two other potential sites was taken by the municipality of Cape Town when the ANC was in power and before it lost a local election to the opposition Democratic Alliance (DA). It is evident, nevertheless, that Green Point was the preferred site for FIFA. For the citizens of the area this raised a number of concerns ranging from the loss of public open space, to adverse environmental impacts, to concerns about additional costs to local tax payers and an influx of undesirable people into the area.

Access to New State Housing by Backyard Dwellers in Langa

Langa township, which was established in 1927, was one of the only three areas in greater Cape Town in which African people were officially permitted to reside during the Apartheid era. Although a proportion of the population were defined as permanent residents, a large proportion (and perhaps the majority), were considered migrant labourers who would eventually return to their designated ethnic homeland in the eastern Cape. During the 1960s and 1970s, Langa comprised low cost houses for the relatively small number of families living legally in Cape Town, together with a series of single-sex hostels to which large numbers of migrant

1. According to the 2001 Census, 75 per cent of the 10,000 people who lived in the constituency of Sea Point, in which the Green Point Common is situated, were white and middle class.

workers were consigned. Gender imbalances, consequently, were extreme and the area had many of the characteristics of a labour camp. Apart from a government-run beer hall, a police station, a school and a clinic, there were very few facilities available for the community. With the progressive unravelling of the Apartheid policy in the 1980s, increasing numbers of women 'illegally' joined their partners in the hostels and brought a more balanced demographic makeup to the area. The greater sense of community was evident in the anti-Apartheid protests, which took place in Langa during the 1980s. This influx, nevertheless, aggravated existing housing shortages. Since no informal housing was permitted by the authorities, many families were forced to rent shacks in the backyards of those occupying formal housing.

With the collapse of Apartheid in the late 1980s and 1990s and the ending of influx control laws, which inhibited the movement of black people into the cities, there was a large and rapid influx of people into greater Cape Town. As a consequence of the already severe housing shortages in the metropolis, the majority of these newcomers were compelled to live in burgeoning informal settlements on the peripheries of the city. With the passage of time and as land became scarce in the large informal settlements such as Khayelitsha, desperate newcomers began erecting shacks on the verges of established townships such as Langa. The rapid growth of an informal settlement on the outskirts of Langa began in the mid-1990s and rapidly gained momentum thereafter. The settlement, known as the Joe Slovo Camp (named after the ANC stalwart and first Minister of Housing in the Mandela cabinet), skirted the N2 freeway from the airport into the centre of Cape Town.

In May 2005, the National Department of Housing announced the launch of the Gateway Housing Project as part of a broad programme to eradicate shack dwellings in the major cities of South Africa. Following this, the City of Cape Town, on the advice of the National Minister of Housing, announced that the houses would be allocated on a 70:30 basis to the residents of the informal settlement and to the backyard dwellers respectively. To the occupants of backyard shacks, many of whom had been on the municipal housing waiting list for 10, 15 or even 20 years, this allocation was inherently unjust, particularly, they argued, as they had at no stage been consulted on the allocation process. Aggravating this state of affairs, shortly after the announcement of the project, a fire swept through the Joe Slovo Informal Settlement leaving some 8,000 people homeless. Rather than being permitted to rebuild their homes, these people were placed in temporary accommodation and were informed that they would be the first to be moved into the new dwellings. For the backyard dwellers, this proposal could not be accepted without a challenge to the government.

Access to New State Housing by the Residence of the Joe Slovo Informal Settlement

As with most informal settlements in South Africa, as intimated, the Joe Slovo Settlement had its origins in Apartheid policies, which restricted the migration of African people into urban areas. A number of informal dwellings were built on the outskirts of Langa Township in the late 1980s but these were subsequently destroyed by the authorities. In 1993, with the imminent collapse of the Apartheid government, households began settling in the area once again. With the advent of democracy in 1994, settlement in the area grew apace and by 2003 there were some 5,451 dwellings in the area. (Development Action Group, 2007). Rudimentary services were provided by the City of Cape Town.

In September 2004 when the National Minister of Housing first announced the government's intent to upgrade the informal settlement, the community of Joe Slovo understood that they would have the opportunity to move into new accommodation. The upgrading was intended to be done in phases and it was understood that residents would need to be temporarily relocated to a 'temporary relocation area' (TRA). However, the fire in January 2005 disrupted plans to temporarily relocate the residents to a TRA. It was now a matter of urgency to relocate households displaced by fire and although efforts were made to place them in the immediate vicinity of Langa, opposition from surrounding communities and indeed from the residents of Langa themselves, resulted in their removal to Delft, a suburb some 15 kilometres away. Those relocated were given reassurances that they would be permitted to return to Joe Slovo once the Gateway Project was completed.

The completion of the first phase of the Gateway, as discussed above, pitted the residents of Joe Slovo against the backyard dwellers of COLACOCO. Although COLACOCO ultimately lost the struggle for equal access to the Gateway accommodation, in effect both communities lost out, because the dwellings on offer were beyond the means of those who wished to move into them. As a consequence, no more than a handful of the residents of Joe Slovo acquired accommodation. When the second phase of the Gateway project began, the National Ministry of Housing,[2] through a public entity known as Thubelisha Homes, began steps to move a substantial portion of the Joe Slovo community in order to make way for new housing. By this stage, however, it had become apparent to the community that a move to Delft would affect them adversely.

The fact that it was located away from all major employment nodes implied that the inhabitants of Delft had to expend considerable sums on transport simply to get to and from work (an expense which many residents of Joe Slovo wanted to avoid). There were few services in the township, the shelter provided was rudimentary, unemployment was high and so was the incidence of crime. To make matters worse, none of those relocated to Delft during the first round of relocations managed to return to a Gateway home. Faced with this reality, the residents of Joe Slovo resolved to fight any further evictions.

The Processes of Collectivisation

Confronted by government policies, which they believed would impact negatively on their lives, the three communities mobilised to resist. As the case studies illustrate, the ways in which this mobilisation took place, the leadership, which emerged and the strategies which they adopted, differ markedly as did their success in changing government policy.

The Green Point Common Association (GPCA)

Following government pronouncements on the preferred site for the 2010 World Cup stadium, a series of public meetings were convened in a local hall in Green Point by a group of citizens to discuss their concerns about the proposed construction. This loose coalition was subsequently formally constituted as the Green Point Common Association (GPCA), a

2. By this stage, the ANC had lost control of the city of Cape Town to the DA and the National Department of Housing, anxious not to lose control of the Gateway project assumed direct control.

formally constituted entity with elected office bearers. According to its website, the GPCA was 'a community based not-for-profit group, comprising of organisations, tax payers associations, sports and recreation clubs and concerned citizens from the greater Green Point and Cape Town communities.' Through the sharing of knowledge, the coalition's stated aims were to keep 'the general public and special interest groups abreast of events affecting the Green Point Common. (and) to encourage good public governance and vigilant compliance with public policies, legal processes and procedures.' (GPCA, 2006)

From the outset, the GPCA actively sought to mobilise public opinion against the stadium's construction in Green Point. In an early victory, the City's newly elected DA party mayor, placed a moratorium on the planning of the stadium, citing irregularities in the procedures followed by the previous ANC-led council. This decision led to strong protests from both the Central and provincial governments, which cited national interests involved in hosting the 2010 World Cup and the potential threat to this if the process of construction was delayed. Following a series of discussions with the provincial government, the city of Cape Town eventually gave its full support for the construction of the stadium. The eventual alignment of the views of the city and the provinces was driven by several imperatives. In the first instance, a rapid decision to proceed with the construction of the stadium was called for if Cape Town was not to loose the project; in the second instance, the programme of construction held the promise of national funding for infrastructural development and a major inflow of revenue into the city.

Despite the loss of the city's support, the GPCA continued to mobilise and threatened to mount a legal challenge against the construction of the stadium. It particularly encouraged its members to lodge complaints against the provincial government's Record of Decision, which had accepted the findings of an environmental impact study and had given planning permission for the project to proceed. Whilst the GPCA and its affiliates did not, ultimately, succeed in halting or diverting the construction of the 2010 stadium it was successful in extracting concessions from both the metropolitan and provincial governments.

The Coalition for Langa Community Concerns (COLACOCO)

With the announcement of the launch of the Gateway project, a number of backyard dwellers approached the local councillor, appealing him to assist them in securing more equitable access to the housing, which was to be constructed. When this approach failed to elicit any response from the municipality, a letter was sent to the Mayor. In response, the community of Langa was invited to a public meeting with the Mayor held in Tygerberg, at the offices of a municipal sub-structure of the city of Cape Town. The meeting became extremely heated as angry backyard dwellers confronted the Mayor with what they believed to be the unfairness of the 70:30 split. Despite their strong appeals for a 50:50 division of housing units, the Mayor was reportedly unmoved and gave no indication that a more equitable form of distribution was possible. Following this meeting, those who had participated in the consultative meeting with the Mayor established the Coalition for Langa Community Concerns (COLACOCO). Its chairperson was a retired school principal and a resident of Langa of some 50 years standing. The modes of engagement pursued by the Langa coalition, also known as the 'backyard dwellers', were largely limited to formal political channels. These included engagement in ward committees, participation in public meetings and petitioning both senior administrators and political leaders. In addition to the Mayor, the coalition unsuccessfully petitioned the provincial Member of the Executive Council (MEC) for Housing and the National Minister of Housing, on the need to review the proposed housing division. When these measures failed to elicit any positive outcomes, they resorted to protest marches and, in the case of some militant youth, direct action in the form of attacks on hostels.

COLACOCO also widened its concerns to include more equitable distribution of the units being renovated in the old migrant worker hostels. It was maintained that these quarters were under the control of a Hostel Dwellers Committee, which allocated the units to their friends and family, irrespective of how long they had lived in Langa. The concerns of the backyard dwellers, legitimate as they might be, inevitably pitted them against both the residents of the Joe Slovo Camp and the Hostel Dwellers Committee. Relations with the latter group soured rapidly and the prospects of violent confrontations between the two became very real, when supporters of the Hostel Dwellers Committee marched to the home of the

COLACOCO President. The internecine struggles ultimately weakened COLACOCO's case and they were not able to enforce a change in the 70:30 allocation of housing.

The Joe Slovo Task Team

The initial resistance by the Joe Slovo community also entailed approaching the ward councillor to assist them in securing access to low cost housing. When this proved unsuccessful, in September 2006 they delivered a memorandum to the Provincial Minister of Housing, requesting his assistance. Despite vague promises, this intervention also amounted to nothing. This was followed in August 2007 with a march to the national parliament in the centre of Cape Town, wherein the Task Team delivered a strongly worded memorandum to the Minister of Housing demanding that they be consulted on the future development of their informal settlement.

> We demand development in Joe Slovo for its residents by its residents meaning that residents should participate in planning and facilitation of houses. We demand to be involved in the decision making about Joe Slovo. (Joe Slovo Task Team, 2007)

Over and above the demand for genuine participation in planning processes, which affected their lives, the memorandum expressed the community's anger that they were being forcibly removed to Delft, likening the behaviour of the democratic government to that of the Apartheid regime.

> Why is government chasing away Black people from urban areas like the previous administration? Oh please, honourable Minister, we do not want to move to Delft, from one temporary house to another, from SHACK TO TRA. A shack is a temporary house and the TRA is also a temporary house, what difference does this make? During the apartheid regime black people were forcefully removed from District Six, now under democratic government, black people are being expelled closer to urban areas, what difference does that make? (Joe Slovo Task Team, 2007)

When the Minister refused to meet the marchers and sent an assistant to receive their memorandum, a decision was taken to escalate the protest and on 10 September 2007, the community blockaded the N2 arterial highway to the airport. The police were called and in a stand-off rubber bullets were fired, people were injured and others were arrested. The Department of Housing's response, somewhat predictably, laid the blame squarely on the Joe Slovo leadership.

> The protestors today rejected the integration of fully subsidised homes with rental and bonded units, and demanded the construction of one-size-fits-all Reconstruction and Development Programme (RDP) housing. In addition, they rejected their temporary relocation to Delft to allow the development of Joe Slovo to proceed, and demanded the in situ upgrade of Joe Slovo.... Their violent protest followed exhaustive consultations with the community by, among others, Parliament's Portfolio Committee on Housing, MEC Richard Dyantyi, councillors and project developers, Thubelisha. ...The violence that erupted today was therefore unwarranted, intolerable and avoidable. Government cannot allow Cape Town's housing crisis to be manipulated by opportunistic individuals and/or politicians. (Department of Housing, 2007)

The explicit rejection of the demands of the Joe Slovo Task Team was also accompanied by explicit threats against those seeking to resist removal.

> The police and National Prosecuting Authority have been encouraged to maintain law and order by bringing charges against the perpetrators.
>
> Government will use all legal instruments at its disposal to ensure the development of Joe Slovo proceeds without further hindrance.
>
> The names of identified perpetrators of violence will be removed from housing waiting lists. (Department of Housing, 2007)

Shortly thereafter Thubelisha Homes, the state housing agency contracted to build the new houses, acquired a court order to forcibly evict the residents of Joe Slovo. Whilst this was a severe setback for the Task Team, it also forced them into a new arena of struggle, which was to their ultimate benefit. News that the community was to be removed under court orders prompted the Legal Resources Centre (LRC) at the University of Cape Town to offer their services as a friend of the Court. The LRC prepared responding papers and the matter was referred to the

Constitutional Court on the grounds that the eviction contravenes elements of the Bill of Rights and the provisions of the land mark Grootboom case.[3]

Leadership

To an extent, the leadership of any social movement is ascribed, in that it is generally the agency of a self-selected few, which serves to galvanise community concerns and which initiates collective action. In all three case studies, a series of events, both long standing and proximate, served to spur individuals to action and to assume positions of leadership. However, as the orientation of their leaders and the resources at their disposal differed significantly, so too did the strategies which they adopted to achieve their goals. Their experiences are of further interest to the extent to which the different communities opted to make use of the formal participatory channels open to them.

COLACOCO, as representatives of the backyard dwellers, represented part of a long standing community and, to a degree, this lent itself to a more conservative and, it could be argued, more trusting engagement with political and administrative structures. The election of a retired school principal to the chair of COLACOCO is also perhaps reflective of the respect for professional authority and formalism. To that extent, the steering committee placed considerable emphasis on the proper election of office bearers and on accurate record keeping. The proceedings of each meeting were meticulously recorded, in English and registers were kept of those who had attended.

The modes of participation open to the Langa coalition were largely limited to formal political channels. These included engagement in ward committees, participation in public meetings and petitioning both senior administrators and political leaders. When these measures failed to elicit any positive outcomes, they resorted to limited protest action (typically handing over memoranda to political leaders) and, in the case of some militant youth, direct action in the form of attacks on hostel. Significantly,

3. In the Grootboom case, the Constitutional court ruled that the state was bound to find alternative accommodation for anyone compelled to move off state-owned land.

they placed faith in the interventions of their local ANC ward councillor to intercede on their behalf. The councillor, however, distanced himself from these protests, largely due to the fact that he did not want to be seen to be opposing politicians at more senior levels of the governing hierarchy. He also played an active role both in subverting the independence of COLACOCO and in advancing the agenda of the national government.

To that extent, he was instrumental in setting up a project steering committee, ostensibly to bring together all parties with an interest in the Gateway Housing Scheme. Among those invited to participate in the steering committee were the local government councillors, city officials, representatives of the housing company and construction companies, representatives of the Joe Slovo settlement and non-governmental organisations, among others. In its final composition, the steering committee had 30 members, only 2 of whom were representatives of COLACOCO. In this context the views of the coalition formed a small minority among a variety of competing voices, some of which were purely technocratic and bureaucratic in nature (for example, the building contractors) and their impact was minimised.

Through the steering committee, the local government councillor was able to present the idea that the 70:30 split was immutable, since the decision had been taken by higher authorities. Thus the minutes of May 2006 attest that, 'Councillor Gophe clarified the issue pertaining to the 70/30 split stating that the presiding forum cannot change the decisions taken at higher political level. Local concessions could however be entertained within local negotiations' (LPC, 2006a: para 5.2.4). In this manner, the debate on the fairness of the policy was foreclosed, in that the decisions taken by the steering committee were ostensibly based on consensus.

When, as indicated above, the youth element of the community proposed more direct forms of action, following the failure to extract concessions from the authorities, moderation was cautioned by the COLACOCO committee. At the same time, whilst the committee intervened to facilitate the release of those arrested during the invasion, they also disassociated themselves from this action. In fact, in virtually all of their deliberations there was an appeal for reasonable action and an implicit belief that a rationally presented case, delivered through formal channels, would elicit a favourable response.

The community of Joe Slovo has a two-tiered governance structure, a 15 member Task Team, which is the deliberative body and a sub-committee, which assists in popular mobilisation and other activities supportive of the resistance. From the outset, Task Team's approach was more confrontational than that of COLACOCO. In response to the rebuttal of their initial demands by local and provincial government officials, the Task Team quickly abandoned formal consultative channels. The recourse to a more militant form of rights claiming can be traced back to the experiences of the Task Team's leaders, several of whom had been activists in the Eastern Cape during the anti-Apartheid struggle. Whilst the public face of the Task Team was a young man engaged in postgraduate studies, the chairperson (his brother) was a veteran of the struggle, experienced in confronting the state.

In contrast to what might be perceived in official circles as the COLACOCO leadership's 'responsible' approach, the leaders of the Joe Slovo community adopted a more confrontational and aggressive approach to the state when confronted with the prospect of relocation out of Langa. Following a futile engagement with the ward councillor, the Task Team responsible for mobilising the community led a march to parliament and delivered a strongly worded memorandum to the National Minister of Housing demanding that they be consulted on the future development of their informal settlement. When the minister refused to meet the marchers and sent an assistant to receive their memorandum, a decision was taken to escalate the protest and the community blockaded the N2 arterial highway to the airport. The police were called and in a stand-off rubber bullets were fired, people were injured and others were arrested.

As an organisation representing a middle class community, the GPCA was able to draw on the professional skills of its members. The chairperson was a retired lawyer, with a good network with an array of professionals and this facilitated the association's ability to marshal information on the prescripts of the city's planning regulations, whilst knowledge of the legal redress possible and the demonstrable financial means to follow this route, meant that the government (at all three levels) had to take the challenge which they posed, seriously. In addition, the individuals mobilising in opposition to the stadium manifested a high degree of homogeneity in terms of socioeconomic standing (predominantly white and middle class), level of education and political affiliation.

The Role of Intermediaries

The leadership of the three social movements is further distinguished in the extent to which they formed alliances with and benefited from the assistance of external agencies. Whilst, as indicated, the GPCA had a strong base of professional expertise from which to draw, it also sought to mobilise public opinion in its favour. It did so in the first instance by forging alliances with local tax payers' associations but, as shall be seen below, it also actively made use of the media to present its case to a wider audience.

The case of COLACOCO is significant for the fact that its leadership opted to proceed alone. This was partly due to the fact that they believed that by engaging with the authorities through the designated channels, their concerns would, ultimately, be addressed. The fact that they were in competition with other sections of the Langa community for public housing also meant that the prospects for the formation of alliances were reduced.

The Joe Slovo Task Team, in contrast benefited significantly from the support of external agencies, partly due to their own initiative and, partly due to the fact that their impending removal became a cause *célèbre* for the anti-evictions movement both nationally and internationally. These included, in the first instance the Western Cape chapter of the Anti-Evictions Campaign, Abahlali baseMjondolo (a national NGO), Slum Dwellers International and others. These affiliations increased the organisational skills and resources available to the Task Team, not least, as shall be reasoned below, in their access to the media. Whilst the Slovo Task Team eschewed any form of engagement with COLACOCO, solidarity links were also established with members of the community who had been moved to Delft. They had also formed an alliance with community organisations in the neighbouring suburb of Khayelitsha. The publicity generated by the Joe Slovo Task Team's defiant stance drew the attention of national and international NGOs and the assistance proffered by these organisations culminated in a legal challenge to their forced removal, which went as far as the Constitutional Court.

The Use of the Courts

As has been observed in other contexts, the use of litigation has enabled social movements to go beyond the formal mechanisms of participatory democracy and to challenge the state in an arena which was traditionally seen to be at the heart of the establishment (Duarte, 2004). This tactic is not new and it is evident that throughout the civil rights movement in the United States, leaders made use of both the courts and protest activity (Jaynes and Williams, 1989; Klarman, 2004). However, while resorting to litigation was reserved in large part to assert the need for fundamental rights on the part of disenfranchised communities, it is increasingly being deployed as an integral component in the armoury of mobilising social movements in defence of a variety of different causes (Hilson, 2002).

Historically, the courts' role in a democratic society has been viewed in terms of two competing models. In the first and mainstream model, courts are viewed as the arbitrators of disputes between private citizens asserting particular rights (Lobel, 2004: 2). In a competing perspective from public law, the judiciary is seen to play an important additional role in implementing social change. According to Lobel, the ongoing debate between these two views of the judiciary's role in a democratic society has obscured a third model of the courts' role. The third alternative perspective, he asserts, views courts as forums for protest. Under this model, courts not only function as adjudicators of private disputes, or institutions that implement social reforms but as arenas which political and social movements utilise to agitate for and educate about their legal and political agenda (Lobel, 2004: 2).

Just as studies have reported that the act of protest itself (in the form of marches, demonstrations etc.,) is an empowering one for those participating, so too have others pointed out that resorting to litigation against the state has its own intrinsic value over and above that of enforcing change. As Lobel observes:

> While victory is an important index of success in the first two views of the role of litigation, winning in court is not salient in the forums of protest model. Of course, the litigators and their clients certainly hope, and at times expect to win in court; but

> their objective is broader than courtroom victory. They primarily seek neither the damages awarded to private litigators under the traditional model, nor the injunction of the public law model, but rather to use the courtroom struggle to build a political movement. The litigation can serve a variety of roles, to articulate a constitutional theory supporting the aspirations of the political movement, to expose the conflict between the aspirations of law and its grim reality, to draw public attention to the issue and to mobilize an oppressed community, or to put public pressure on a recalcitrant government or private institution to take a popular movement's grievances seriously. What is decisive is that judicial relief not be viewed as dispositive, such relief is important but not the driving force of the litigation. (Lobel, 2004: 2).

The GPCA's reaction to the perceived threat to their living environment involved popular mobilisation but the modes of engagement with the authorities were significantly different to those of COLACOCO. While the association did formally engage with the political leadership of the city, as well as with planners, environmental impact analysts and other officials, it was always clear that litigation was a powerful tool at their disposal. According to the GPCA's chairperson, a retired barrister, 'The only democratic defence that is open to us is that of fighting for our lives through the court' (Roelf, 2006). He also threatened that the 'entire process will be subjected to a long and drawn out process in the courts ... [and] no sod will be turned.' It is certain, moreover, that had the association chosen to invoke a court injunction, they could have succeed in delaying the construction process to the extent that the World Cup organising committee would have been compelled to select an alternative venue outside of Cape Town. Conceding this, a senior official in the office of the Provincial Premier stated that were the GPCA to opt for litigation:

> Cape Town will have to kiss hosting a semi-final game goodbye ... We will simply not have enough time to fight the case and then start building afterwards. We are now in the do-or-die phase. Construction of the Green Point stadium has to begin right now. Even if the GPCA lose their court case, the time delay will set us back so much that it will be impossible to complete the stadium in time for a semi to be hosted in Cape Town. (Joubert, 2007)

It is also evident that the GPCA was more interested in the concessions which they could extract from the state than with actually halting the construction of the stadium in its entirety,[4] and to that extent, the threat of litigation was successful as a means to an end.

In contrast to the GPCA, the leadership of COLACOCO made no use of legal channels to assert their rights. Thus, at no time were the services of a lawyer retained nor were efforts made to elicit the assistance of a legal aid organisation. It was reported that the coalition felt that they could not afford a lawyer and they were uninformed about the possibilities of accessing legal aid. It is also possible that the hesitancy in securing legal backing reflected an unfounded but nevertheless real confidence in the participatory channels open to them.

In contrast, the Joe Slovo Task Team's success in securing the services of the LRC lifted their struggle onto a new level, where, for once, there was parity in the interaction between state and citizens. The *Heads of Argument* prepared by the LRC on behalf of the Joe Slovo community for submission to the Constitutional Court, presents a finely argued case that places the onus of proof that no alternative to relocation exists, firmly on the state. Citing the Grootboom case as precedent, the argument proceeds as follows:

> The residents have been on the land for a very long period. Some of them have now been there for as long as 15 years. The City is the owner of the land. There is no suggestion that the City has ever attempted to remove the occupiers from the land, or has even told them that their presence on the land is without the consent of the City. On the contrary, the City has acted as one would expect a responsible local authority to do. It has accepted the existence of a de facto situation which arises from the housing crisis in Cape Town. That crisis and its causes were described by this Court in Grootboom. The crisis is the result of apartheid housing policies, not least of them the "coloured labour preference policy" which was imposed in the Western Cape, and the pass (influx control) laws. As a result of those policies, a deliberate decision was made not to provide housing for Africans in Cape Town, in order to minimise African presence and African

4. Personal communication, David Polovin, chairperson, GPCA, 4 March 2007.

> family life in Cape Town. The papers in this case show that the crisis described in Grootboom in 2000 has regrettably not been resolved: indeed, there is evidence that the scale of the crisis has grown larger.
>
> Under the circumstances, the City plainly recognised that to evict people from the land which they had occupied, under circumstances in which there was not any other housing which could be made available to them, would achieve nothing but to cause human misery and social dislocation and conflict. The City therefore accepted the presence of the occupiers on its land, at least on an interim basis, and for that reason provided them with services. (Budlender and Kubukeli, 2008)

The *Heads of Argument* proceeds to present the case for the in situ upgrading of the Joe Slovo informal settlement as the legal entitlement of its inhabitants.

The Use of the Media

While resorting to litigation was a major factor differentiating the strategies deployed by the three communities, so too was their use of the media. As Oliver and Myers have pointed out, the media are not 'passive channels of communication and nor are they neutral or objective observers or recorders of events' (Oliver and Myers, 1999: 39). Knowledge of the media industry and of media processes provides a means for social movements to present their case definitively and to frame their struggle for the public at large. As Oliver and Myers observe, 'Experienced organisers plan events that meet journalistic standards of newsworthiness, write press releases, call reporters, and craft their "sound bites" for the media' (Oliver and Myers, 1999: 43). By shaping the public discourse in this way, they are able to portray their demands as reasonable and justifiable in terms of their rights as citizens.

From the outset, as indicated, the GPCA actively campaigned to win public support for its case through the media. This included establishing a website with an online blog to elicit public debate, conducting media interviews, issuing press releases and writing letters to the press. This process upped the ante, as it were, and created the impression of a sizeable opposition. It is evident that the media assault achieved three additional objectives. In the first instance, it helped to build coherence among the disparate groups comprising the association, by reinforcing a common understanding of the threats posed by the proposed stadium. In the second instance, it helped to intimidate those within the community, such as local hoteliers, who were favourably disposed to the construction of the stadium. By maintaining a coherent focus, furthermore, the association was able to avoid the divisions, which ultimately undermined COLACOCO's actions. In the third instance, the media coverage alerted FIFA to the possibility of a delay in the construction of the stadium and they, in turn, raised their own concerns with the South African government (Mangxamba and Dentlinger, 2006), increasing pressure for a settlement of the GPCA's challenge.

While the actions of COLACOCO drew some media coverage, this was not an orchestrated process but rather an outcome of independent reporting of ongoing community protests. In the early phases of the campaign, steps had been taken to alert the media to the struggle underway and COLACOCO's chaiperson gave some interviews to the local media and appeared on national television.[5] However, once the steering committee was established, it effectively served to muzzle opposing voices. The minutes of the committee's meeting held in May 2006 cite the problem of conflicting reports in the media and invoking the MEC for housing.

> The meeting was advised that the MEC is very concerned with conflicting reports being circulated in the media.... The meeting agreed that none of its members shall liaise directly with the media about issues affecting the social housing program at Langa. The meeting clarified that representatives are permitted to report only to their constituencies as well as principles on progress achieved, however all media liaison must be directed to the MEC until further notice (LPC, 2006b: para.3.7).

It is also evident however, that COLACOCO itself was wary of what it perceived to be misrepresentation of their case, even if this was likely due to poor investigative journalism on the part of uninformed media rather than any evident bias.

The Joe Slovo Task Team, in contrast, made ample use of the media, principally through their affiliations to the Anti-Eviction Campaign and to

5. Personal communication, Siphiwo Tindleni, chairperson, COLACOCO, Langa, 10 February 2007.

Abahlali baseMjondolo (Huff, n.d.) The latter has an effective web page and blogs, which provide regular updates on the Slovo case. This publicity also attracted the interest of a wider public and led to further offers of support. It could also be argued that the noisy marches to parliament, together with the blockade of the N2 freeway served as a further means to publicise the community's cause.

Outcome

The three case studies presented above provide contrasting experiences on the extent to which interest groups in the respective constituencies were able to mobilise their communities in a concerted and sustained manner and on the means that they were able to deploy to that end. In the case of the GPCA, community mobilisation failed to halt the construction of the soccer stadium but concessions were, nevertheless, extracted from the state. These include a commitment to retain the common as a recreational area; a commitment that the stadium will not be surrounded by a village which might subsequently be sold off as housing; the allocation of alternative land for the Metropolitan Golf Course to compensate for land lost in the construction of the stadium; and a commitment by the city to compensate or employ the club for a loss of earnings and to cover staff costs until such time as it is again fully operational. (Dentlinger, 2007)

For the members of the COLACOCO, hard lessons were learnt about the efficacy of formal democratic channels for engagement with the state. Significantly, the movement failed to adapt to the circumstances and to adopt new strategies once the formal channels failed to deliver favourable outcomes. The inability of the movement's leaders to yield any tangible returns, furthermore, ultimately lead to the disillusionment of its members and culminated in the dissolution of the coalition.

The Joe Slovo Task Team, in contrast, proved to be more responsive and rapidly changed tactics when confronted with an unresponsive state. The recourse to direct protest action and subsequent litigation meant that they forced the authorities to engage seriously with their demands. Although the Constitutional Court ruled in favour of their removal (on the grounds that this was necessary for the construction of new dwellings), it also instructed that 70 per cent of the new houses to be built on the site should be reserved for Joe Slovo residents. The community has rejected this ruling, insisting that any upgrading of the housing in the area must take place in situ, implying that they will not even accept temporary relocation whilst construction is underway.

In none of the case studies was there any recognition on the part of the state of the legitimacy of the demands of the communities involved and in all instances their protests were portrayed as irresponsible, unreasonable and against the public good. That a compromise was reached with the GPCA was therefore not a reflection of the state's acceptance of the validity of their claims but an indication that the state had been forced to make concessions to avoid both losing face internationally and the possibility of significant financial loss. Similarly, the stand-off with the Joe Slovo Task Team was forced upon the local and national state through litigation. By the same token, in the zero-sum game of state-citizen contestation, no steps were taken to assuage the demands of the backyard dwellers by constructing alternative housing for them elsewhere in Langa, rather than in the Gateway Project (something COLACOCO had proposed). To that extent, the case studies illustrate, somewhat starkly, that challenges to the hegemony of the state cannot be advanced on the basis of moral rectitude, by following the right channels, or solely on the basis of rights enshrined in the Constitution. This reading of events posits an essentially adversarial relationship between the state and citizens and suggests that the state will only concede to popular demands when forced to do so. In this context, the role of citizen leaders, their ability to mobilise and their ability to select strategies that will extract concessions from the state becomes critical to the advancement of democratic rights on the part of ordinary citizens.

References

Budlender, G. and K. Kubukeli (2008). Counsel for the Applicants represented by the Task Team "Heads of Argument on Behalf of the Residents Presented by the Task Team" Chambers. Cape Town, July.

Dentlinger, L. (2007). "Ratepayers to Cough Up R140m More for Stadium", *Weekend Argus*, 24 February.

Department of Housing (2007). "Department of Housing Issue a Stern Warning against Violent Protesters in Joe Slovo Informal Settlement", Press release Issued by: Department of Housing, 10 September. *http://www.info.gov.za/speeches/2007/07091114451002.htm*

Development Action Group (2007). *Living on the Edge: A Study of the Delft Temporary Relocation Area.* May.

Duarte, M. (2004). "Protesting Through Law: The Emancipatory Power of Law at the Service of Social Movements", Paper presented at the *Annual Meeting of the Law and Society Association*. Renaissance Hotel, Chicago, IL.

GPCA (2006). *Who We Are*. Green Point Common Association. *www.greenpointcommon.co.za/pages/about.asp?subnav=1* (accessed 24 May 2009).

Hilson, C. (2002). "New Social Movements: The Role of Legal Opportunity", *Journal of European Public Policy* 9(2)

Huff, A., (no date). "Itemba Liyaphilisa: Redefining Development through the Joe Slovo Anti-Eviction Struggle", Unpublished Paper, Abahlali BaseMjondolo webpage *http://www.abahlali.org/node/3149#attachments.* Accessed on 5 March 2009.

Jaynes, D., and R. Williams (1989). *A Common Destiny: Blacks and American Society*. Washington, DC: National Academies Press.

Joe Slovo Task Team (2007). "Memorandum of Joe Slovo Residents, to the National Minister of Housing. From: Joe Slovo Residents", Date: August 03, 2007, RE: Communication for service delivery in the Housing Department of the National Minister.

Joubert, P. (2007). "No Easy Green Light for Green Point", *Mail and Guardian*, 26 January.

Klarman, M. (2004). *From Jim Crow to Civil Rights: The Supreme Court and the Struggle for Racial Equality*. New York: Oxford University Press.

Lobel, J. (2004). "Courts as Forums for Protest", *Bepress Legal Series*, *Working Paper* 213, *http://law.bepress.com/expresso/eps/213*

LPC (2006a). "Minutes of the N2 Langa Project Committee Meeting 17 February 2006", Langa Housing Offices, Minutes on letterhead of Cape Town Community Housing Company.

———. (2006b). "Minutes of the N2 Langa Project Committee Meeting 11 May 2006", Langa Housing Offices, minutes on letterhead of Cape Town Community Housing Company.

Mangxamba, S. and L. Dentlinger (2006). "Get Cracking, FIFA Boss Tells SA", *Cape Argus*, 7 December.

Meyer, D. (2004). "Protest and Political Opportunities", *Annual Review of Sociology* 30, August.

Mott, A. (2004). "Increasing Space and Influence through Community Organising and Citizen Monitoring: Experiences from the USA", *IDS Bulletin* 35(2), April.

Oliver, P., and D. Myers (1999). "How Events Enter the Public Sphere: Conflict, Location and Sponsorship in Local Newspaper Coverage of Public Events", *American Journal of Sociology* 105(1), July.

Roelf, W. (2006). "Residents May Sue to Stop Stadium Plans", South African Press Association, 12 April.

Young, I.M. (2002). *Inclusion and Democracy*. Oxford: Oxford University Press.

4 Using Participatory Spaces for Improving Housing and Urban Services

Diadema, São Paulo, Brazil

Patrícia L.N. Cobra and
Lizandra Serafim

Introduction

Industrialisation of the Great ABC region[1] of Brazil in the 1970s brought with itself a number of problems. The sudden migration of people from other parts of Brazil to work in the industries created tremendous pressure on infrastructure and urban services simply failed to keep pace with the burgeoning population. There were simply not enough houses to accommodate the large number of people. As a result, people occupied unused public areas building their own temporary houses. A movement for housing was born in these conditions and it tried to address the housing concerns of people settled in the industrial region. This movement had several achievements to its credit for improvement in urban services and houses. Simultaneously, democratisation of Brazil in 1985 paved the way for the creation of participatory spaces through which people's demands could be channelised. The opening of various participatory spaces threw up several challenges like non-preparedness of communities to use these spaces, negotiations with the state and other social actors for getting resources etc., which the housing movement also found difficult to handle. In this situation, the state stepped in to take up the role of mobilising the communities. So a unique collaboration between the state and the community organisations and the movement was seen in enabling people

1. ABC region includes the municipalities of Santo André (A), São Bernardo do Campo (B), São Caetano do Sul (C).

to use these participatory spaces. Once their capacity had been built, people used these spaces not only to put up their demands to the state but also to influence policymaking and project implementation.

The use of the participatory spaces demonstrated the collaborations, conflict, contest, leadership among various social actors and the state. It also showed how these spaces could be used to avail urban services and houses, integrate citizen's perspective in city plans and ultimately ensure the accountability of the state.

Diadema has been chosen as a case study as it was located in the ABC region, which witnessed a tremendous increase in industrialisation and hence its effects. The housing movement was quite strong here, which ultimately built the base for using participatory spaces created in democratic Brazil. The dynamics of making these spaces vibrant and effective is quite apparent in this zone. The case study also shows quite effectively how participative spaces ensured citizens' perspective in housing plans, monitoring of the expenditure on houses, citizens' participation in city development plans and infrastructure projects. This study is based on secondary literature and interviews with the leaders of community organisations, the housing movement and government representatives.

Context

The city of Diadema is located in the southeast corner of São Paulo's metropolitan region[2], in an area known as the Great ABC, which includes the municipalities of Santo André (A), São Bernardo do Campo (B), São Caetano do Sul (C), Diadema, Rio Grande da Serra, Ribeirão Pires and Mauá.

The Great ABC, one of Brazil's main industrial zones, was formed in the beginning of the 20th century for the export and import industry. It lies on the railway route connecting the São Paulo countryside to Santos harbour. In the 1950s, the railways started declining as the mode of transport as motorways started replacing them, becoming the main carrier for industries in the country.

2. São Paulo's metropolitan region is composed of 39 municipalities where approximately 18 million people live.

As motorways were prioritised, automobile production received a strong thrust. The priority given to individual automobiles in the country's process of economic and industrial development directly influenced urban structuring and the organisation of the national territory.

The opening of the Anchieta highway, which expanded the connection with Santos harbour, marked a new phase of industrialisation of the Great ABC, characterised by the installation of large industrial parks, with companies such as Ford, General Motors, Volkswagen and Mercedes Benz and others mostly dedicated to automobile assembly and the production of automobile parts. In this context, the Great ABC region consolidated itself as São Paulo reinforced its position as the country's main industrial zone.

However, in the early 1950s, Diadema remained a modest industrial centre harbouring small industrial establishments and service businesses, generally complementary to the automobile assembly factories. Workers working in these industrial establishments resided in Diadema. In the 1960s and 1970s, Diadema and São Bernardo do Campo went from moderate industrial growth to high growth in the ABC region, when the number of industrial establishments increased at a very fast pace. These new industries further increased the labour workforce in the municipality. The construction of Imigrantes highway connecting São Paulo's metropolitan region to the Santos area in 1971 formed a new axis of growth and Diadema fell on this axis.

Actions by local and state public authorities further stimulated industrial growth in Diadema. Diadema's territorial planning laws marked 60 per cent of the city's area as industrial zones, borrowing the state legislation's definition of 'Predominantly Industrial Use Zone' (*Zona de Uso Predominantemente Industrial*, or *ZUPI*). 'The local authorities stimulated the formation of an industrial park [also] through the exemption from municipal taxes, which, together with the absence of well located land in the neighbouring municipalities, provided the city with a rapid proliferation of industrial enterprises.'[3]

Diadema's and the whole of ABC's high industrial growth rates spurred an internal migration movement, attracting large numbers of people from São Paulo's countryside and from other states, especially those

3. Coelho (2008).

in the north and northeast regions of the country. As well as being well located, Diadema offered low priced plots, even though they were informal, lacked infrastructure and basic community equipment and in some cases, were located in risky areas. At that moment, Diadema had the highest population growth in the region. From 1960 to 1970, the population grew from 12,308 to 79,316 inhabitants, a 544 per cent increase. In the same period, the number of people working in the city's factories went up from 632 to 9,622, or a growth of 1,422 per cent.

The Great ABC's process of industrialisation and the population growth that stemmed from it were accompanied in the 1960s by dense occupation of the territory, which happened in a quick, disordered and unequal way, in the manner similar to São Paulo's metropolitan region. According to Coelho, the pace at which workers arrived and urban land was occupied was greatly superior to the speed at which urban infrastructure was installed and essential public services were offered. The speedy and dense occupation of the territory thus resulted in a city full of illegal or irregular plots of land, *favelas* (slums) and other types of informal settlements with precarious houses that lacked basic infrastructure.

In the beginning of the 1980s, most of Diadema's streets were unpaved and most of the population did not have access to water, sewage and public light networks. In that period, 30 per cent of the streets were paved. Out of the 52,364 existing houses, only 26,623 (51 per cent) had tap water and 7,418 (14 per cent) were linked to the sewage network. Infant mortality was 82.93 per thousand live births. Diadema had 128 *favelas*, which occupied 4.2 per cent of the city's area and housed 34 per cent of its population. Besides a lack of infrastructure, ownership was insecure, legal irregularities affected 72 per cent of the city's plots.

History of the Housing Movement

The rapid growth of population in Diadema created severe pressure on infrastructure and access to urban services like houses, water, sanitation and health. The municipal government and state government were unable to cope with the sudden increase in demand for urban services resulting in tremendous dissatisfaction among people. In the early 1970s, they started demanding an improvement in the living conditions, which were also articulated by popular and trade union organisations. Trade unions and popular organisations had come into existence in the early 1970s due to the industrialisation of the area and had played a crucial role in ensuring social guarantees. Their close involvement in taking up the people's demands added critical weight to the struggle in Diadema.[4]

The CEBs [*Comunidades Eclesiais de Base* or basic ecclesial communities] and the Church also played a very important role in the development of leadership and in the organisation of movements. The Church and the trade unions not only mobilised the people but also organised actions like metal workers' strikes and alternative proposals to the lack of social policies by the local and national governments.

According to Boni[5], a leader of the West Association, Diadema's housing movement emerged from the trade unionist movement in the beginning of the 1980s. In that period, workers' demonstrations were violently repressed and outlawed by the military dictatorship[6], bringing the CEBs, which in that period were not being spied upon by the Brazilian political police and the trade unionist movements closer together. In this way, trade unionism became more involved in housing problems like evictions, lack of infrastructure, high population density and lack of housing. Moreover, these problems affected trade unionists as they also lived in *favelas* and informal settlements. So there are innumerable instances where we find that wives of trade unionists were active in raising these demands. The links between the movement for housing and urban services and trade unions were quite deep, which resulted in mutual collaboration and help.

The trade unionist movement assisted the struggle for housing, helping organise communities and local leaders and providing materials (buses, pamphlets etc.). Initially, the housing movement was not an organised popular movement. In fact, it was localised and sporadic, largely led by the groups of neighbourhood associations that fought singly for improvements in their *favelas* or clandestine lots. The trade union leaders helped the new leaders in mobilising their communities by door-to-door

4. Baltrusis and Mourad (1999): 43-44.

5. Declaration obtained in an interview carried out on November 8th, 2004.

6. Brazil lived under a military dictatorship between 1964 and 1985.

campaigns, disseminating pamphlets and calling the population to attend assemblies or demonstrations for a better quality of life. People reciprocated the trade unionist movement's help by participating in the demonstrations organised during the workers' strikes. According to leaders Cida and Toninho[7], the cooperative relationship between the trade unionists and the housing movements strengthened both the actors and is existent even today.

Another important feature of the housing movement in the late 1970s was the active participation of women. They not only participated in but also led a number of neighbourhood associations. According to Ronaldo Lacerda[8], a leader of a neighbourhood association, East Association, in the beginning, inhabitants of occupied areas or irregular plots organised themselves locally and demanded solutions for their local and urgent needs from the city's government. 'Generally, popular participation began with the mobilisation of essentially females, who got organised in order to gain the attention of the state or the municipality, or even of the national government, for their demands. These demands were always sectoral, mainly restricted to the neighbourhood and were generally related to problems with access to tap water and electricity, construction of houses, improvements in education and health care etc.'[9] The dominance of women leadership can be seen from the actions and functioning of association "Our Fight Our Land" (Box 4.1).

There were a large number of such neighbourhood organisations in Diadema, which were merged into the *Associação dos Favelados* (Association of Slum Inhabitants), which raised the demands for improving housing, poor infrastructure and pathetic urban services. These associations, trade unions and the Church were the main actors of the housing movement in Diadema, which built considerable pressure on the government for housing, improvement in urban services and most of all, democratisation.

---

7. Declarations obtained during a workshop carried out on September 11th, 2008.
8. Declaration obtained in an interview carried out on October 16th, 2008.
9. Bisiliat (2004): 102.

Box 4.1

Association "Our Fight, Our Land" (Nossa Luta, Nossa Terra)

This association was formed by people who were paying rent and living in the *favelas* and irregular plots in Diadema. Like the other associations in town, the associates fought for better quality conditions in their neighbourhoods, later, for the construction of social interest housing, the only way they could have access to a house and could stop paying rent.

The leaders of this association, right from the start, were women. According to them, women appeared as natural leaders because they felt the problems more intensely. 'The demands came out in daily life, the housewives faced difficulties in their routines, we lacked water to make food and do the laundry, it was difficult to take the kids to school and there was no light for the kids to study', says Vera, president of the association.

The female leaders also highlighted the fact that women have determined and strong personalities, which contributes to their becoming natural leaders. The association president also points out that women had jobs with flexible timings, which permitted them to dedicate part of their time to the fight for housing, participating in meetings, assemblies and demonstrations.

Nowadays, all the coordination positions in the "Our Fight, Our Land" association are occupied by women.

Creation of Participatory Spaces

Diadema's housing movements also gained impetus from the social actors who were active in other parts of the country, such as those pertaining to the *Movimento Nacional pela Reforma Urbana* (National Movement for Urban Reform), which, during the writing of the new Federal Constitution in the second half of the 1980s, presented a proposal for a popular amendment, which spawned the Urban Policy Chapter inserted in this document.

The country's political conjecture, together with strong activism from leftist leaders and the engagement of Diadema's population, culminated in the election, in 1982, of the first mayor from the newly formed *Partido dos Trabalhadores* (PT—Workers' Party). In that election, the *Associação de Favelados* had a strong militant role, working in the election campaign for PT in the areas they represented. It is worth noting that the original formation of PT was linked to the trade unionist movement and the emergence of popular urban movements.[10] With PT in the local government, the population's demands were incorporated into public policies.

With the democratisation of Brazil in 1985, a number of spaces of participation like housing councils, meetings and conferences convened by municipal and state governments, participatory budgeting, managing municipal council funds, forums for the preparation of city development plans etc., were created for citizens. These spaces provided tremendous opportunities for participation in policymaking and the monitoring and implementation of projects. A brief discussion on the participatory spaces would indicate the nature and scope of popular participation.

The management councils were the spaces created by the 1988 Constitution for citizens' participation in policymaking and monitoring of programmes. Such councils were established sectorally e.g., education, health, housing, environment etc., in each municipality. Each municipality could form the councils as per their requirement. In São Paulo municipality for example, there were as many as 16 management councils. These councils were collective bodies of members from different constituencies like citizens, professionals, service providers and government institutions. These bodies generally comprised 50 per cent of the representatives elected directly by the people, 25 per cent elected by professionals and the remaining 25 per cent by service providers and government institutions. These councils acted as the 'deliberative, supervisory and consultative bodies whose main role was establishment, follow up, control and evaluation of public policies.'[11]

The origin of the participatory budget was associated with civil society's effort to establish peoples' control over public policies and the government budget, with the existence of a new legal and institutional framework created by the 1988 Constitution and with left-wing parties (Worker's Party), which wanted to establish popular participation in

10. One of the main founders of PT, a great national leader, was Luis Inácio Lula da Silva, president of Brazil for two consecutive mandates (2003-2006 and 2007-2010).

11. Instituto Polis and Ford Foundation (2008): 189.

governance.[12] The participatory budget has been tried in different ways in different municipalities but the processes are directed towards a 'cycle' which is repeated annually. The cycle starts in the first half of each year and culminates in the delivery of the Annual Budgetary Bill to the Municipal Legislature in September-October. The process starts with meetings in districts or regions where people put forward their priorities of budgetary allocations in their areas. For example, they may prioritise health, education, infrastructure depending upon their needs. These demands are discussed in the plenaries, which comprise representatives elected from the districts or regions. Thereafter, these demands are also negotiated by the representatives with the government, which then puts it up as part of the investment plan to be incorporated in the Budgetary Bill later. This bill has to be approved by the Municipal Legislature Chamber. The cycle ends with the monitoring and implementation of budgetary works.[13]

Similarly, popular participation in city development plans was ensured through negotiations and dialogues between community organisations and municipal governments and construction agencies. People were also involved in managing funds for the construction of houses as well as in the actual construction of houses and infrastructure.

Meetings and conferences convened annually or biannually by the ministries or the government departments, for dialogue on the public policies are also avenues for popular participation.

These participatory spaces were used extensively in the housing movement of Diadema. The movement shows us that even with scarce resources it is possible to improve local housing policies through the participation of the city's inhabitants in the discussion, design and implementation of programmes and projects. It can contribute to the improvement of the quality of life of citizens with better infrastructure and urban services in inhabited areas. According to Coelho, the study of this experience shows that the existence and effectuation of collective spaces for dialogue between public authorities and collective political subjects make the debates, decisions and division of responsibilities between

12. Ibid: 112.

13. Ibid: 113.

administrators and groups organised around housing policies more democratic.[14] These spaces contribute to the education and empowerment of the citizens who are taking actions aimed at the promotion of their own development. Furthermore, they help to integrate peoples' perspective into governmental actions.

The movement along with democratic movements in the early 1980s resulted in the adoption of social participation instruments, such as the municipal housing council, participatory budgeting and participation in the formulation and implementation of public policies in Diadema.

The democratic spaces for dialogue between the government and civil society, organised and mobilised the demand for the fulfilment of social rights, contributed to the co-authoring of policy decisions, sharing of responsibilities and to the establishment of pacts between the government and social actors in public policy management. However, mere creation of participatory spaces was not enough; initiatives were launched by both civil society and the government to make these spaces vibrant and effective.

Making Participatory Spaces Vibrant and Effective

The housing movement was successful in institutionalising a number of participatory instruments but the citizens were still not well versed with the functioning of these institutions. Hence, their capacity had to be built for making effective use of these participative spaces. The movement had to play a very critical role in enhancing the capacity of citizens. It found a unique partner in its endeavour, the state. It has been observed normally in the developing democracies that the state creates institutional spaces of participation but does not play an active role in promoting the use of these spaces. However, this was not the case in Diadema. The state played an active role not only in mobilising the citizens but also making the movement aware of the processes of city development plans and management of municipal funds. This enabled citizens to use participative spaces like participatory budgets, meetings and conferences, municipal council funds for housing and participation in city development plans. Through active participation, they were successful in including the common man's perspective in housing plans and protecting their interests.

14. Coelho (2008): 144.

At the outset, let us discuss the state's role in building the capacity of citizens for using these participatory spaces.

State as the Enabler of Participation

Responding to the demands for housing and urban services of the communities that lived in the city, the technicians of the first PT administration (1983-1988) carried out multiple actions in an attempt to integrate the areas occupied by *favelas* into the rest of the city. 'The municipal government could have fulfilled the [very specific water and electricity] demands but what's interesting is that the technicians spoke about urbanising *favelas*, which was virtually unheard of at the time and which represented a revolution, because it implied a total transformation of the *favela*, to get rid of the heaps of shanties in order to open the streets, to install a subterranean network of water pipes and electricity, leaving the surface for the movement of cars, ambulances etc. This was way beyond people's expectations, who wanted water and light.'[15]

Due to the great scarcity of financial resources, 'the way found to urbanise Diadema's *favelas* was a slow process—which spanned multiple government authorities, establishment of services so that the population could gain access to tap water, sewage, electricity, [as well as] paving streets, building stairs and opening access to the city's main avenues.'[16] Due to the lack of resources from the state and federal governments, these projects were carried out in partnership with the inhabitants, in a system of collective effort (*mutirão*). Citizens participated in state-led projects aimed for improving the infrastructure in Diadema.

During the whole process of *favela* urbanisation, popular participation was crucial, not only in the collective efforts of construction but also in the organisation of the housing nuclei. In fact, collective organisation was a pre-condition set by public authorities for starting the construction work. The housing nuclei falling in the zone of urbanisation were to be organised as inhabitant commissions, which would serve as interlocutors between the community and the municipal government in the process of urbanisation. Playing a key role in the organisation of the *favelas*, the municipal

15. Bisiliat (2004): 86.

16. Coelho (2008): 125.

government's team urged the communities to participate, organise and elect the inhabitant commission for accessing urban services like tap water and electricity. Thus, the municipal government worked to encourage self-organisation of the communities.[17]

Besides *favela* urbanisation, the officers from the municipal government introduced the topic of land regularisation in the housing policy agenda and in activities with the housing movement. After a wide mobilisation of the inhabitants on the issue, the municipal government and the housing movement collaborated in pressurising the municipal legislators to approve the use of the concession of real right of use (*Concessão do Direito Real de Uso*). This instrument 'aimed to provide occupancy rights to the population living in a *favela*, which occupied a public area (...), that is, it warrants social use of the property while it remained public.'[18]

However, for granting these land titles, *favelas* had to have been urbanised or had to be in the process of urbanisation and also had to have legally instituted associations of inhabitants and an inhabitants' commission.[19] Once formed, these associations became signatories to the 'concession of real right of use' contract; and each family received an equal part of the estate. The period stated for use of these areas was 90 years.

The success of the urbanisation policy and the regularisation of areas occupied by *favelas* was due to popular participation during the whole process, be it through the commissions and associations or through collective efforts to build infrastructure. At first, this participation was encouraged by the public authorities, who played the role of educators. After this effort at educating people, urbanisation and regularisation of *favelas* became the main claims of the *Movimento por Moradia* (Movement for Housing), which started to define the agenda of the municipal government, indicating the most urgent demands to be fulfilled.

It is worth noting that, in the first two administrations, popular participation occurred via the commissions of inhabitants of urbanised *favelas* or the *Associação de Favelados* but in the third PT administration

17. Bisiliat (2004): 86.

18. Mourad (2000): 32.

19. Reis and Liso (1998): 128.

(1993-1996), this association was divided by the public authorities into four associations referring to the geographical regions of the municipality (North, South, East and West). Each one of these associations included smaller associations with specific names and leaders.

According to Coelho, this division into territories was carried out to help guide the strategies of the municipal government's technical teams, as well as the organisational strategies of the communities, which defined regional priorities.[20] Diadema's leaders generally agreed with this division, however, Boni, a leader of the West Association, believes that this division into territories was a manoeuvre by the public authorities to make the movement more vulnerable and dependent on the public authorities. However, in the whole process of *favela* urbanisation, the active role of public authorities cannot be denied and their role spanned from organisation and mobilisation, to defining the agenda and directions of the communities associations or commissions. It is important to note that these agendas were not retrograde in nature but were progressive, which paved the way for housing and urban services for the inhabitants of Diadema.

Facilitating Participation in City Development Plans

Besides paying considerable attention to investments in infrastructure, *favela* urbanisation and land regularisation, gradually the municipal government also focussed on territorial planning. Diadema's third popular PT administration (1993-1996) prioritised the development of the City Master Plan (*plano diretor*) and sought popular participation in designing the plan. In addition, communities were mobilised to build pressure for the legislative approval of the plan. However, the scarcity of urban land in Diadema made the possibility of housing units for low income families a difficult proposition.

Due to this scarcity a proposal emerged to create an urban policy, the Areas of Special Social Interest (*Áreas Especiais de Interesse Social,* or *AEIS*), aimed at expanding access to urban land for the construction of housing units for the poorest social groups. This policy reserved some portions of urban territory for the construction of Social Interest Housing (*Habitação de Interesse Social*). Two types of AEIS were proposed by the

20. Coelho (2008): 70.

municipal government: AEIS-1 was for occupied areas to be urbanised and regularised, continuing the urbanisation programme which had been started since the first government; and AEIS-2 was for empty areas to be used exclusively for the construction of new housing units for the low income population.

The AEIS-1 were areas occupied by *favelas* and irregular plots, which were to be integrated with the rest of the city and, most importantly, ensure security of ownership of housing units for the inhabitants through land regularisation. The AEIS-2 were underused areas, or unused areas, which had to be negotiated for by the popular movements and the municipal government, for building social interest housing for lower income groups.

Getting this urban policy approved was a difficult task; hence, an intense process of education and negotiation was necessary. In addition, there were misunderstandings among the housing movement and municipal government over the concept of a land bank, which was to be appropriated for AIES-2. The movement believed that the land for AIES-2 would be bought by the municipal government through negotiation with private owners from the empty areas or unused areas of the city. As the municipal government did not have enough funds for this purpose at that time, they proposed that the movement bought the land directly from its owners. The movement was concerned about the difficulties of negotiating directly with the owners as they felt that the owners would not be willing to negotiate and would only sell the land for high prices.

To deal with this misunderstanding, the municipal technicians conducted workshops to explain that the idea of a land bank would be extremely costly for the municipal government, because it would make it necessary to carry out expropriations of high-priced plots and estates, which the city could not afford. 'In this sense, the municipal government technicians attempted to convince the housing movement about the benefits of the AEIS as a way of fulfilling the housing demands of the low income population without cost for the city, and they were successful. Convinced of the unfeasibility of a land bank, the housing movements adhered to the proposal of increasing the availability of land through the implementation of AEIS.'[21] Once more, municipal technicians played the

21. Carvalho *et al.* (2005): 11.

role of instructors and information multipliers, educating the housing movement's leaders on the policies that could help in ensuring a better quality of life in the cities.

Frequent interactions between the *Movimento por Moradia* (housing movement) and municipal technicians led to collaboration between the two in deciding the criteria for the inclusion of families in the housing units on AEIS. They decided that the families to be included in AIES should have an income of 10 Reals (approximately 5 dollars) or less; should not have any estatc property and must be residents of the city. Furthermore, the families should be organised into legally constituted associations, which would be responsible for the AEIS land acquisition contract. The movement also suggested areas for the application of the policy. The whole process ended in the demarcation of 36 AEIS in unoccupied private areas, amounting to 750,000 square metre of land located in urban areas with some infrastructure. The next step was the integration of AEIS areas into the City Master Plan.

However, this integration was resisted by the landowners and business segments, who argued that implementing this policy would make economic development of the city unviable, since a great part of the demarcated areas were located in the old industrial zone. This resistance could only be tackled by popular pressure. The debate for approval of the City Master Plan including AEIS continued to rage among people. The presence of a large number of housing movement activists in the municipal assembly also created pressure on the representatives to approve the City Master Plan.

Due to intense popular pressure, the City Master Plan was approved in 1994, composed by urban policies, which allowed urban income redistribution, included market sectors, promoted the deconcentration of earnings and the redistribution of opportunities.[22] The approval of this City Master Plan was considered a great victory by the housing movement.

It ultimately paved the way for the construction of houses for the poor income people in the city of Diadema. The first area negotiated for AEIS by the housing movement was a 96,000 square metre private estate called Sanko. In this area, four housing associations promoted the construction of

22. Rolnik (1998): 105.

housing projects with resources from the *Companhia de Desenvolvimento Habitacional e Urbano* (Housing and Urban Development Company), or CDHU. Each association chose the type of construction that it deemed most appropriate for its associates. Some projects were built by CDHU and one of them was built by the system of collective effort and based on a blueprint developed by a technical assistance team hired by one of the housing associations. The *Secretaria Municipal de Habitação* (Municipal Secretariat for Housing) helped the inhabitants by designing an urban project and carrying out the construction work for basic infrastructure equipment.

CDHU in close collaboration with the communities was able to build 1,250 housing units in the city. The construction process took nearly 10 years, with several incidences of popular (communities) participation in the projects. One of these symbolic moments happened in 1998, when CDHU did not deliver the resources for construction. To overcome this hurdle the associations involved in Sanko camped in front of CDHU's headquarters. After great pressure from the movement, as well as with the help of the municipal government and state representatives, the resources were made available for the project. The delay in the delivery of these resources delayed the completion of the new housing units. The last units were delivered in October 2008.The Sanko housing units are not entirely finished yet. Some public infrastructure and public spaces like parks are still being demanded by the communities.

One important programme, titled the Legal Aid Service (1989-1992) organised by the state helped in the formation of entities, associations, commissions etc., for strengthening society's participation in the elected bodies. This programme supported the associations so they were institutionalised and registered with all legal requisites, so that they could participate in the development of the processes of urbanisation and land regularisation of the nuclei located in AEIS.

The experiences of participation in Diadema's city development plans again reflect the critical role played by the state in including citizens in the housing policies, the integration of housing policies in city development plans and the participation of communities in the construction of houses and infrastructure. The state played the role of educators and mobilisers and even set the agenda and directions for the communities. However, once the capacity of communities had to be built, they negotiated with the state to protect their interests as can be seen in the case where CDHU delayed the construction of houses. The close collaboration between the state and the communities finally led to the delivery of houses for the poor income people, improvement in urban services and integration of housing policies in the city development plans.

Citizens' Voice in Managing Municipal Fund for Housing

For arranging the resources for AEIS, a municipal fund to support social interest housing (*Fundo Municipal de Apoio à Habitação de Interesse Social*) or FUMAPIS was instituted by law. The FUMAPIS was managed by the FUMAPIS Council, which evolved from the commissions of informal housing nuclei. The main role of the council was to decide upon and monitor the way in which resources from the FUMAPIS were used in the implementation of Diadema's housing policies. Coelho says that housing funds were a result of the strong mobilisation organised mainly by the *União dos Movimentos de Moradia* (Housing Movements Union) and the *Central dos Movimentos Populares* (Central Popular Movements) created at three government levels.[23] A strong base in the movement made FUMAPIS Council participative in nature having representation from all three groups, the executive, legislature and the popular housing movement.

The Council thus proved to be an institutional space for permanent discussion and deliberation on housing issues, contributing to the inclusion of social groups, which had not participated in the processes of formulation, implementation and decision-making of housing policies. In this way, close interaction in the institutional spaces brought hitherto left out social groups closer to the popular housing movement.

One good example of participation in managing FUMAPIS's resources could be seen in the construction of the Jardim das Praias. This area was demarcated as AEIS and the housing movement tried negotiating for the sale of the land with the owner but no deal was struck. Confronting this impasse, the FUMAPIS Council took the decision to buy the land with

23. Coelho (2008): 82.

resources from FUMAPIS.[24] It was not the decision of the Council alone, in fact, pressure from the communities closed the deal or it can be said it was a collective decision of the community. According to Ronaldo Lacerda, a leader from Jardim das Praias, the families to be settled in this area were organised and participated in the movement's meetings, putting pressure on the council members to approve the release of funds for the area. Lacerda shows how the community based organisations prepared people for participation in the functioning of the Council. (See Box 4.2) This involvement and organisation of the community proved crucial for obtaining the resources. Interactions with the inhabitants of the communities, which were largely unorganised, showed that they did not have access to various channels of participation as they did not represent the majority of the community. Thus, the councils provided opportunities of participation to new social groups. As a result of their actions, the Council was able to acquire an area in Jardim das Praias, which was divided into 362 plots distributed among four housing associations from different regions of the city and to families living in risky areas.

Close collaboration between the state and communities does not mean that there were no conflicts or confrontations between the two. One such confrontation could be seen in Diadema, when the housing movement used political strategies, such as the occupation of estates and warehouses, to put pressure on the government in 1997, when their demands for housing were not heard. According to Lacerda[25] the occupations carried out during this period were political actions of the housing movement, which demanded democratic public policies that warranted the right to adequate housing.

Reacting sharply to confrontations, the government diminished the importance of the Municipal Housing Council, suspending its meetings, as well as FUMAPIS. It is important to note that the deactivation of the Municipal Housing Council and FUMAPIS provoked reactions from housing associations, which defended democratic management. In this period, these associations, together with popular movements, invested in community education, leadership development and the strengthening of

24. Later, the money invested returned to the Fund because of an appeal made by the Federal government.

25. Declaration obtained in an interview carried out on October 16th, 2008.

collective organisation, all of which contributed to leverage the political struggle. Some of the commitments made by the government in 1996 were saved with great difficulty, after great popular pressure.

Box 4.2

Ronaldo Lacerda, Leader of the East Association and President of the Freedom Pro-Housing Association (Jardim das Praias)

Ronaldo Lacerda was first engaged with the housing movement through an invitation he received from an elder leader to participate in an assembly in the *favela* he was born in. According to him, his initial motivation was to fight for better living conditions in the area e.g., basic services such as water and electricity supply and the guarantee that they would not be evicted from the area. Gradually, he got more engaged with the housing movement and started participating in assemblies and demonstrations. He soon realised that the housing problems went beyond his neighbourhood. His personal motivations became collective, leading to the realisation that the housing problem was not only about acquiring water and electricity for one house but it was a global problem. This perspective enabled him to look at the housing problems not in isolation but jointly with other regions.

In the 1990s, he was a part of the group of families that participated actively in buying the Jardim das Praias area. He participated in the negotiation process and in the building of the settlement and houses, not only as a neighbour but also as a representative of the East Region Association. Thus, he emerged as a leader in the east region.

At the same time, Ronaldo and other community members founded the Freedom Pro-Housing Association, which works specifically in the Jardim das Praias neighbourhood. The association organises the community in demonstrations for other demands such as green areas and promotes professional capacity building and workshops to build leadership.

With the aim of fighting for better housing conditions in Diadema and a clear understanding of the housing problem, the public services and infrastructure it requires, Ronaldo became a candidate for the Municipal Legislative Chamber in the last municipal elections but did not gather enough votes to be elected. He is now a member of the FUMAPIS Council, President of the Freedom Pro-Housing Association and owns a small fabric factory.

These conflicts were resolved when a more democratic government came to power in 2001 and it reactivated the spaces of participation and deliberations of housing policies. The Council was reselected and the meetings resumed and these processes again generated debates and actions around housing issues.

The FUMAPIS Council also generated considerable competition among representatives of local society, as it was a strategic space through which resources could be channelised for housing. Social representatives competed among themselves to get elected to the Council. According to Elza Cunha Alencar,[26] a social technician from the Housing Secretariat, the election to the Council was regionalised. It meant that representatives came from each of the four regions (North, South, East and West) of the city. Each region sent one official representative and one extra representative—a substitute for the official when he or she could not participate in a meeting—for the Council. These elected representatives competed in this democratic space for financial resources, which would be used for fulfilling the housing demands. They deliberated over policies of collective interest related to housing and the city's priorities.

Through the Council, the movement also secured some programmes, which helped in the organisation of the housing movement. One of them was the Programme to Support Housing Associations, which resumed its relations with the housing associations by promoting partnerships and agreements with CDHU and *Caixa Econômica Federal* (CEF, a state-owned federal bank), to enable solutions for housing demands.

It is worth noting that the institution of participatory channels and the creation of democratic decision-making spaces to manage housing policies did not mean the elimination of conflict. The deliberations on the issues of conflict led to more intense discussions and debates among the communities, ultimately resulting in better solutions of the problem often with consensus. Citizens' voices were, thus, articulated through community based associations, which were able to influence the FUMAPIS councillors and were able to win resources for housing in their areas.

Participatory Budget—Mechanism for Prioritising Housing

The participatory budget (*Orçamento Participativo*, or OP) was another instrument, which made considerable contribution in allocating budgets for housing in Diadema. OP was instituted in 1994 in the city with the aim of discussing the priorities in the municipal government's annual

26. According to interview done in February 2009.

budget. It helped in fulfilling the demands of the inhabitants of the city's different neighbourhoods. The processes of OP were open to all the inhabitants of the city. The OP started with convening assemblies in the city's neighbourhoods where the inhabitants' demands were discussed and representatives for the higher (regional) plenaries were selected. These representatives discussed the communities' demands with the Mayor on a monthly basis, which were later taken up by the municipal government. In OP in Diadema, inhabitants gave priority to housing, which was also discussed in the regional plenaries resulting in increased allocations for housing in the municipal budget.

According to Coelho, the housing sector due to prioritisation in the OP of Diadema started to gain more prominence in the distribution of resources from the municipal budget. The investments made directly by the city significantly increased, amounting, in 1995, to seven per cent of the budget. It is worth noting that many construction projects for the urbanisation of *favelas* were deliberated upon in the assemblies of the OP and defined as priority investments to be made with municipal resources. This fact shows the close connection between Diadema's municipal budget's democratic management processes and those of its housing policies. This connection was also important for the installation of urban equipment and infrastructure in the social interest housing projects implemented in estates and plots located within AEIS-2, negotiated by the housing movements' organisations.

Thus the participatory budget not only helped in the completion of projects related to infrastructure and housing but also the training of the communities in the participatory processes as these were becoming regular spaces for negotiations with the government. It also helped in better and organised articulation of the demands of the inhabitants of Diadema.

Meetings and Conferences as the Instruments of Popular Pressure

Meetings and conferences were organised annually by the government at three levels, federal, provincial and municipal. These were also important instruments for creating popular pressure for policymaking and implementation. These meetings and conferences were convened by ministries or the government departments for discussing public policies among the people. It witnessed the active participation of different social segments such as business owners, trade unions, non-governmental organisations, public managers, members of parliament and members of social and popular movements. These participatory spaces were the outcomes of the popular movement for democratisation in Brazil. Meetings and conferences convened by the municipal governments for discussing the housing demands were used as a forum for demanding the regularisation of *favelas* and other precarious and informal settlements and the construction of new housing units for the low income population. Moreover, suggestions for municipal housing policy were also made in these forums. The Diadema experience shows that these meetings made important contributions in the revision of the City Master Plan. Similarly, in the fourth municipal housing meeting, suggestions were made related to the provision of subsidies in the design of the Municipal Housing Plan (*Plano Municipal de Habitação*) and the Target Plan (*Plano de Metas*) for 2006-2012.

Meetings and conferences convened by the government, as can be seen, from the case of Diadema, served as important spaces for raising concerns e.g., health, education, housing etc., of the people and policy advocacy. Citizens have used these spaces to good effect in Brazil.

Results

The effective use of participatory spaces by the community organisations and the housing movement along with the support of the state resulted in many victories in the struggle for housing and urban services.

The most evident victory was the improvement in the living conditions of the city's inhabitants. The *favela* urbanisation programme, for example, changed the physical characteristics of the city. During the first 13 years of municipal governments led by the Worker's Party (PT), the housing and urban policies significantly altered the city's urban and housing characteristics. With the projects for the *favela's* urbanisation in 1996, 60 per cent of the city's houses were linked to the sewage network, 95 per cent had tap water and 96 per cent of the streets were paved. In 1995, out of the 197 existing *favelas*, 121 were entirely urbanised and integrated in to the city, with access to public services and equipment. In 2006, 161 of the 207 *favelas* in the city were completely urbanised and integrated into the city, 32 more are in the process of urbanisation, 6 with smaller located interventions and 8 were to be relocated because they were in areas of risk.

The *favelas'* urbanisation programme had resulted in tremendous improvement in the lives of the inhabitants of Diadema. The infrastructure built in the *favelas* helped improve other sectors, such as health and public security. With the improved sanitary conditions, collective health improved with a significant drop in diseases among the citizens. The urbanisation works also created conditions for the appropriation of the public spaces previously abandoned and badly illuminated. Organised and well-illuminated areas inhibited delinquent action, bringing down the rate of violence in most of the areas.

The implementation of the AEIS also brought considerable benefits to the people. The inhabitants of Sanko and Jardim das Praias said, 'gaining access to adequate housing in urbanised locations improved people's lives'. They said that they had relief from paying rent, which substantially increased their income. Furthermore, adequate housing meant that inhabitants had formal addresses. According to Manuel, an inhabitant of Jardim das Praias, having an official address helped one obtain better employment. This scenario helped children gain better opportunities to study, complete more years of formal education and access better living conditions.

The land regularisation of some housing nuclei meant that families acquired the ownership of their houses and certain guarantees against evictions. The regularisation also increased access to credit for some of the residents, who could use the ownership title as a guarantee for financial institutions. This shows the importance of complete land regularisation to all the urbanised *favelas* in Diadema.

Interviews with the inhabitants of the *favelas*, which had been urbanised and received land regularisation investments, showed that the results of these actions went way beyond physical and urbanistic improvements. The insertion of the housing nucleus in the city, for example, generated awareness about rights in its inhabitants, to the detriment of 'favoured' relations, which were normally established among the inhabitants of the urban settlements and representatives of the local authorities. Furthermore, working together in participatory spaces and construction generated a feeling of camaraderie among the urbanised and regularised neighbourhoods. The perception developed among the inhabitants that the neighbourhood and the housing units deserved permanent care and it prepared them to struggle for their rights.

The great achievement of the housing movement in the city of Diadema was the construction of participation spaces that enabled the inhabitants to participate in the decisions about the housing policy. This participation happened in all of the policy phases, from the definition of laws and proposals until the implementation of infrastructure work and housing units. These spaces also granted transparency to the development of the policy and programmes.

The urbanisation, regularisation and housing construction programmes also helped in the organisation of the communities. The Jardim Maria Tereza housing nucleus, for example, participated in this process of popular organisation. This nucleus emerged in the 1970s, when workers at the region's industries occupied a public area. The living conditions were very precarious, without public lighting, infrequent water supply, lack of a sewage system, with unpaved, potholed streets and alleys, among other problems. Facing the demands of Jardim Maria Tereza's inhabitants, the municipal authorities encouraged the creation of a commission of inhabitants, invested in urban infrastructure, provided construction materials and helped the community in the construction executed through a collective effort system.

After these improvements, however, some community leaders were lost and the inhabitants were demobilised. The community removed itself from the housing movement and the nucleus was no longer internally organised. Today, this community is trying to get reorganised but, according to an inhabitant, it is difficult to ensure the participation of the population, which is no longer the same that fought for urbanisation. These challenges have been faced by the housing movement in a number of locations in Diadema. According to Lacerda, after getting houses with adequate infrastructure, the population demobilises, leaving the inhabitants' association depleted. According to Zuleika, a technician at the

Municipal Housing Secretariat, 'after the inhabitants got their plots and built their houses, participation ended. They could not see that the struggle had to move on, that they still needed to get Basic Healthcare Units (Unidades Básicas de Saúde, or UBS), day care centres, among several other things.'

In some of the housing nuclei, such as Jardim das Praias, the inhabitants' association or the nucleus commission still encourages the participation of the community, in their struggle in other areas, such as education, health and sports. According to Lacerda, the movement must involve the community in these struggles so that new leadership emerges, inspiring young people to participate in discussions and political actions related to claims for spaces for leisure and sport activities.

The housing movement is now greatly concerned with thinking about housing policies being integrated with other social policies, such as economic development, education and security. According to leaders Cida, Toninho and Lacerda[27], the housing movement is dedicated to the topic of integration of housing policies with other social policies, such as health, education, economic development and public security. The need for linking those as well as other social policies is increasingly important in the daily lives of the communities. According to Lacerda, the choice to resume the discussions on housing policies in a way that is integrated with other needs of Diadema's population is a way of strengthening the social struggle for housing involving the social groups that have already got their own houses and need to mobilise to improve the living conditions in the neighbourhoods where they live. The endeavour is to build on the success of the housing movement and expand the struggle to other fields like health and education. All the learnings of citizens' participation in the institutional spaces should also be used in other fields.

Conclusions

The struggle for improving housing and urban services in Diadema took a distinct turn when the participatory spaces were institutionalised after the adoption of a democratic Constitution in 1988. Citizens in the

27. Declarations obtained in a workshop carried out on September 11th, 2008 and in an interview carried out on October 16th, 2008.

post-1988 period needed to learn the methods of using spaces effectively for putting up demands for housing and urban services. Surprisingly, this role was taken up by the state. The state collaborated with the housing movement and community organisations for organising them into inhabitant commissions, encouraged them to scale up their demands to the organisation of *favelas* and land regularisation instead of limiting their demands to basic services, facilitated popular participation in city development plans and managing municipal funds for housing. This close collaboration between the state and people prepared the latter for dialogue and negotiation, which proved to be very useful in the use of participatory spaces. It also provided a perspective and vision for a city among the inhabitants. One critical question, which this collaboration raises, is whether it led to the domination of participatory spaces by the state or it led to the co-option of social actors by the state. In this case study, we find that the state played the role of mobiliser, capacity builder and envisioner but it did not dominate the participatory spaces. Neither were the social actors co-opted by the state. People not only set the goal and objectives of the participatory spaces as seen in AEIS and FUMAPIS Council but also confronted the state when their demands were not met. Other participatory instruments like participatory budget and meetings and conferences were also used to prioritise and create pressure for demanding housing and urban services. The case study amply demonstrates the processes and the results of participatory spaces, which can be an important democratic experience for not only the people of Brazil but also the people of developing democracies.

References

Baltrusis, Nelson Laila e Mourad Estudo de Caso Diadema (1999). In Raquel Rolnik, *Regulação Urbanística e Exclusão Territorial*. Revista Pólis 32, São Paulo: Instituto Polis.

Baltrusis, Nelson. O Plano Diretor de Diadema 2001—uma breve avaliação. In Laura Bueno, Machado de Mello e Renato Cymbalista. Planos Diretores Municipais. Annablume, São Paulo, 2007.

Baltrusis, Nelson, Laila Nazem Mourad e Yeda Maria Inoue Akemi (2003). *Agentes de planejamento urbano a participação popular na elaboração do plano diretor de Diadema*. X Encontro Nacional da Anpur, Belo Horizonte.

Bisiliat, Jeanne (2004). Lá onde os Rios Refluem. Diadema 20 anos de Democracia e poder local. Editora Fundação Perseu Abramo, São Paulo.

Carvalho, Maria Albertina, Mariana Mencio, Paula Pollinie, Renato Cymbalista (2005). Sistematização do Plano Diretor do Município de Diadema – SP. São Paulo. Relatório de pesquisa.

Coelho, Marta Cirera Sári (2008). *Espaço de Direitos É mais que Direito a Espaço. O processo de Urbanização de Favelas em Diadema (1983-2008)*. São Paulo, PUC-SP: 2008. Dissertação de mestrado.

Fonseca, Silmara Cristiane (1999). *Diadema e o Grande ABC: expansão industrial na economia de São Paulo. In R.B. Fonseca, (Coord.). Impactos urbanos e socioeconômicos dos investimentos em* transporte na Região Metropolitana de São Paulo. Universidade Estadual de Campinas/Núcleo de Economia Social, Urbana, Regional (Unicamp/Nesur), Convênio Metrô-Fecamp. (Projeto de Pesquisa).

Fundação João Pinheiro (2004). *Déficit Habitacional no Brasil Municípios selecionados e microrregiões geográficas.*

Instituto Polis and Ford Foundation (2008). *The Challenges of the Democratic Management in Brazil—Participation.*

Prefeitura Municipal De Diadema (2000). *Diagnóstico sobre a Capacidade Institucional do Município de Diadema no setor habitacional para atendimento às populações de baixa renda.*

Prefeitura De Diadema (1996). *Habitação cada dia melhor. Integração e Cidadania.*

———. (1996). *Habitação cada dia melhor. Plano Diretor de (1994).*

Mourad, Laila Nazem (2000). *Democratização do Acesso à Terra Urbana em Diadema.* Campinas, FAU-PUCCAMP. Dissertação de mestrado.

Reis, M. e C.H. Liso (1998). "A Concessão de Direito Real de Uso na regularização fundiária", in Fernandes, E. (org.). *Direito Urbanístico*, Del Rey, Belo Horizonte.

Rolnik, Raquel (coord.) (2000). *Programa de Capacitação de agentes locais para a atuação em processos de Regularização Urbanística–AEIS*. AlterMidia, Setembro. Vídeo.

———. (coord.) (1998). *Impactos da aplicação de novos instrumentos urbanísticos em cidades do Estado de São Paulo*. Relatório final de Pesquisa, Faculdade de Arquitetura e Urbanismo da PUCCAMP, FAPESP e Lincoln Institute of Land Policy. Campinas.

5 Improving Urban Services through Citizens' Action, Dharamshala, Himachal Pradesh, India

Bhavita Vaishnava

Introduction

In recent years India has been witnessing a fast pace of urbanisation and has become one of the fastest growing economies of the world today. According to the 2001 population census results, India's urban population amounted to 286,120,000 inhabitants, almost the equivalent of the entire population of the United States of America.[1] Though this rapid growth of urbanisation has led to economic and infrastructural development in certain mega cities of the country, it has on the other hand resulted in unplanned and haphazard growth in small and medium towns posing a great challenge to the state and local governments. As the cities grow in terms of area and population due to rural-urban migration, it leads to deteriorating urban services as a result of the growing pressure on existing resources. The mushrooming of slums and squatter settlements lacking the most basic amenities like water supply, sanitation, sewerage etc., is a common feature of urbanisation in almost all the growing cities of the country.

It is in the above mentioned context that the role of urban governance comes to light. In India, urban local bodies (ULBs) are the primary administrative units that cater to basic urban services and infrastructure in the cities. Though the history of local governance goes back to 1726 with the establishing of Mayor's Courts in the Presidency towns of Madras, Bombay and Calcutta, it came into prominence in 1992, when a major step

1. M-Gnanou and M-Ebrard (2007).

towards the decentralisation and empowerment of local governance institutions took place with the enactment of the 74th Constitutional Amendment Act (CAA). The Act classified ULBs into municipal corporations (*nagar nigam*) for larger urban areas with a population of more than one million, municipal councils (*nagar palika*/municipalities) for smaller urban areas and city councils (*nagar panchayats*) for transitional areas. The central idea of this amendment was to break down huge structures of urban governance into small bodies with ample functions and power to facilitate a process of bottom-up development. Hence, this amendment was to provide space for ordinary citizens to participate in the decision-making process and governance system of the country. The 74th CAA and the various follow-up actions including the reforms towards effective implementation of its provisions, have given wide-ranging responsibilities and functions to the ULBs and their elected representatives.

The municipal bodies are vested with a long list of functions delegated to them by the state governments under the municipal legislation. These functions broadly relate to public health, welfare, regulatory functions, public safety, public works and development activities. Public health includes water supply, sewerage and sanitation, eradication of communicable diseases etc.; welfare includes public facilities such as education, recreation, etc.; regulatory functions related to prescribing and enforcing building bye-laws, encroachments on public land, registration of births and deaths, etc.; public safety includes fire protection, streetlighting, etc.; public works measures such as construction and maintenance of inner city roads, etc; and development functions related to town planning and development of commercial markets. In addition to the legally assigned functions, the sectoral departments of the state government often assign the ULBs with various functions such as family planning, nutrition and slum improvement, disease and epidemic control, etc.

However, the provision of water supply and sewerage in several states has either been taken over by the state governments or transferred to parastatal agencies. It is also a shared responsibility in many states. These agencies usually undertake land acquisition and development works and take up remunerative projects such as markets and commercial complexes, etc. The municipal bodies in most cases have been left only with the functions of garbage collection/disposal, streetlighting, maintenance of inner city roads, registration of births and deaths, etc.

Today the municipal bodies are facing a peculiar situation where the demand for services has been rising due to urbanisation and urban growth but on the supply side, the local resource base has been constantly declining. Ineffective local governance, inefficient management practices, poor planning processes, lack of periodical revision of municipal tax rates/ user charges, poor information systems and record management are some of the basic weaknesses in the present municipal administration system. Many municipalities in India, particularly those belonging to small and medium size cities are poorly staffed with unclear and fragmented staff responsibilities. In addition, their capabilities and motivation to deal with the increasing complex urban needs are extremely low. Faced with such a situation the ULBs are becoming increasingly dependent on higher levels of government for their operation and maintenance requirements. This has serious repercussions on the availability and quality of basic services in the urban areas of the country.[2]

As far as citizens' participation in development activities in urban areas is concerned, it is relatively less as compared to the rural setup. In urban areas though, spaces for participation exist in the form of ward committees as per the 74th CAA. These ward committees (*mohalla samitis*) can play an important role in the systematic growth of towns as well as access municipal services in a better manner. The responsibilities of the ward committees, as provisioned in the CAA include the following.[3]

- Maintenance of civic services.
- Drafting of annual budgets.
- Slum improvement.
- Formulation and execution of development schemes.
- Monitoring the implementation of development.
- Granting approval and financial sanction to plans and municipal works.
- Scrutiny of monthly progress reports.

---

2. Mathur (2004).
3. Mohanty (2008).

But the provision for ward committees is restricted to municipalities having a population of three lakh or more. Till date, even this provision has not been fully operational in most of the municipalities leaving the citizens to the mercy of elected councillors and municipal officials. In the absence of any legal sanctity to the *samitis*/ward committees formed thus so far, they have been viewed at best as citizens' own local initiatives to make the municipalities more accountable.

Spaces for participation also widened with the launch of the Jawaharlal Nehru Urban Renewal Mission (JNNURM) by the Government of India in December 2005 across 63 cities in the country. The mission aims to create 'economically productive, efficient, equitable and responsive cities'. Citizen participation under the Mission is ensured through the Community Participation Law (CPL), which aims at institutionalising citizen participation and introducing the concept of area *sabhas* (consisting of all the registered voters of a polling booth) in urban areas. All the area *sabhas* are linked to the ward level committee through area *sabha* representatives, who are chosen by the community. Thus, the mission creates a minimum of three tiers of decision-making in urban governance, namely, the municipality, the ward committee and the area *sabhas*. Apart from the above, participation is also provisioned by involving citizens in municipal functions like setting priorities, budgeting provisions, exerting pressure for compliance of existing regulations, etc.

The following case study depicts how some of these 'invited' spaces provided by the government as well as spaces 'created' by citizens were used to hold the municipal authorities accountable for basic services in Dharamshala. It also reflects the various processes of community mobilisation and collectivisation undertaken by PRIA to facilitate citizens' engagement in accessing municipal services.

The Context

Dharamshala, the headquarters of Kangra District lies on a spur of the Dhauladhar Ranges, the Pir Panjal region of the outer Himalayas. The town commands majestic views of the mighty Dhauladhar Ranges above and the Kangra Valley below. It is divided into upper and lower towns with a difference of some 457 metres (1500 ft) between them. Lower Dharamshala comprising the Kotwali and Kachehri is a busy commercial centre, whereas Upper Dharamshala or 'Mcleodganj' with the suburbs of Mcleodganj and Forsythganj is a tourist destination and the residence of His Holiness, the Dalai Lama. The city enjoys multiple roles as the district headquarter of Kangra District, the capital of the Tibetan Government in exile as well as a hill station. The town was established as a cantonment-cum-administrative centre and acquired its current multifunctional character due to the coming up of regional offices, trade and commerce, tourism, education and financial institutions and hospitals.

As the town is a major tourist destination, it attracts more than one lakh Indian and foreign tourists every year. The floating population of Dharamshala on a peak day is about 5,000. Though this enables great tourist potential for the town, it also poses a threat to its natural ecology as increasing tourism and commercialisation result in a dearth and subsequent depletion of natural resources. With the growth of tourism, a number of commercial and business establishments have also evolved in the town and are major contributors to solid waste generation. Also in the early '90s an increasing amount of industrially produced consumer goods were sold in Dharamshala that led to the generation of non-biodegradable waste in the city. An inefficient waste collection system resulted in the accumulation of waste in streams and hillsides due to the continuous dumping of garbage by the residents.

Solid waste in general, consists of dry refuse such as ashes, dust, food waste, packaging in the form of paper, metals, plastics or glass, kitchen waste, discarded clothing and furnishings, garden waste, etc. In advanced countries, solid waste may also contain heavy articles like unused cars, televisions, refrigerators, VCRs, VCDs, music systems, etc. It is a critical service on account of the high organic content in waste and the tropical climate of the country; the uncollected and indisposed waste can result in various kinds of diseases and present serious health risks. Therefore, its frequent collection and disposal is absolutely essential in cities and towns.

Compared to other countries, the solid waste generation in India's urban areas is not large in quantitative terms. Studies show that it varies between a low of 294 grams to a high of 484 grams per capita per day, the variation being explained by a variety of reasons including the size of cities, their functions, household income and the level of economic development. In most cases however, waste collection is not being done adequately and on an average roughly 40-60 per cent of total waste generated remains uncollected, which is one of the biggest sources of environmental degradation in human settlements. It contributes to the pollution of the entire environment, air, water and soil.

In most cities, solid waste is collected from bins and transported to dump sites on the periphery of the city. The indiscriminate dumping of waste in the nearest available low lying area often causes damage to the soil. Very few cities practice scientific methods of sanitary landfill or convert the waste into compost or energy. This is largely due to the fact that solid waste is not separated prior to collection. The physical characteristic of solid waste collected by municipalities is not readily suitable for recycling into compost or energy.[4]

As far as the status of solid waste in Dharamshala is concerned, the town generates about 10-12 tonnes/day and the municipality is able to collect only 70-75 per cent of it. This is due to the hilly terrain and steep slopes that make it difficult for municipal vehicles to collect garbage from certain areas that are difficult to access. There is no proper system for disposal and waste is often thrown on the hillside and in open drains. The reasons for the indiscriminate disposal of waste as per the municipality are:

- Lack of civic sense and awareness among the community.
- Limited municipal resources i.e., manpower and finance.
- Lack of coordination and communication within the municipality and other line departments.

The municipality has four vehicles out of which one is provided by the Tourism Department and 37 *safai karamcharis* out of which 16 are men and 21 are women. The municipality has provided 70 containers and 35 dumpers at various locations for the collection of waste in the town.

With regard to waste recycling, it is one of the municipalities in the state, where a waste treatment plant has been installed. This was made possible because of the constant pressure by the municipal council on the

4. Mathur (2004).

state government for the same. The collected waste is divided into dry and wet waste at the disposal site and composting of the same is done through 20 compost pits. This system is called STAC i.e., Sulabh Thermophilic Aerobic Composting. The contract for the waste treatment has been given to Sulabh by the state government.

The poor status of urban civic services in Dharamshala reflects the grim reality of the inaccessibility of services by the community and lack of appropriate initiatives by the concerned authorities. Given below is a brief description of some of the problems faced by the community with regard to municipal services in their areas.

- In Ward no.3, door-to-door collection of waste has not yet started and people usually throw their garbage in open areas around their houses. Open defecation is also a common practice, as most of the households do not have private latrines.
- In Ward no.8, Col. M.G. Sharma mentioned the problem of defective water meters, which show higher readings than normal. Though the people in the community have complained about this to the authorities, no significant action has been taken to resolve the issue as yet. Apart from this, he also spoke about the absence of streetlights on the road that connects the ward to the town.
- Prem David a citizen of Ward no.10 spoke about the poor quality of water especially in the rainy season. He said that the water was extremely dirty and muddy and could not be used for domestic purposes. As far as garbage collection is concerned, he mentioned that the municipal council does not provide a door-to-door waste collection service and people generally throw the garbage in open drains or on the hill side. He also said that the poor monitoring of the *safai karamcharis* is a major issue in most of the wards. As there is lack of supervision of their work, they often throw the collected garbage into the open drains (*nalas*), which is a source of many diseases and health problems for the residents living near by.

Considering the dismal state of sanitation in the town, local organisations and the community joined hands to devise measures to confront the problem. Given below are some of the initiatives taken up by local organisations to solve the problem.

The Tibetan Welfare Society

In 1994, the Tibetan Welfare Office (TWO) initiated the 'Clean upper Dharamshala' project. One of the main objectives of the project was and still is, is to enable a clean environment in Mcleodganj. The project started in Mcleodganj with three so called 'green workers' who collected recyclable waste from individual doorsteps. Later, an open truck was purchased in order to collect and transport non-recyclable and other mixed waste to the disposal site in lower Dharamshala.

Gamru Youth Brigade Club

The Tikka Gamru Garbage initiative began in the summer of 2003 through the collaborative efforts of Cross-Cultural Solutions (US) and the local Tikka Gamru residents. The Gamru Youth Brigade Club provides door-to-door collection of garbage in Ward no. 3 for 92 households. Nine dustbins have been placed and one worker is engaged in the door-to-door collection of waste on a regular basis. They regularly sensitise the community on the issue of waste disposal and management.

Thus, it can be said that citizens and community based organisations (CBOs) in the town were already taking steps to solve the problem in their own unique ways. Collective as well as individual action by citizens to raise their voices in accessing basic services existed in different areas but was dormant. The need of the hour was to bring together these various initiatives in different areas and collectively demonstrate the strength of civic engagement and participation. It is at this point of time that Society for Participatory Research in Asia (PRIA) acted as an intermediary organisation in mobilising the communities, strengthening citizens and their collectives and capacitating them to negotiate with the government authorities. The citizen leaders that emerged out of the process further took charge of identifying and addressing emerging issues. The processes of community mobilisation adopted by PRIA are mentioned in the following Section.

Process of Community Mobilisation

As a well-established democratic theory argues that though individual citizens who effectively exercise their rights and entitlements by voting, making demands on public institutions or engaging in the community's public life, help transform political institutions into democratic ones; associations on the other hand, are the schools of democracy that play a critical role in producing these civic and active citizens. Associations in this way make an important contribution to the quality of democracy.[5] In pursuance of the same, the process of formation and mobilisation of ward committees, women's groups and youth groups was initiated in different wards. Along with this, the citizens were sensitised towards their right to participate in development activities undertaken by the ULBs. Active citizens from the community were identified and capacitated to take up leadership roles in accessing urban civic services. Somc of the initiatives are listed below.

Identification and Strengthening of Citizen Leaders

The role of citizen leaders is essential in mobilising local communities and ensuring the tenets of inclusion and participation to promote ownership of the communities over the different development processes. Their role can be put into two broad categories of society building that includes social mobilisation of the community, overcoming social exclusion and managing differences/divisions within the communities and engaging governance institutions that comprise raising their voice on issues of concern, negotiating with different stakeholders on behalf of the community and also ensuring one's credibility within the community.[6]

Active citizens from the community were identified during the process of community mobilisation and collectivisation as citizen leaders. They were ordinary citizens from the community like ex-servicemen, retired government officials and school teachers etc., who enthusiastically participated in community meetings and played a major role in influencing others from their area to participate as well. These citizen leaders were then capacitated on different issues of development, especially those related to urban governance and civic engagement through trainings and capacity building exercises. They were further equipped with leadership skills to effectively voice the concerns of society, put forward their demands before

5. Houtzager *et al*. (2007): 9.

6. Ganai (2004).

the government authorities and act as representatives on behalf of their communities.

Exposure Visit to Pithoragarh

Solid waste management (SWM) is a part of public health and sanitation and according to the Indian Constitution falls within the purview of the State List. The activity being local in nature is entrusted to the ULBs. The ULB undertakes the task of solid waste service delivery, with its own staff, equipment and funds. Yet, most ULBs have not been able to handle it because of a shortage of staff, funds and technical expertise; as a result, one can witness garbage littered around most urban locations. However, a few examples of efficient SWM practices exist in some areas and Pithoragarh is one of them. Active community participation and efficient municipal services have resulted in effective sanitary conditions in Pithoragarh for which they have also received awards from the state government.

To learn about the processes of community mobilisation and participation in SWM in Pithoragarh, citizen leaders, elected representatives, government officials and representatives from CBOs were taken to the town for exposure visits. The objective of the visit was to enhance the participants' knowledge on community organisation and sensitise them on the issue of SWM. Learning about the procedure, composition and role of *mohalla swachata samitis* (MSSs) i.e., neighbourhood cleanliness committees in urban governance and their linkage with the municipality was also on the agenda of the visit.

Dr. Dinesh Joshi, Director, Himalayan Study Circle (HSC) was the local resource person for the exposure visit. Sharing his experiences, he said that Pithoragarh with topography similar to that of Dharamshala faced similar sanitation problems. The community was not aware about sanitation issues and there was a lack of motivation and will on their part to participate in community meetings and discuss their issues at the ward level. Lack of financial resources and coordination between the municipality and other departments was another major problem. Considering the situation, some citizen leaders were identified and oriented by HSC on sanitation issues and also mobilised to participate and engage with government authorities. Following this, the citizen leaders interacted with elected representatives, officials of the municipality and representatives of CBOs on the need to manage waste in the town. They also facilitated in building linkages with the municipality and community. As a result of their efforts, 40 MSSs were formed in every ward.

Thereafter, the municipality itself launched massive awareness generation drives for mobilising citizens, Civil Society Organisations (CSOs) and CBOs to make them aware of the sanitation issues affecting their locality and to make them participate actively in the SWM initiative. Gradually, citizens stopped throwing waste on the streets and in their backyards and arrangements were made for the door-to-door collection of garbage by *safai karamcharis*. MSSs had the responsibility of monitoring the *safai karamcharis*, the door-to-door collection of garbage and the functioning of vermin compost pits. In the course of time, the formation of the MSSs proved to be a successful model as it achieved the desired results and sanitary conditions in the town have improved since the last 2 to 3 years.

The interaction with the MSS members was an enriching learning experience for the participants as it made them aware of the significance of citizen leadership and community participation in effectively managing solid waste in their area.

Formation of *Mohalla Samitis* (Ward Committees)

Various endeavours were made to sensitise and mobilise citizens about their role in urban governance through active participation in ward committees. These initiatives led to the formation of ward committees in Ward nos.2, 3, 5, 7, 8 and 10 in the town. Simultaneously, regular interface with ward councillors and elected representatives was also organised, so that they realise the importance of these committees and develop a mutual relationship with their members. Though some of the ward councillors were quite keen to form ward committees most of them were reluctant, as they did not want to be monitored by the community. During the meetings for the formation of these committees, the community envisaged the following roles for them:

- Performance monitoring of the key municipal services and urban sanitation.

- Performance monitoring of SWM by ward committees in 25 per cent of the wards.
- To ensure proactive disclosure under RTI Act Section 4 in Dharamshala, Kangra, Nagrota Bagwan and Palampur municipalities.

In the wards where these committees could be formed, a series of meetings were held on the status of various urban services like solid waste, sewerage, water supply etc. Through these meetings, the members tried to raise emerging issues and confronted the concerned ward councillor but they were successful only in a few areas where the councillors were active and supportive. Thus, the initiative of organising citizen's action and collectivisation through the formation of ward committees could not be mainstreamed in terms of being accepted by all the ward councillors.

Mobilisation of *Mahila Mandals* (Women's Groups)

The decentralisation of power to local governance institutions in the country through the 73rd and 74th CAA in 1992 and 1993 has enhanced the role of the local community and promoted the tenets of true democracy and people's participation at the grassroots level. This can also be witnessed in the mobilisation of democratic structures like youth groups and women's groups across the country.

The mobilisation of existing women's groups and the formation of new ones has been a major initiative in the process of accessing urban civic services in Dharamshala. With the formation of these groups, the women of the area got a platform to collectivise and share the issues of concern. This also helped them to come out of the confines of their homes and participate in the development activities around them. The women's groups in Ward nos. 8, 7, 10, 3 and 4 have been able to highlight emerging local issues concerning urban civic services like water, sanitation, drainage, sewerage, solid waste disposal and electricity in their wards. Through their myriad efforts, they have solved these basic problems in some of these wards by creating a pressure group at the ward level.

Household Survey on Basic Urban Services

A household survey was undertaken to assess the standard of municipal services through the members of women's groups and ward committees in Ward nos.2, 3, 5 and 8 of the town. The survey proved to be a platform for healthy interaction on the issues and challenges of urban services faced by the community. It also facilitated the process of awareness generation in the community about municipal services on one hand and their effective monitoring by the community on the other. The survey brought to light the true picture of municipal services with regard to the above mentioned services.

The survey revealed that a majority of households received water from private connections. The water supply was generally clean and free from impurities except in a few wards. A significant percentage of households had private latrines as compared to a negligible proportion of households (3.47 per cent) who used public latrines and had to walk more than 250 metres from their houses. As far as sewers are concerned, a majority of households felt that the municipal sewers were not cleaned at all. Nearly 54 per cent of the households said that they faced the problem of water logging, which occurred more than five times in a year. Most of the households used community bins for waste disposal, which was collected twice or thrice in a week by municipal staff. With regard to the rating of these services, most of the households rated these services as 'average' to 'very poor'.

Thus, the survey was unique, as in it was conducted by common citizens of the town. It not only helped them to gain an insight into the status of municipal services but also empowered them to take up such community based monitoring initiatives.

Media Engagement

The association and contribution of the media played a crucial role in strengthening awareness generation and mobilisation drives on urban services. The event management team of *Dainik Jagran* (a national daily) launched a cleanliness drive in the town with the support of concerned CSOs working on SWM/garbage collection and similar issues. The emphasis of the initiative was to generate awareness within the community on SWM issues, how the problem could be resolved through collective efforts by CSOs, common citizens and the media. This association facilitated healthy discussions and sharing on relevant issues and its coverage in the local newspapers helped in developing a common understanding among the people.

On 25th July 2007, a rally on cleanliness was held in Dharamshala, which saw the participation of different stakeholders like CSOs, youth groups and the representatives of the government like the then Transport Minister G.S. Bali. This rally was widely covered by the local media and helped in generating awareness on the significance of SWM and cleanliness.

Apart from being proactively involved in organising and covering such events, the media also highlighted and followed the events related to the preparation of the detailed project report on solid waste management for Dharamshala, specifically the consultation that was held with different stakeholders.

The media's support was sought in all the major endeavours to create widespread awareness among the communities related to the developments in the field of SWM and other municipal services.

Right to Information Mobilisation Drives

The Right to Information Act enacted by the Government of India in 2005 is a benchmark in the history of people's action and participation as it confers upon common citizens the right to seek information and hold the government accountable for its actions or inactions. The Act promotes transparency of the government mechanism on one hand and people's participation on the other. In light of the above, a number of mobilisation drives like rallies, workshops etc., with local communities in ward meetings and elected representatives were undertaken in the town. These initiatives were conducted to sensitise the community on various aspects of the Act and acquaint them with its different procedures and processes. They were informed about the procedure of filing an application so that in the near future they could utilise the Act as an instrument to gather relevant information from the authorities.

The mobilisation drive was taken up in the form of meetings and discussions with ward committees, women's groups, youth groups and the different resident welfare associations of various wards in the town. Along with this, information, education and communication (IEC) materials were also used to raise the community's awareness about the Act. Sensitisation programmes were held in different educational institutes like the B.Ed colleges, law colleges and other private institutions to raise awareness among students and the youth. Apart from the community, elected representatives were also sensitised to ensure better service delivery from the supply side. The mobilisation drive on RTI was an endeavour to strengthen the ongoing efforts for accessing urban services as it entitles the community to seek information on the same.

All the above initiatives geared towards community mobilisation emphasised the element of inclusive participation of the local communities and involvement of citizen leaders as well as other stakeholders. This helped in ensuring their ownership over these processes making it more sustainable. Though these initiatives could influence participation at the grassroots level, they were not free from constraints and challenges. Some of them are listed below.

Lack of Awareness in the Community on the Issue of Basic Services, Health and Sanitation

- Indifference of local organisations towards the problem of solid waste.
- Hostility of elected representatives towards community participation and engagement.
- Lack of cooperation and support from the ULB and municipal officials.

Role of Citizen Leaders in the Process of Community Mobilisation

As mentioned in the previous Section, citizen leaders were identified and strengthened by PRIA to facilitate the process of community mobilisation. These citizen leaders played an instrumental role in demanding accountability from the municipal authorities and accelerated the process of availing basic services in the town. Citizen leaders were successful in mobilising local communities and also influencing the authorities regarding different urban services. Given below are some of the reflections of cases where citizen leaders acted as community mobilisers and facilitated the process of participation and civic engagement.

- Mr. Prem David has been an active member of Ward no.10 and has been participating in the development activities (urban governance-improving basic services) of the ward since the very beginning. He mentioned that initially, the ward witnessed myriad problems related to basic civic services like solid waste disposal, sanitation and poor drinking water but now through the efforts and participation of the local community, many of these problems have been resolved. He had played a crucial role in mobilising the community around the issue of people's participation through his consistent involvement in facilitating the formation of a ward committee. The ward committee thus formed helped in creating a pressure group at the ward level to resolve the emerging issues efficiently. He pro-actively participated in the household survey and resource mapping of the ward to trace the available resources and identify the gaps in the existing system.
- The Navjagrati Youth Club in Gamru village has set an example of how collectivisation by the local communities in the form of youth groups can mobilise and motivate citizens to participate in development activities in a proactive manner. The youth club was formed in 2005 in Ward no.3 of Gamru village with a membership of approximately 25 members from different *mohallas* of the ward. The club has since then taken up the task of community mobilisation on different issues and organised a number of awareness generation programmes and community meetings in the area. The household survey to scan the situation of waste management, covering approximately 250 households could not have been conducted successfully without the support and cooperation of the youth club. As the process of door to door collection of waste had not started in the area as yet, the club formed a 'Green Team' under which the members of the club collected waste from houses and disposed it in the containers provided by the municipal council. Apart from this, they also organised multistakeholder dialogues with doctors, government officials and community members to create a platform for

discussions and sharing. The various endeavours and dialogues of the youth club with the local authorities in the past few years have led to the construction of a water tank, community centre and dispensary in the area, which has been a major achievement for the club.

- In Ward no. 8, under the leadership of Col. M.G. Sharma, streetlights were installed in the area. The main road connecting the ward to the town was extremely dark due to the absence of streetlights, which made the route prone to accidents and posed a great threat to the lives and the security of daily commuters. Though this issue had been reported to the concerned authorities no concrete steps were taken until Col. Sharma spoke to the local media and an article on the same was published in the newspapers. As an effect of this article and the subsequent pressure created by the Housing Board Welfare Society and other such societies from the ward, the situation improved and streetlights were put in place. Apart from this, Col. M.G. Sharma mentioned the problem of defective water meters and his ongoing effort to address the problem with the local administration along with the community. Other social concerns like raising demands for the construction of a community centre for sociocultural purposes etc., are also being taken up under his guidance in the ward.

In the above three instances one can see that the citizen leaders and local groups played the role of catalysts in identifying and addressing emerging local issues and amplifying the voice of the communities.

Results of the Process of Community Mobilisation and Collectivisation

This section highlights the outcomes and achievements of the various community mobilisation processes conducted in the town of Dharamshala. It reflects the potential strength that ordinary citizens possess, which can be exhibited through their collective action and participation in governance issues. These outcomes have been categorised into two, i.e., those that led to enhanced accountability of the government institutions and those that increased the community's accessibility to basic services. These outcomes can be explained as follows.

Outcome I: Ensuring Accountability through Active Citizen Participation

There are different means through which accountability can be exacted from the state and one of the most significant among them is through citizen participation and engagement. This requires the active involvement of communities in raising issues and voicing them effectively at an appropriate time.

In this case also, citizen participation through the use of RTI Act, different mechanisms of social mobilisation and state-citizen relationships led to the creation of an enabling environment for ensuring accountability and transparency by the authorities. These can be elaborated as below:

- Self-disclosure on RTI in Dharamshala and Kangra municipalities and the promotion for the same in Palampur and Nagrota Bagwan.

To ensure proactive disclosure on RTI Act in Dharamshala municipality, efforts were made to create better understanding of the concept, the need and importance of the Act and its provisions especially Section 4, which deals with the preparation of the self-disclosure manual. The efforts proved successful when the executive officer of the municipal council of Dharamshala agreed to prepare the same. The process began with the collection of relevant data and incorporating it into the required format. However, the task involved numerous challenges like inappropriate or insufficient delivery of financial data and data related to ongoing schemes in the municipality. These issues were tackled by approaching the vice-president of the municipality, as the executive officer was unable to dedicate time to procuring data from the concerned authorities and going through the manual for its finalisation. In spite of all these challenges, the document was completed as per the available data.

On the other hand, efforts were also on in the Kangra Municipality to promote self-disclosure and the executive officer ensured his willingness to prepare the document to create a model in the state of Himachal Pradesh. In Nagrota Bagwan and Palampur municipalities, the executive officer provided the required information that had to be mentioned in the document that resulted in the completion of the manual.

Preparation of Detailed Project Report on Solid Waste Management

Taking into account the increasing discussions and activities around the issue of solid waste at the ward level, the municipality decided to prepare a Detailed Project Report (DPR) on SWM. On 30th November 2007, a dialogue between CSOs, citizen leaders, ward committee members, municipal council officials and elected representatives was organised to proceed further on the methodology of the DPR's preparation. This dialogue was a kind of an orientation for the participants on the concept of DPR, its methodology, data that needed to be collected and the role of elected representatives to ensure the successful completion of the initiative.

The consultation with citizens was the most important part of the DPR's preparation process. To create the citizen's interest in DPR formation and ensure their active and meaningful participation, ward level meetings were organised in different wards of the municipal council where ward councillors took the initiative to organise the same. Ward councillors were involved in making these ward level consultations effective. The focus of these meetings was to motivate citizens to play an active role in the DPR preparation process. Suggestions on the segregation of wet and dry waste, collection and disposal of waste etc., were gathered through focussed group discussions (FGDs) on these issues. During these consultations, some important issues such as privatisation of services, imposition of user charges and willingness of the citizens to pay user charges were also discussed.

A number of meetings were held with the president, vice-president, executive officer and junior engineer of the Municipal Council of Dharamshala. During the discussions, the main emphasis was on the importance of citizen's participation at every stage of the DPR's preparation. Representatives of the municipal council, government officials, sanitation workers, *vyapaar mandal* (trade unions), retired army officials, active citizens, students, media persons, taxi unions etc., were also interviewed for their suggestions on DPR.

Regular meetings with various stakeholders such as ward representatives, members and citizen leaders were organised to increase their level of participation in the project. Suggestions provided by the citizens were incorporated to create a sense of ownership for the plan. Hence, the DPR was prepared by the municipality with the consensus of concerned stakeholders, which reflects its sense of responsibility and accountability towards the citizens of the town.

Outcome II: Improved Service Delivery through Active Citizen Participation

The myriad efforts of citizen leaders, local collectives like youth groups, ward committees, women's groups and intermediary organisations led to the creation of a demand for quality services from the concerned authorities. The examples demonstrate the magnitude of effect that citizen participation and ownership can have on governance issues. The following paragraphs illustrate some of the major achievements that could be accomplished due to the involvement and engagement of citizens in accessing improved basic services.

- Construction of a community park: The members of Ward no. 8 were able to facilitate the construction of a park in their ward after regular meetings of the ward committee and with support of the ward councillor. This was possible due to their active participation and involvement in the entire process. On similar lines, they were also able to resolve the issue of poor delivery of electricity in certain parts of the ward with the support of the local media.
- Improved waste management services: Active citizens in Ward no. 7 led to improved waste management services in the ward. Complaints made by citizens regarding street sweeping and the collection of garbage from primary/secondary collection points resulted in the appointment of a private contractor for the service. Six labourers were assigned the work of sweeping the streets, cleaning the drains and the collection of garbage from primary and secondary collection centres by using *rehris* (carts) as a vehicle for transportation.
- Infrastructure development: With regard to infrastructure development, *kuchcha* (unpaved) roads were upgraded to concrete ones in Ward no. 7 near the bus stand. A small bridge was also

constructed at the same site. The constant efforts of the citizen leaders led to the installation of 9 streetlights, 4 public taps and 3 water tanks in the area. Similarly, in Ward no. 3, the attempts of the Navjagrati Youth Club, led to the construction of a water tank, dispensary and community centre for the residents of the ward.

- Transparency in government departments: Mr. Atul Bharadwaj, a local activist has filed more than 50 RTI applications on different issues in Dharamshala. Through these applications, he has been able to stir the local as well as the state government into action on different fronts. His most important application has been to the forest department seeking information regarding the construction of a hotel and multistorey building on forest land in Mcleodganj, which was supposed to be used as a local bus stand and parking space for other small vehicles. This application disclosed the discrepancy and corruption within the state government in terms of violations of sanctions. This in turn led to the Supreme Court giving orders for the demolition of the buildings on forest land. In another application, he had sought information from the DSP's (District Superintendent of Police) office regarding the number of cases filed and their procedure for addressal. This led to the process of scanning and completion of records by the department for the same.
- Formation of Rotating Monitoring Committee: Mobilising citizens in Ward no. 10 proved successful with the formation of a Rotating Monitoring Committee. The responsibility of monitoring, thus, did not fall on a few people but was spread out among the concerned residents. The task of the monitoring committee was to stand guard near the *nala* (drain) every morning (the time when most people threw garbage) and keep a check on the defaulters. This was done with to sensitise citizens about the importance of a clean and healthy environment. The formation of the committee led to reduced cases of garbage disposal in the *nala* and instilled a sense of civic responsibility in the citizens towards their town. As an effect of this initiative, citizens also planned on involving the municipality in dealing with the problem of garbage disposal in their ward.

Through the above examples, one can see the strengths of participatory governance either through individual or collective efforts.

They also present a picture of the different ways in which the citizen-state relation exists at various levels, irrespective of their nature of participation i.e., individual or associational.

Conclusion

The above instances highlight the significance of people's participation and the changes that it can bring about in the governance system of any given society. The case study also illustrates the role intermediary organisations play in stimulating civic engagement and enhancing the capacities of ordinary citizens to actively participate in decision-making processes. The various examples of community mobilisation and demanding accountability mentioned in the case study reflect the use of different spaces of participation. These range from traditional forms of participation like rallies, meetings etc., to more recent ones like the use of media and monitoring exercises by citizens. One can also witness that both 'invited' and 'open' spaces were used by citizens at different junctures.

The formation of women's groups and ward committees is a reflection of citizen's participation in 'invited spaces'. These are state-created institutional spaces that have the potential for creating inclusive spaces but are often restricted by institutional design and social environment. They are often unable to completely change the landscape of discrimination, exclusion and marginalisation. This can be easily witnessed in the case of women's groups, where the participation of women reveals both the challenges as well as advantages of institutional spaces. While women look at participation as their entry into public space, the patriarchal view promotes a version of participation which is largely family centric and complacent to the decisions of the male members.[7] There are instances where women's groups were discouraged from taking up sensitive issues like alcoholism etc., to protect the interests of the male members and certain influential sections of the society.

Instances where citizens collectively monitored services in Ward no. 10, youth groups took over the charge of collecting garbage on their own and individual citizens contacted the media to highlight local issues bring

---

7. Mohanty (2006): 81.

to light the use of 'open' spaces by citizens and community based organisations.

Apart from spaces for participation, the case study also illustrates the different aspects of state-citizen relationship. It can be said that though citizens in the town were not satisfied with the quality of services provided by the municipality, they mostly dealt with them through peaceful means and maintained cordial relations with the government. However, 'direct relations' with the government were encountered in places where active citizens like Atul Bharadwaj took a leading role in exercising the RTI Act in an effective manner. The same can also be witnessed in associational participation where the Navjagrati Youth Club members accessed their entitlement over urban services in the form of the construction of a water tank, dispensary and community centre in their ward. 'Direct relations' to government come closest to the ideal of civil citizenship—that is, individual citizens can knock on the door of public bureaucracies to appeal decisions, demand better treatment or petition for improvements in services. These kinds of relationships are most likely when citizens have sufficient legal and effective equality in their interactions with public officials.[8]

The Navjagrati Youth Club also adopted a pattern of 'detached relations' with the authorities when they collected waste on their own through the Green Team. Here detached relations can be defined as relations where the individuals organise with friends, family or community members in local areas to collectively self-provision basic goods. On the other hand, in Ward no. 8, through the example of Col. M.G. Sharma one can understand the aspects of 'brokered relations' with the government where he took the help of the local media to highlight the issue of electricity. Brokered relations are the ones where active citizens seek the intervention of powerful third parties to obtain a response from public agencies.[9]

Thus, the case study is an example of how citizens' voice was strengthened under the facilitation of an intermediary organisation, which

8. Houtzager *et al.* (2007): 11.

9. Ibid: 19.

led to enhanced civic engagement and participation of the communities. The citizen leaders that emerged out of the process could successfully influence their counterparts in claiming citizenship by participating in different development activities in the town.

References

Ganai, Salma (2004). "Concept Note on Understanding Citizenship and Citizen Leadership", based on *Strengthening Citizen Leadership Writeshop*- 27th-31st January, PRIA, regional support partners, Lucknow.

Houtzager, P., A. Acharya and A.G.Lavalle (2007). "Associations and the Exercise of Citizenship in New Democracies: Evidence from São Paulo and Mexico City", *Working Paper* 285. UK: Institute of Development Studies.

M-Gnanou, K. and F. M-Ebrard (2007). "Urbanisation in India: From Megacities to Urban Villages", *http://www.ifpindia.org/ecrire/upload/press_ifp_website/indiapolis_articlerelu.pdf*, accessed on 28th April 2010.

Mohanty, R. (2008). "Collective Mobilisation: Mobilising Knowledge and Participation for Social Change", *Participation & Governance* 1(2), July.

———. (2006). "Citizen Participation in Development: Issues of Identity, Inclusion and Voice", in R. Mohanty and R. Tandon (ed.), *Participatory Citizenship, Identity, Exclusion, Inclusion*. New Delhi: Sage Publications.

P. Mathur, M. (2004). "Municipal Finances & Municipal Services in India: Present Status and Future Prospects", *www.developmentfunds.org/*, accessed on 28th April 2010.

6 Women Leaders and Intermediary Organisations in Khayelitsha, South Africa

Lisa Thompson and Ina Conradie

Introduction

It is well documented that poverty affects women in both urban and rural contexts in socioeconomic, political and psychological ways (Sen, 1999, Sen and Grown, 1987; Parpart, 1995; Mohanty, 2007; and Mahmud, 2010). The focus of this paper is to find out how women living in urban poverty are empowering themselves politically, claiming leadership positions and participating in ensuring socioeconomic and political rights. Our aim is to unravel women's understanding of their individual and communitarian political identities and how this relates to a more universal understanding of citizenship, citizen action, activism and the role of civil society. This paper explores the forms of community organisation that articulate with intermediary institutions, here understood as civil society organisations (CSOs) that position themselves as the interface between communities and government. The paper looks specifically at the South African National Civic Organisation (SANCO), a social movement that has both a national and local presence. The paper explores how effectively citizen leaders have been able to articulate their demands within SANCO and what the constraints and political opportunities have been. This second theme explores the ways in which citizens of Site-C in Khayelitsha, Cape Town, realised their new democratic rights within a specific context. This included the particular social fabric of Khayelitsha (largely Xhosa speaking and migrants from the previous Eastern Cape homelands), where most of the inhabitants live in poverty.[1]

1. Formal employment is low in Site-C and economic need is universal.

This research is seen as a necessary process of unravelling the complexities of political participation and protest surrounding democratic spaces of local governance and policy mandates on service delivery. Through focus groups and one-to-one interviews with women leaders in Khayelitsha (Site-C), some of the findings of the survey have been re-examined as they pertain to gendered democratisation and development processes. The paper also explores processes of collective action within which the women leaders position themselves. How do they interface with the local government through official 'invited spaces' as well as self-created or 'invented spaces' such as street committees and SANCO.

In the exploration of the first theme, women's understanding of political identity and understanding of citizenship, citizen action and the role of civil society, a brief description and analysis of interviews undertaken with women's groups who have recently become part of income generating projects (IGPs) (Conradie, 2009) have been provided. The women volunteered to take part in the selection and setting up of the projects through street committees (hereafter SCs). Between 2007 and 2009, focus group interviews were done with three groups, *viz.*, sewing, catering and home based care. Individual interviews were conducted with the leaders of the IGPs as well as community outreach projects (like that of Iliso, run by Vivian Zilo), as well as the ward councillor (Theresa Bottoman), and where possible representatives of civic organisations (such as the Khayelitsha Development Forum (KDF), which is funded by the government but run at the community level).

Of the women interviewed in focus groups, most were residents of Khayelitsha for upwards of 10 years and in some cases as long as 20 or even 25 years (i.e., since Khayelitsha was set up as a 'dormitory township by the previous Apartheid government). Prior to their involvement in the IGPs they were unemployed or underemployed, hence their willingness to become involved in the IGPs. Bulelwa's personal history was an example of the kind of chronic poverty that was common as the Khayelitsha survey data shows.

> In 2002 the government grant came. My husband then got a disability grant because he suffers from asthma. It then became better. Now I live away from my husband. He is in Umtata in the Eastern Cape and I am here but we are not divorced, we just stay

> in different places. The twins are schooling here, and I've also taken in two other girls. One of them is the child of my first born daughter; the other is the daughter of my sister. With the changes in Site C, we will get a built house. I still have no job, that's why I came to you to join the amakozikazi (Bulelwa, interview, 2007).

Bulelwa, as of August 2009, was surviving on two child support grants (a monthly income of R540) with which she had to feed a family of five. Yet, she was successful in obtaining a house through the Peoples Housing Project (PHP) scheme. Like Bulelwa, the IGP participants represented a broad spectrum of ages and backgrounds, most were married and had children but a minority of the women who attended the focus group interviews were single with one or more dependents. The aim was to probe their understanding of their political and economic location and what constraints and opportunities had been presented to them by the new democratic dispensation, as citizens located in Khayelitsha, so often characterised as a 'dormitory suburb' in Cape Town.[2] Many of the inhabitants, mostly migrants from the Eastern Cape, had lived there for many years (between 15 and 20 is common) (Thompson and Nleya, 2008; Conradie, 2008).

Khayelitsha in the Political Context

Although there are numerous large apartheid townships near the big cities of South Africa, built to enforce racially separate development, Khayelitsha, meaning 'New Home', is different. It was designed and built in the death throes of the apartheid movement, when it was very clear that the policy of keeping African people permanently out of Cape Town would not work. The government of the day nevertheless decided to locate the largest African township in the Western Cape in a swamp near the sea, where people were moved to from 1984 onwards. Currently it houses approximately one million people, although this number is disputed, as census surveys are not easy in an area with so much informal housing.[3]

---

2. Khayelitsha was established in the 1980s to house black African migrants in urban areas in terms of the previous Apartheid government's policy of racial segregation. Today Khayelitsha is a sprawling urban area, still characterised by poor services and infrastructure and still predominantly made up of rudimentary housing known as 'shacks'.
3. The 2001 census estimates of 350,000 are contested for Khayelitsha as too low.

The historical development of the area is pertinent to this exploration. For many years but increasingly during the 1970s and 1980s, people moved to Cape Town from the more rural and poorer Eastern Cape in search of work. The men came first and often worked on contract. The women followed to be with their husbands but were sent back to the distant Eastern Cape every day, their plastic houses broken down in the night and early morning by military bulldozers. They however kept coming, as a form of resistance and because of economic reasons and settled in an area called Crossroads. There a civil war broke out between government aligned traditional groups and ANC aligned 'Comrades'. During this period, the people were moved from the virtually destroyed Crossroads to Site-C, after their four traditional leaders[4] had agreed to the move and had also obtained their agreement. These leaders each had jurisdiction over the group of people that moved to Site-C with them, although their authority dissipated soon after 1990.[5] The resistance to being moved back to the rural area was also successful; in 1986, the government gave in and withdrew the 'influx control' legislation.

Site-C was one of the three original 'suburbs' of Khayelitsha in 1984/1985, where people got a tent, half a plot of sandy soil, a shared toilet that worked on the bucket system and a shared tap for more or less every 12 households. Only now, in 2008/09, were houses built to replace corrugated iron and wooden shacks and services were being upgraded, in a slow but gradual process.

Given this history and the strength of organisations like the SANCO in Khayelitsha in the late 1980s and early 1990s, how had the people's understanding of their political identity and action changed over time? In particular, how did their understanding of citizenship find expression in forms of association within the community as well as with the state? The continuities that might exist between these earlier 'invented' (or self-created) political spaces and those currently being observed both at the level

4. They were Mr. Maqhula, settling with his people in Section A, Mr. Mali Hosa of the New National Party in Section B, Mr. Fulani in Section C and Mr. Nyande in Section D.

5. Interview with Thozama Mnxulu, July 2009.

of civil society as well as more formal spaces of representation[6] were explored.

Democratic Governance, Processes of Collective Action, Leadership Development and Facilitation in Mobilisation

To understand grassroots perceptions of political identity, citizenship and citizen action one needs to remember that the term civil society is used in a variety of different ways. As Lewis (2002: 570) says, civil society is used variously as a loose analytical category as well as in terms of the processes of political engagement between the state and societal actors. NGOs, community based organisations (CBOs) and other organisations are often categorised as part of civil society as well as its representative, although it is clear that in many contexts NGOs are not faithful to the interests of the constituencies they purport to represent. The 'usefulness' of the term civil society has also been debated in the African context, on grounds of among other things its initial use being to describe a specific sociopolitical historical situation peculiar to Western Europe. African scholars like Mamdani (1996) and others have argued that civil society is a term that has been used to define African political society from the time of colonisation and hence is useful in understanding the dynamics of inclusion and exclusion, or what Comaroff and Comaroff (1999) have called the 're-remembering' and 're-imagining' of civil society in the West and in other contexts such as Africa (Lewis, 2002: 582-584). We use the term civil society to refer both to organisations representing civil society, as well as looser forms of associational life, using the Gramscian notion of the relationship between society and the state as both mutually constitutive but also as an arena of contest (see also Cornwall and Coelho, 2007). In doing so, we recognise that the state and civil society are not rigid categories. This helps for example to understand the complex adaptation of SANCO to democratic politics and governance, as well as the way in which

6. The concepts of self-created or invented spaces and formal or invited spaces are used extensively in the Citizen Development Research Centre (CDRC) hosted at the Institute for Development Studies at the University of Sussex. The CRDC international research network of research institutions based in Bangladesh, Mexico, India, Brazil, South Africa, Nigeria, Kenya and Angola have explored the different contexts within which such spaces are used and the ways in which they develop stronger and more democratic civil society (see for example, Kabeer, 2005; Cornwall and Coelho, 2007).

this has affected civic organisations. It was a revelation to discover in our last round of fieldwork, just how closely SCs are still bound to SANCO's central organising structures and how SANCO has been influenced by both recent political and socioeconomic developments. The history of both SANCO and organisations like the KDF serve to highlight the fuzzy nature of the relationships between civil society groupings and the government in the present context of Khayelitsha, impacting on the understanding of both political identity and civic action. SANCO is perceived largely as an ANC based organisation and its relationship with the ANC has made its intermediary role in grassroots communities initially very clear, as it was seen as part of the liberation struggle and a 'legitimate' form of grassroots organisation and affiliation, to its current status, that of an organisation struggling to define a role for itself that is critical yet distant enough from government (Seekings, 1996; Zuern, 2004 and 2006; *The Star*, 2009). Since the formation of the Congress of the People (COPE) in December 2008, SANCO's relationship with the ANC has become even more of an issue, as both women leaders and the communities to which they belong have chosen to associate with or join COPE. As Seekings (2007) and Zuern (2004) emphasise, SANCO has struggled to redefine itself as distinct from the ruling party. In Khayelitsha, in July 2009, this caused SANCO to split into two rival organisations, each calling themselves SANCO.

As Zuern (2004: 3) says of SANCO, 'SANCO has been variously defined as a "social movement", a "civil society actor" and an "institution in a state of decay". These competing definitions are significant, because the choice of definition represents not just a position in academic and political debate, but sharply contrasting models for popular activism and organisation.'

Zuern (2004: 3) goes on to analyse the continuum of action that SANCO is said to represent in respect of these definitions—'from "a vibrant, participatory social movement" to "a stifling institution" as a either a "hegemonic" or "counter hegemonic" actor, and whether it really "...supports the ideals of participatory democracy it rhetorically champions."'

To begin with, an attempt was made to understand how the women in the IGP groups understood their relationship with civic organisations on the one hand and the government on the other. The current sociopolitical structures in Site-C are represented in the accompanying diagram.[7] Both survey and qualitative fieldwork emphasised the importance of SCs as the building blocks of associational life in Khayelitsha and this is strongly confirmed by research in Site-C. Recent research indicated that the SCs do report on all matters of significance pertaining to the street (or block) at a SANCO General Committee meeting held every Tuesday. All the women in the three focus groups interviewed stated that they were members of SCs and that SCs were very important for getting things done in Khayelitsha, from resolving issues of criminality, to addressing issues and problems with services, unemployment, the problem of HIV/AIDS orphans and the likes (interviews December 2008; July/August, 2009). Thus in terms of redefining its role post Apartheid, it is clear that SANCO has found a niche for itself as a forum within which communities can express grievances related to their daily political or socioeconomic wellbeing.

A SC may consist of anything between 15 or more members who all live in the same area, mostly a street but sometimes the area is divided in a different way. In Site-C, they meet once a week as a SC, then once in the same week representatives of the SC meet as a block committee and then representatives of these committees report to the SANCO General Council in the same week.

Sometimes a SC member might have to deal with a crisis outside of a meeting. One Sunday morning Xoliswa, chairperson of her SC, could not go to church as an old man who had lived for 18 years in a nearby shack came to see her in tears. He was about to loose his 'house' as the former resident of the plot had come to reclaim it and the old man's file had disappeared during one of the frequent changes of service providers. The new claimant had the legal documents to prove his case but the old man also had a claim, in terms of his long occupation, which was legally valid. Moreover, he had nowhere else to go. Xoliswa negotiated with all parties until a compromise was reached. The old man would be allowed to stay if she could secure another plot for the new claimant from the housing and political authorities.

7. The information in the diagram was provided by our interviewees—see references and Monaco (2008).

Does the way this issue was handled represent a political opportunity? Were the old man's democratic rights exercised in a way they would not have been without these events, facilitated by a SC member on a Sunday morning? Did Xoliswa's agency make a difference to the success or failure of this case?

To all these questions, the answer would be affirmative, which would confirm that in this case the SC fulfilled a role in facilitating democratic rights. In this case, the deliberation could not precede the action, due to the urgency of the matter. It could be said to be an example where democracy was instrumental in enforcing a human right and that the agency of Xoliswa as a member of the SC was essential to this enforcement.

In another example, three children were left alone in their house after their mother, a single parent, died of AIDS. Xoliswa went to the local State Welfare Department to find out what could be done for the children but there were no relatives to care for them and the Welfare Department was overwhelmed by similar cases and insufficient resources. The SC considered all possible options and recommended that the children should stay on in the house under the supervision of the eldest child, a girl of 17. When she turned 18, the state would put the other children in her foster care so that she would have an income to support them. The SC also took it upon themselves to keep an eye on the children's welfare and to ensure that their needs were met.

In this case, the State Department failed to provide for a family in need and it was the SC that took up on the welfare function, in the South African context, acting as an advice office. Although the outcome in this case provided a shelter for the children, neither their rights nor their needs were met. They were nevertheless provided with basic security by means of a pragmatic but unsatisfactory solution.

In a last example, there were a number of short-term employment opportunities as part of the government's Public Works Programme, brought to the SANCO meeting by the councillor. In this case, when the project money was disbursed through the City Ward Forum, the councillor asked each SC to select those with the greatest need, so that they could get work first. KDF used a similar method, SCs were asked to nominate those in need to Ward Development Forums (WDFs). Although this deliberation had an economic outcome, it said less about economic opportunities than about a cultural value known as *ubuntu*—we are human through our humanity. However, one should not over-romanticise this process, as more research is needed to be able to understand whether or not communities feel employment opportunities are fairly granted by the civic leaders.

Broader questions on what citizenship and democracy meant to the women's groups collectively and individually were most frequently answered by reference to what developmental opportunities the government was providing either through services such as housing, electricity and water and sanitation and state grants, in particular child support grants, disability grants and pensions. In a number of instances, these grants were the mainstay of their income. Nerooi says, '... there are a lot of changes now, we can go to Department of Social Development and ask for assistance, now departments may assist you financially. You can go to the City Hall and get someone to listen to you.' (Focus Group Interviews, July 2007)

On the question of how democracy was working for them, Bulelwa's (of the home based care group) answer in August 2009 repeated much of the information of previous focus group work, 'I am getting a house now, but there is no employment, I have no job, my husband is not working and my first born is not working.' Nontsikelelo adds, 'I am single, I have three kids, I am not working, we are suffering.'

Aside from the above, notions of political identity related specifically to party political and associational life in the SCs and the relationship between political identity and socioeconomic position remained inextricably interwoven. In 2007, most of the women still belonged to the ANC but recent events have seen the groups reorienting their political affiliation. As mentioned, this has led to some upheaval in SANCO, with the SANCO organising structure now split into the 'old' and the 'new' SANCO, with two chairs, two committees and in some areas two sets of street committees, partly as a result of political allegiances and alliances, as well as accusations of undemocratic election processes and corruption. As Vivian (who is a member of both KDF and the 'new' SANCO) puts it,

'When we go to KDF we say we keep politics out of it, we look at what the community needs to develop...we don't want fighting with each other,

KDF try to keep politics out, there is lots of politics in SANCO although we are trying to get things done...' (Vivian, Interview, 31 July 2009)

At this point, a more detailed discussion of the relationships between the civic and sociopolitical structures in Khayelitsha to better understand the power dynamics in which the SCs are functioning is needed.

Current Civic and Sociopolitical Intermediary Organisations and their Roles *vis-à-vis* the Community as well as the State

As the Figure 6.1 on the organisational structures shows, there are three main axes of public participation in Khayelitsha. On the right are those pertaining to the Cape Town City Council (CTCC) or municipality, where ward councillors are elected by the citizens of an area on a party-political basis to represent their concerns. There are two such ward councillors in Site-C, Nontsomi Bili, an ANC member and the other, Theresa Bottoman, an ex-ANC member who has just moved to the new political party COPE (Congress of the People).

Each ward councillor can then form a ward forum with up to 10 community representatives to represent the social, political, economic and other needs of her ward. Theresa for instance has people advising her on social needs, health issues, education, early childhood, disability, religious issues, etc. Each of these representatives again represent an organisation or organisations or a group of people, whether NGOs, CBOs, churches, or similar groups. They discuss the problems on the ground and make recommendations about the spending of money allocated by the CTCC to the area. The final decision in this regard rests with the councillor but she always works in consultation with the members of the forum. Some councillors can of course fail to consult widely and act wisely on the recommendations of community members but the CTCC has a reputation for running a tight ship and holding its staff accountable.

The second axis on the left is the KDF and its ward development forums (WDF). The KDF is well known and recognised for its good organisation and reputation for getting things done.[8] The KDF was created

8. It functions under the chairmanship of Zamayedwa Sogayise and Michael Benu is the secretary.

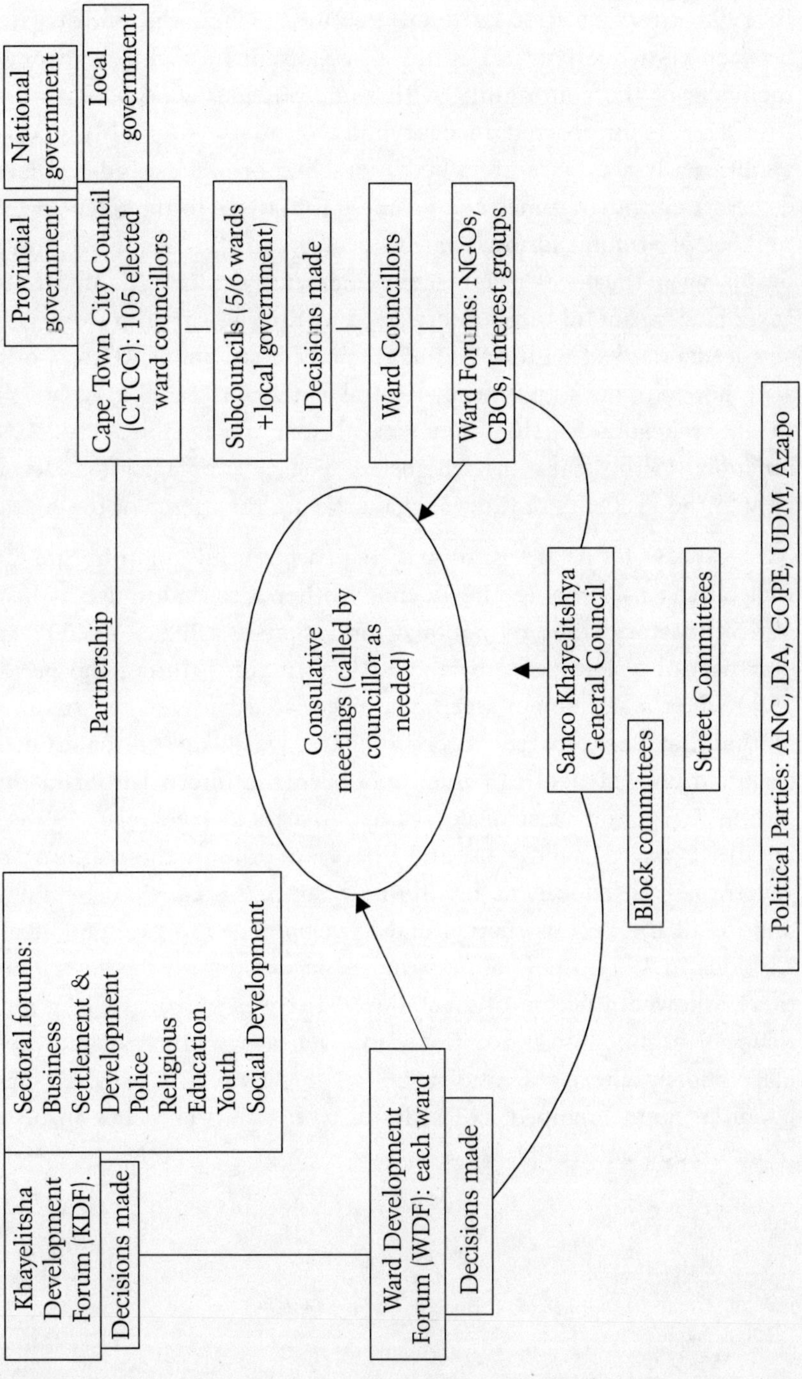

Figure 6.1

Civic & Sociopolitical Structures in Site-C, Khayelitsha, August 2009

in 1994 after the first national elections, when the political tensions between erstwhile political enemies in Khayelitsha had to be contained, by members of the community 'with some outside help.' The result is that 'the KDF is interested in everybody'[9] and is ostensibly very overtly apolitical. It acts as a civic body, which coordinates and regulates civic development programmes and business initiatives in the township. It has a number of sectoral forums, as can be seen in the Figure 6.1 and in turn liaises with the local government and with the CTCC on all issues of governance. Among those interviewed in Khayelitsha, the women's groups and leaders talked with respect and appreciation about KDF's work. Some said they were not as politically neutral as they professed to be but said that in an area such as this that was almost impossible. The KDF then functions in the realm of civil society as a civic organisation, accountable only to the residents of Khayelitsha—'We are the agents of the people'.[10]

SANCO forms the third axis. It is a powerful group in Site-C and in Khayelitsha as a whole and in many other areas, although it has had a difficult history since its national formation in 1992. SANCO's national organisation was created by the ANC structures during the period after 1990 when a settlement was being negotiated between the ANC and the Nationalist Party, partly to channel the work and contribution of the manifold civic structures, which had been the internal front of the ANC during the period of struggle against Apartheid (Seekings, 1997; Zuern, 2004). It played a powerful and important role in the planning of local government development for the new South Africa, even helping in the drafting of the Reconstruction and Development Programme but after the elections in 1994, many of its strongest leaders joined the government and there followed a period of great flux. This was exacerbated by reports of financial decline and corruption. However, a new membership drive took place shortly afterwards and in 2004, the National Chairman claimed a potential membership of 6.3 million, with 4,300 branches in 56 regions (Zuern, 2004 and 2006).

---

9. Interview with Michael Benu, 3 December 2008.
10. ibid.

The main constraints for SANCO as a civil society organisation and political watchdog now seem to be its close alliance to the ruling ANC; in Site-C we were told by one citizen leader that SANCO is '100 per cent ANC.' This could mean that SANCO is seen to contain trouble on the ground when there is political protest about lack of service delivery, rather than to act as a voice for those seeking better services. Or it could also mean that SANCO endorses protests directed at non-ANC led local governments, as is currently the case in the Western Cape, with the Democratic Alliance firmly in power after the April 2009 elections. Either way, its role as a civil society actor may therefore be compromised, although it is seen to play a very valuable role as a kind of 'advice office', which points people in the direction of resources (Zuern, 2004). It is clear from the interviews with women leaders in Khayelitsha that the question of '100 per cent ANC' also implies a lack of tolerance for other political parties. This is consistent with Seekings' (2007) observations on the ruling ANC's lack of tolerance, also with SANCO attempting to distance itself and/or function as a political party in its own right in the 1990s. The ANC's lack of tolerance of opposition and dissent is thus evident in the way in which SANCO has been able to use political opportunity structures to position itself in relation to the state.

SANCO can then be said to have been constituted in its preformation stage by numerous organisations and unions loosely aligned in a social movement for liberation, most of which functioned under the coordination of the United Democratic Front (UDF) from the time of its launch in 1983. After the formation of SANCO in 1992, it became a civic organisation with an overt political role. Its role in civil society was thus compromised, if one assumes the independent nature of civil society organisations during this historical phase (Lowe, 1999).

In the Site-C situation, SANCO is seen by the interviewees as a very important local organisation, where people who have lived together during difficult times work closely together, in spite of political differences. They deal with issues of daily life and of development and try to work together to improve the lives of those who often live in abject poverty, in an area where the whole community, with a few rare exceptions, live far below the poverty line. It is linked to the other organisations in the area through the practice of joint plenary sessions between SANCO, KDF, City Ward Forums (CWF) and councillors who meet once every three months but aside from this discursive deliberative practice, it has no structural linkage to the other organisations. Yet, 'it knows everything' (Bottoman, July 2009). The interviewees were of the opinion that in general the SANCO branch in their area could work with all political groups, although they had a strong ANC alliance, because they dealt with developmental rather than political issues and were accountable to the people they were elected by. Although all indications are that if this is so, the difficulties caused by political divisions will also apply to SANCO and there may be occasions when these constrain the work of the organisation.

Issues which were dealt with on the right hand side of the chart concerned mainly municipal services and amenities, whether these dealt with health care, education, recreation or any other service. Although local government (representing different political parties) and the City Council (under the opposition Democratic Alliance) work together, there is often duplication of services and party political differences mean that these are not always resolved without acrimony. In Site-C, the two ward councillors of the CTCC represent the ANC and COPE respectively and SANCO supports the ANC, as explained before. The result, according to the secretary of one of the WDFs, Vivian Zilo, is that, 'the structures are good, but they don't always function well because they are blocked by politics in the community' (Zilo, July 2009).

Decision-making happens at different points of the chart. In the CTCC structure, it takes place at the sub-council level, with local government structures taking the responsibility for decision-making arrangements. The ward forums of this structure have only advisory powers (Monaco, 2008: 78).

The discussions, which are brought to the SCs by their members, ideally representing each household in the area, on the other hand are concerned with much more dynamic, day-to-day problems. These cases are first discussed at the SC. 'We are each other's family' said one of the interviewees in this regard.

At the SC level, most members are women, who have been living in close proximity for decades, so this is not surprising. Most of the other problems are taken to the weekly SANCO General Council meeting for

Site-C, where they would also be discussed for the purpose of finding local solutions but some of these issues might need to be referred to the WDF or when it concerns municipal services, to the CTCC ward forums. At this level, most of the executive members are male.

SANCO's decision-making powers therefore cover local and relational issues and the observations in fact confirm that they often function as advice offices as the Black Sash did during the pre-1990 period, in offering people counsel or referring them to a different resource, depending on the problem. They have no jurisdiction over 'hard' issues however and only make recommendations.

The real decisions on local development issues are taken at the Khayelitsha WDF level and these are important forums in the area. Some decisions will be transferred to the KDF and they might refer these for specialised attention to the sectoral forums. The KDF, clearly, is the body with the highest authority in terms of development issues in the civic structures in Khayelitsha and ultimately decides on who gets what in terms of employment opportunities.

Deliberative Discussions in Khayelitsha

At the centre of this whole process is a purportedly very democratic practice, according to the ward councillor, Theresa Bottoman. Whenever a new issue of general importance arises, the ward councillor will first call a public meeting by means of using a loudspeaker and attendance at these meetings is usually high. People are informed about the issue and general discussions take place.[11] This practice also occurs in the organisation of SC meetings, where the local leaders call the street together to discuss issues.

At other times, the councillor calls a meeting to discuss issues with the different substructures and depending on the issue, she asks the members of the WDF, the municipal ward forums and/or the SANCO General Council to a consultative meeting, often all of them at the same

11. On the day of our interview with Bottoman there was going to be a public meeting on the proposed reconstruction of the central road through the area. People from the community would be needed to help with the manual labour and short-term job opportunities would therefore exist. The community would be consulted about these from the start, so that these opportunities would be allocated through general consultation and agreement and in a transparent manner.

time. These consultative sessions form the basis of the councillor's work in her constituency and she says that she takes very few decisions on her own, although sometimes she does. According to Bottoman, the decisions on a community issue would rather reflect a long, consultative discussion and many different points of view, woven into a consensus position (Bottoman, 28 July 2009).

Interviews yielded different perspectives on reaching an agreement in a meeting. Both interviews and the experiences of one researcher show a clear bias towards lengthy consultation and consensual decision-making, although one of the interviewees was emphatic that voting was used much more regularly these days to resolve disputes. Bottoman emphasised an implicitly agreed order in how people were given the floor, older men first, then older women and then generally the men before the women, older people before young people (Bottoman, Interview, 28 July 2009). Women in the focus group interviews mentioned that women nowadays speak equally with men, though younger people still respectfully awaited their turn. 'It's 50/50' stated Xoliswa, one of the women leaders very firmly, 'because we are a democracy now'.

One should not naively believe that the consensual culture discussed here is always applied in a just and fair way, or is never manipulated to serve interest groups. It is subject to the same amount of corruption as any other political mode in which human beings operate but maybe with greater visibility and transparency, as the discussions occur in public. It is also unclear from the interviews conducted to this point, just how consensual decision-making will remain with the fracturing of political identities along party political lines as well as civic contestation in relation to leadership positions. The split in SANCO is already a sign that different forms of political association and deliberation have been made possible.

Strategies of Engagement

If we reflect on the strategies of engagement that are used by communities and women leaders in Khayelitsha, a complex picture emerges. Engagement opportunities are numerous and there are a number of overlapping ways of ensuring that an individual or community problem is attended to. SCs function well to ensure a forum for grievances of a day-to-day nature, as well as for more intractable issues such as crime and unemployment. According to the citizen leaders, the relationship between the various intermediary organisations such as SANCO and KDF are good and the rivalry and power brokering seems to be contained by continuous dialogue and consultation. The relationship between these organisations and ward councillors and the local government is also ostensibly functional and effective, particularly in Site-C. Further research is required to examine the extent to which these power dynamics affect specific projects and policy decisions. A positive example is that as recently as August 2009, a local government development initiative in Khayelitsha that was initially going to use outside contractors was persuaded through the SANCO/KDF/CWF plenary to appoint leaders within the community as project managers. Two of the women leaders, Vivian and Xoliswa, were appointed as managers after lobbying for community based management.

What is not clear is that if the community organisations are ostensibly working so effectively through intermediary institutions why is there still so much protest in townships like Khayelitsha? As recently as July 2009, government officials were speculating again about a 'third force', that is some unnamed intermediary form of organisation inciting people to violent action against the state. The interviewees, as well as the 2007 survey data indicate that protest is a last resort strategy for those in communities where public services such as streets, lighting and housing as well as basic services like water and sanitation have been lacking for as long as 25 years (Thompson and Nleya, 2008, 2009 and forthcoming). 'People are tired of promises and tired of waiting' states ward councillor Theresa Bottoman and many of the women leaders echo the same sentiment.

Strategies for engagement thus appear to range from grassroots involvement through SCs and organisations like SANCO and KDF, to taking to the streets and blockading major roads. How intermediary organisations like SANCO position themselves in relation to these choices remains unclear. 'We don't protest we discuss things' states Xoliswa (Interview, July 2009). Yet, protest action remains endemic.

Outcomes and Conclusions

If political freedom implies the ability to take actions, which increase opportunities, then communities in Khayelitsha find themselves free to participate in a number of spaces that have been created by intermediary organisations that enable them to do just this. The case study area, Site-C definitely offers significant scope to citizens but within certain conditions. If one works with the elected councillors, who have considerable power to allocate resources and to make decisions, there are many opportunities, as specifically Ward no. 87 councillor Bottoman, whose work we know, works in a participatory way with emphasis on collective decision-making. Some of the respondents were unsure whether she would serve everybody equally now that her political affiliation had changed. She assured us that she would. Also within the KDF structures, opportunities exist but these are more of a coordinating and facilitating nature.

The main constraint faced by people in Site-C was debilitating poverty and in this regard, these structures seem to be able to only take supportive measures. Occasionally some public works positions become available in the short term but every year thousands of young people leave school with little chance of formal employment and very little seems to be done about it.

The work of the SANCO SCs offer people both a political, individual and communitarian democratic and development experience. Meeting those needs in a supportive way plays a vital and very positive role and the nature of this township is fundamentally shaped by these services. The relationship between SANCO and the ANC opens up both avenues for cooptation and collaboration as well political protest.

The multi-party nature of the political landscape in Khayelitsha is a new and dynamic feature, which creates more complexity and the possibility of conflict but simultaneously more political opportunities.

The changes in the nature of participation in decision-making structures and procedures in recent years are worth noticing. Women are elected to leadership positions alongside men, although the top structure of the KDF is still male. Women also report a sense of freedom to participate on an equal footing. Some very significant changes have therefore occurred since when four traditional leaders were the voice for this community 25 years ago, albeit under cooptation by the apartheid government.

In conclusion, in civic and sociopolitical matters the citizens of Site-C have both the opportunities to raise their personal and social concerns at different forums and to exercise their civil rights to obtain better services and resources. However, it is not clear to what extent it is possible for the average urban township woman (or man for that matter) to exercise influence in these structures without resorting to party political affiliation, a dilemma faced by SANCO nationally, provincially and locally and currently evident in the split in SANCO in Khayelitsha. To the extent that access to participation depends on political allegiance, the freedom to participate may not be all that it initially seems.

References

Alvarez, S., E. Dagnino and A. Escobar (eds.) (1998). *Cultures of Politics/Politics of Cultures: Revisioning Latin American Social Movements*. Boulder CO: Westveiw Press.

Amin, S. (1993). "Social Movements at the Periphery", in P. Wignaraja (ed.), *New Social Movements in the South: Empowering the People*. New Delhi: Vistaar Publications.

———. (1976). *Unequal Development*. New York: Monthly Review Press.

Appadurai, A. (2002). "Deep Democracy: Urban Governmentality and the Horizon of Politics", *Public Culture* 14: 21-47.

Arrighi, G., T. K. Hopkins and I. Wallerstein (1989). *Anti-systemic Movements*. London: Verso.

Ballard, R., A. Habib and I. Valodia (eds.) (2006). *Voices of Protest, Social Movements in Post-Apartheid South Africa*. University of KwaZulu Natal Press.

Castells, M. (2003). "Global Informational Capitalism", in D. Held and A. McGrew (eds.), *The Global Transformations Reader*. Cambridge: Polity Press.

———. (2003). "The Rise of the Fourth World", in D. Held and A. McGrew (eds.), *The Global Transformations Reader*. Cambridge: Polity Press.

Castells, M. (1997). *The Power of Identity: The Information Age*. Oxford: Blackwell.

Comacho, D. (1993). Latin America: A Society in Motion", in P. Wignaraja (ed.), *New Social Movements in the South: Empowering the People*. New Delhi: Vistaar Publications.

Comaroff, J.L. and J. Comaroff (1999). "Introduction" in J.L. Comaroff and J. Comaroff (eds.), *Civil Society and the Critical Imagination in Africa: Critical Perspectives*. Chicago: University of Chicago Press.

Conradie, I. (2009). "New Democratic Spaces in Khayelitsha, Cape Town: Deliberative Democracy and Capabilities", Paper presented at the HDCA Conference. September 10–12. Lima, Peru.

Cornwall, A. (2004). "New Democratic Spaces? The Politics and Dynamics of Institutionalised Participation", *IDS Bulletin* 35(2).

Cornwall, A. and V.S. Coelho (eds.) (2007). *Spaces for Change? Participation, Inclusion and Voice*. London: Zed Books.

Cox, R. (1987). *Production, Power and World Order, Social Forces and the Making of History*. New York: Columbia.

Cox, R. (ed.) (1997). *The New Realism: Perspectives on Multilateralism and World Order*. Tokyo: United Nations University Press.

Dahl, R.A. (2003). "Can International Organisations be Democratic? A Sceptic's View", in D. Held and A. McGrew (eds.), *The Global Transformations Reader*. Cambridge: Polity Press.

Edwards, M. and J. Gaventa (eds.) (2001). *Global Citizen Action*. Colorado: Lynne Rienner and London: Earthscan.

Escobar, A. (1996). "Imagining a Post-development Era", in J. Crush (ed.), *The Power of Development*. London: Routledge.

Kabeer, N. (ed.) (2005). *Inclusive Citizenship: Meanings and Expressions*. London: Zed Books.

Lewis, D. (2002). "Civil Society in African Contexts: Reflections on the Usefulness of the Concept in Development and Change" 33 (4).

Lowe, Chris (1999). "Civil Society, the Domestic Realm, History and Democracy in South Africa", in Jonathan Hyslop (ed.), *African Democracy in the Era of Globalisation*. University of Witwatersrand Press.

Mahmud, S. (2010). "Why do Workers in Bangladesh Fail to Mobilize?" in L. Thompson and C. Tapscott (eds.), *Citizenship and Social Movements: Perspectives from the Global South*. London: Zed Books.

Mamdani, M. (1996). *Citizen and Subject: Contemporary Africa and the Legacy of Late Colonialism*. Princeton: Princeton University Press.

Mehta, L., L. Thompson and N. Nleya (2009). "Water Rights and state Management in India and South Africa", in L. Thompson and C. Tapscott (eds.) (2009). *Citizens and Social Movements: Perspectives from the Global South?* Zed Press: London (in press).

Mohanty, R. (2007). "Gendered Subjects, the State and Participatory Spaces: The Politics of Domesticating Participation in Rural India", in V. Coelho (eds.), *Spaces for Change: The Politics of Citizen Participation in New Democratic Arenas*. London: Zed Books.

Monaco, Sara (2008). *Neighbourhood Politics in Transition: Resident's Associations and Local Government in Post-Apartheid Cape Town Uppsala*. Sweden: Uppsala University.

Mushakoji, K. (1993). Foreword in P. Wignaraja (ed.), *New Social Movements in the South: Empowering the People*. New Delhi: Vistaar Publications.

Newell, P. and J. Wheeler (eds.) (2006). *Rights, Resources and the Politics of Accountability*. London: Zed Books.

Nyamu-Musembi, C. (2005). "Towards an Actor Oriented Perspective on Human Rights", in N. Kabeer (ed.), *Inclusive Citizenship: Meanings and Expressions*. Zed Books: London.

Parpart, J. (1995). "Post-Modernism, Gender and Development", in J. Crush (ed.), *Power of Development*. London: Routledge.

Seekings, J. (2007). "Sanco: Strategic Dilemmas in a Democratic South Africa", *Transformation* 34(1).

———. (1997). SANCO: Strategic Dilemmas in a democratic South Africa in Transformation, 34.

Sen, A. (1999). *Development as Freedom*. Oxford University Press: Oxford.

Sen, G. and C. Grown (1987). *Development, Crises and Alternative Visions*. New York: Monthly Review Press.

Stammers, N. (2009). *Human Rights and Democracy*. Pluto Press.

———. (2005). "The Emergence of Human Rights in the North: Towards Historical Re-evaluation", in N. Kabeer (ed.), *Inclusive Citizenship: Meanings and Expressions*. London: Zed Books.

Stavenhagen, R. (1997). "Peoples Movements, the Anti-Systemic Challenge", in R.W. Cox (ed.), *The New Realism: Perspectives on Multilateralism and World Order*. Tokyo: United Nations University Press.

Steady, F.C. (2002). Engendering Change through Egalitarian Movements: The African Experience, in C.N. Murphy (ed.), *Egalitarian Politics in the Age of Globalisation*. London: Palgrave.

Stienstra (1999). "Of Roots, Leaves and Trees: Gender, Social Movements and Global Governance". in M.K. Meyer and E. Prugl (eds.), *Gender Politics in Global Governance*, Boston: Rowman and Littlefield.

The Star (July 24, 2009). "Residents vent Frustration over Inaction on Services".

Thompson, L. and N. Nleya (2008). "The Policy Implications of the Millennium Development Goals and Service Delivery at the National and Local Levels", *Africanus*, 2008/9 (December).

———. (2009). "Survey Methodology in Violence Prone Khayelitsha, Cape Town, South Africa", *IDS Bulletin* 39(6) (July).

———. (2009). "Passivity or Protest? Understanding the Dimensions of Mobilisation on Rights to Services in Khayelitsha, Western Cape", in B. Von Lieres and V.S. Coelho, *Mobilising for Democracy?* London: Zed Books (forthcoming).

Wignaraja, P. (ed.). (1993). *New Social Movements in the South: Empowering the People*. New Delhi: Vistaar Publications.

Zuern, E. (2004). "Continuity in Contradiction? The Prospects for a National Civic Movement in a democratic Sate: SANCO and the ANC in Post Apartheid South Africa", Paper prepared as part of a project entitled *Globalisation, Marginalisation and New Social Movements in Post Apartheid South Africa*, Centre for Civil Society and the School of Development Studies, University of KwaZulu, Natal.

———. (2006). "Elusive Boundaries: SANCO, the ANC and the Post-Apartheid African State", in R. Ballard, A. Habib and I. Valodia (eds.), *Voices of Protest: Social Movements in Post-Apartheid South Africa.* Pietermaritzburg: UKZN Press.

7

Engaging Community in Rehabilitation and Reconstruction Planning, Bhachau Town, Gujarat, India

Alice Morris

Introduction

India has shared the growth pattern and rapid urbanisation with some of the fastest growing regions in Asia. The country has witnessed around 8 per cent growth in GDP in the last couple of years and has planned to achieve a target of over 9 per cent growth by the end of 11th plan period. India's urban population is also increasing at a faster rate than its total population. With over 575 million people, India will have 41 per cent of its population living in cities and towns by 2030 AD from the present level of 286 million and 28 per cent.[1] The contemporary urban scenario in India revolves around issues related to access to basic services, livelihood, health, education etc. As the demand for these services is multiplying because of increasing pressure on urban areas, there is an immediate need for urban planning and management[2] at all levels of urban governance.

Urban planning and infrastructure provisions have traditionally been supply-driven and expert-led, giving mixed results. Such planning often does not reflect local reality, needs and development priorities. Participatory planning is different from traditional planning in that it envisages the participation of people as stakeholders in the planning process. It takes into

1. UNDP and MoHUPA (2009).
2. Annexure A-7.1.

consideration the interests and concerns of all sections of the society to ensure their participation in the entire process. It is seen as an important tool for decentralisation and effective implementation of the 74th Constitutional Amendment Act.

The purpose of participatory planning is to create a platform for learning rather than plunging directly into problem solving. The process is expected to enhance the following:[3]

- Identification of the felt needs of the people.
- Bringing forth consensus.
- The empowerment of local disadvantaged groups.
- Integration of local knowledge systems into project design.
- Two-way learning process between the project and local people.
- Political commitment and support.
- Accountability in local governance.

Participatory planning is fast gaining acceptance as an effective tool for facilitating inclusive participation and governments all across the world are endorsing the same. The Government of India's recent thrust to upgrade urban infrastructure and basic services through a comprehensive scheme, the Jawaharlal Nehru National Urban Renewal Mission (JNNURM) by developing city development plans (CDPs) through a community consultative process is a step forward in recognising the participatory method of urban planning as a precursor to any sustainable city development strategy.

In the light of the above, the following case highlights the significance of participatory urban planning in the rehabilitation and reconstruction of the town of Bhachau after its devastation due to the earthquake of 2001 in Gujarat. It illustrates the significant role played by the government bodies, intermediary organisations as well as local citizen leaders in the planning process. The case study is divided into four sections, which aim to reflect the condition of the town right after the earthquake, processes of mobilisation and collectivisation adopted by intermediary and community based

3. Thomas and Bendapudi. (n.d.)

organisations (CBOs), nature of relationship among the involved stakeholders and the outcomes of the entire process respectively.

The Context

Bhachau is a city and a municipality in Kutch district in the state of Gujarat, India. Bhachau town at the time of the earthquake had a population of 18,000 covering an area of 750 acres and was divided into 7 administrative wards according to the 1991 Census. The main market area is spread over 100 acres, which includes residential arcas as well. Forty-five per cent of the population is engaged in primary activity and an equal number in the informal sector and services. Only 10 per cent of the population is engaged in manufacturing. Bhachau is known as the Haridwar of Kutch since it is the first town on entering into Kutch.

Bhachau was developed on a trade route that connected Chirai Naka and Vondh Naka. The fort was established on the hill as a checkpoint to keep an eye on the road. The initial town grew between Chirai Naka, Vondh Naka and the fort. In the next stage, it developed towards the south and across the main spine. Areas like Himmatpura, Navibhachau and Junavada were developed. Vadinagar and other areas developed as satellite townships, which were later incorporated in to the main town. In the last stage, Bhachau extended beyond the railway line, towards Saraswati society, Bhavanipura and even today, newer areas like Navagam are growing fast and are a part of the ongoing process of development.

The old city though crowded, is beautiful because of the variations of scales and breaking of monotony in different ways. The arrangement of its built-form, the road junctions (*chowks*), open spaces, the majestic *darwazas* (gates) are very significant. People of the town identify themselves with certain locations, crossroads and monuments. The old settlers identify themselves with the *'Kote Vistar'*, which is the central area of the town. The new settlements have an existence of their own and identify themselves with different points in the town and have formed their own systems. There are three main *chowks* where people meet, Jaimataji Chowk is used by the entire town, whereas Mandvi Chowk where two roads meet is mainly a traders meeting point. The Chirai Naka and Kharia Dham crossroads is also an important meeting point.

On 26 January 2001, a massive earthquake (magnitude of 7.7 on the Richter scale) struck Gujarat. The district of Kutch was one of the worst affected areas. Kutch has 10 towns of which 4 i.e., Bhuj, Anjar, Bhachau and Rapar were the worst affected by the earthquake and among them Bhachau suffered the most severe damage. All the buildings in the town had collapsed or were damaged beyond repair. The historical monuments were also damaged and the *darwazas* were destroyed. More than 10,000 buildings collapsed killing approximately 2,000 people. The estimated loss in the municipal town of Bhachau for residential buildings was worth Rs. 237.3 crore, for commercial establishments Rs. 22.4 crore, for government property Rs. 11.6 crore and for other infrastructure Rs. 22.7 crore, with the total loss estimated at about Rs.294 crore.

Life in the town was hit hard and the entire socioeconomic structure of the town collapsed leaving the people helpless, traumatised and without work and shelter. The community buildings, water tanks, hospitals and communication centres had turned into rubble, severely crippling life support systems. With the loss of life and property, the people's livelihood options were also destroyed. In order to reorganise the socioeconomic life of survivors, the post disaster recovery actions in Bhachau were identified carefully. The post disaster recovery work was instrumental in strengthening local leadership as the affected people collectively or individually tried to facilitate the economic, social and physical development of the area with a long-term vision to reduce future vulnerabilities.

Immediately after the devastation, rescue and relief started pouring in from different parts of the country and the world. The first phase of relief concentrated on providing immediate help to people. After the immediate relief the process of calculating losses started. During the immediate rehabilitation and reconstruction period after the earthquake, the proper assessment of damage and consequently relief was a challenge for the stakeholders, even though the government had set up guidelines for this. The compensation amount was determined based on damage assessment, status of land ownership and proof of residence. Unfortunately, these criteria saw 1767 families left out, in the absence of a legal title to land or proof of residence. Most of these families had migrated to Bhachau during the last few decades in search of economic engagement. Being poor, they could hardly afford to buy or rent a house in the town and settled at the periphery, mainly in low-lying or hilly areas. People who had lost their ration cards, widows, the poor and other marginalised households also could not gain access to relief. It was difficult to ensure equitable distribution of compensation and the dissemination of correct information to people regarding the helping agencies, the nature of compensation and criteria for getting compensation etc. and people were facing problems in accessing this vital information.

The Government of Gujarat (GoG) announced a rehabilitation package within 20 days for the four towns (Bhuj, Bhachau, Anjar and Rapar). To plan the settlements properly, the government came up with a development plan scheme. As per the package, new Area Development Authorities were set up for each town. The development plan for Bhachau was to be prepared by Bhachau Urban Development Authority (BhADA) and the Urban Development Department, GoG. The responsibility of preparing the plan was given to Dalal Consultancy Firm. Since the Asian Development Bank (ADB) was to fund the infrastructure development in Bhachau it had clearly articulated that community participation was mandatory in the process of the development plan's preparation. The GoG's rehabilitation package had also stated that the plans would be prepared with people's participation. The consultants and BhADA gave priority to soliciting people's opinion on the plan with the belief that the people's involvement in the planning of their own town was very important. During the process of formulating the plan, there was a need to keep the community together to ensure the people's participation in building a vision for their city. The consultants while preparing the draft plan held community level discussions, interviews with important stakeholders, associations and trusts, community based organisations like Bhachau Punarvasan Samiti etc. and interacted with other organisations working in the area. The plan was prepared based on a survey conducted among 600 households, a traffic study and an estimate of future infrastructure needs.

The Bhachau Punarvasan Samiti was a group of citizens residing in the inner city and their focus was on its rebuilding in the direction they wanted. Their aim was to influence the plan in a way that their interests were protected and so they made a plan for the city from their perspective and submitted it to the consultants. This was incorporated into the final plan. They were also mentioned in the plan document. On the other hand, there were some sections of society, which were excluded from the plan because of their marginalised status. It soon became clear that many small *bastis* (slums) had either been neglected or had not even been included in the plan. In Rabarivas (Ward no.3) 150 households, 700 households in Junavada (Ward no.7) and Vadinagar and a number of households in Sitarampur and Himmatpura (Ward no. 6) were left out from the plan. In Vadinagar out of 170 households, only 30 per cent had entitlement to the land and households without land titles were excluded. The new plan depicted a forest area in place of the existing settlement of Junavada. The plan did not acknowledge their existence and hence no action was proposed for their rehabilitation.

After preparing the draft plan, Dalal Consultants held a public consultation on June 12, 2001 at Bhachau for soliciting people's opinions on the plan (Box 7.1). Following this, the plan was put up at the Additional Collector's office for the community to comment on and give their suggestions. Even though the consultation was organised, the participation of many stakeholders like tenants, slum dwellers, informal business holders and women was very low. Neither the community nor the civic agencies working on the rehabilitation and reconstruction of the town were satisfied by the process adopted for preparing the draft development plan.

The key concerns included lack of stakeholder participation like that of tenants, slum dwellers, informal sector, women etc. and the use of inappropriate tools and methods to consult and share information with people. The consultations held were centralised and excluded the needs and priorities of many communities and groups. There was simply no attempt to build a common vision for the town. Although the rehabilitation and reconstruction process was guided by the involvement of people in the decision-making process, it was realised that the plan actually benefited only a small proportion of the population and there was a need to protect the interest of all citizens, particularly the vulnerable groups.

Box 7.1

Key Features of the Development Plan

- Since 40 per cent of the people live in the Kote Vistar, which is the heart of the town, the focus of the draft plan had been in detailing out the plan for this area.
- Any person having a residential plot of more than 50 square metre would have to bear a 10 per cent reduction in size.
- There would be no reduction in size of the commercial plots and residential plots which were less than 50 square metre.
- The characteristics of the two main chowks—Mandvi Chowk and Ashapura Chowk would remain the same.
- A new system of road hierarchy was planned where the main roads would be 14 metre, the connecting roads 9 metre and the internal roads would be 6 metre to enable better connectivity between areas and access to all plots.
- Provision would be made for open spaces in the town and on the roadsides.
- The area's topography would be taken into consideration while developing the plan.
- The plan would be in conformity with the existing land use pattern.
- Much of the development would be towards the north and east.
- Development would be restricted in the zones of poor foundation.
- The industrial area would be located in the eastern part along with the Transport Nagar.
- Land under agriculture and forest would be preserved.
- Water pipelines and sewerage lines would be given due attention.
- The entire plan would be implemented in phases based on priority and need.

Process of Mobilisation and Collectivisation

At this point of time when there were differences in opinions among groups regarding the rebuilding and relocation of the town, UNNATI (a voluntary organisation with a mission to promote participatory principles, gender equity and social justice in the process of development) facilitated a process of participatory planning for Bhachau town. The interventions thus focussed on trying to find out people's opinion on resettlement, addressing the concerns of relocation *versus* in situ reconstruction, land use, community infrastructure and access to the poor, special needs of women, the disabled and cultural groups. Stakeholder consultations were facilitated to remove ambiguities and arrive at a consensus using the future search conference methodology. Linkages between town planners, architects and other technical persons were fostered to make a people-centred plan for the town. People's participation was also sought in monitoring the process to ensure that minimum standards were being followed during reconstruction. UNNATI mobilised the citizens, particularly the poor and those excluded from the plan, who were largely living outside the inner city area. A series of meetings and discussions were held with the community to inform them about what was happening in the town and to motivate them to come together to participate in the process to ensure that the plan was inclusive and reflected the needs and priorities of the people (Box 7.2).

Box 7.2

Interventions by UNNATI after the Disaster

- Observing and responding to the governmental process of relief & rehabilitation in the town. Conducting community consultations, critical review and evaluation of the government schemes and feedback of the community on the same.
- Documenting and making development plans for the town in terms of land use, spatial linkages, public private spaces, infrastructure etc. Identifying issues, problems and bottlenecks in the same.
- Facilitating the process of revaluation, re-modification, re-adaptation and reconstruction of the town by evolving solutions for identified issues, problems and bottlenecks.
- Generating awareness within the community on rehabilitation processes, impacts, issues, seismic safety, etc.
- Integrating disaster mitigation plans with town planning—in aspects of physical planning and community organisational capacity.

The various initiatives taken up by UNNATI in Bhachau are further explained below.

Multistakeholder Dialogue

A multistakeholder consultation was organised on August 25, 2001 jointly by UNNATI and local groups to discuss the draft development plan. The consultants were asked to present the development plan to the stakeholders of the town. Around 190 people including senior representatives from ADB, the Gujarat Urban Development Authority, BhADA and Dalal Consultants were present at the consultation along with members of the Bhachau Punarvasan Samiti. The consultation was successful in bringing forward the views of the citizens. The stakeholders articulated their expectations from the development plan and the community raised many concerns.

The issues that came up during the dialogue were confusion about the status of Navagam, the forest area shown in the plan in place of the Junavada settlement, the relocation of Vadinagar institutional area in place of the existing Rabarivas, lack of provisions such as fodder markets, veterinary facilities, agricultural stock keeping, seed banks, extension facilities and market linkages etc. The people pointed out that inlet of Bhattiya Talao had been blocked because of the dumping of debris cleared from the collapsed buildings. They were concerned that this could affect the natural drainage of the town and obstruct the local watershed resulting in various problems.

It was also pointed out that the town plan had a fragmented approach and the focus was only on widening of the roads in the core town of Bhachau. The residential areas surrounding the main markets form the core town, where the widening of streets and relocation of some houses and shops had been proposed to relieve congestion. The people were concerned about the economic activities of the area, which were highly competitive and their viability depended on their proximity to the main *bazaar* (market). They feared that once their plots were acquired for the widening of roads, many of them would be forced to shut down their business. The attempt to relieve the congestion from the core town did not take into account the prerequisites for the survival of these microenterprises and hence endangered their existence. Therefore, community representatives suggested a review of the road system to find out whether certain roads were actually required or not.

Exposure Visit

There was a Bhuj Development Council (BDC) in Bhuj, which comprised group of citizens engaged in the development of the town even before the earthquake occurred. This council played a major role in the rehabilitation process of Bhuj. With this model in mind, the idea was to facilitate a similar group in Bhachau. *'Nagarik Phahchan'* (knowing the citizens) was organised in which 15 citizens were taken to Bhuj to meet the members of the BDC and to understand how they functioned. At Bhuj, they also got the opportunity to observe a community consultation. It helped to build the group's confidence and enabled them to voice their priorities and preferences.

Formation of the Nagrik Sahyog Kendra (Citizen Support Cell)

In January 2003, the Nagrik Sahyog Kendra (NSK) was set up by UNNATI in collaboration with Gujarat State Disaster Management Authority (GSDMA) and the Development Authority, BhADA to facilitate participatory urban planning and provide support to rebuild the town in a participatory manner. It was given space in the BhADA office to carry on its functions and activities. Through the NSK, many activities were undertaken, such as, regular '*falia* (cluster) meetings', publishing of a popular newsletter '*NagarVani*' (voice of the town), meetings with various government authorities like the district administration, Gujarat Urban Development Company Limited (GUDC), GSDMA, etc. The bulletin issued by NSK opened up spaces for the citizens to raise their concerns and also to access information related to the rehabilitation process. Gradually it was also used as an instrument to share the status of rehabilitation in the town particularly in the poorer and backward areas.

One of the most important roles that NSK played was that it developed a good reliable database on different issues, taking the citizens and authorities in confidence, which formed the basis for many decisions during the process of modification and citizen concerns. This became an effective interface between the government and citizens for facilitating the rehabilitation process in Bhachau town.

Apart from the above, groups were also formed and oriented to support the rehabilitation process after the earthquake. Leaders were groomed and capacitated to mobilise the community to participate in the process of development planning in the city.

Promoting Community Based Rehabilitation and Livelihood Opportunities

Community based rehabilitation of vulnerable groups like widows, single women, orphans and the differently abled was taken up extensively. As part of this initiative, vulnerable groups were provided support to access basic services, medical care, psychosocial care, shelter and legal support to gain control of their property and inheritance. An exercise was conducted to map the loss of on-farm and off-farm livelihood among the poor communities. Support was provided to embroiderers, weavers, block printers, dyers, snake charmers and vendors to restart their work. These groups were also provided support to link to potential markets.

Assessment of the Reconstruction Process

Quick assessments were taken up regularly to help in understanding local needs and determining the direction of the reconstruction process. Information on government policies and programmes, standards and processes to be followed during rehabilitation were shared, so that the community could analyse the trend and pace of the rehabilitation process. Since, reconstruction is a complex process, inter-institutional linkages among NGOs, government and local governance institutions like the *panchayat* and *nagar palika* were also facilitated.

As a result of the various interventions by UNNATI along with the citizens and local community groups, a lot of development was witnessed at the grassroots level. The multistakeholder consultation led to modifications in the draft development plan and the settlements at Junavada were given their earlier place in the new plan and the residential zone was demarcated. Vadinagar was brought back to its original location. The size of the proposed institutional area was reduced and Rabarivas was accommodated at its existing location.

For the citizens' group this was their first success but they did not stop here. They realised that external support was important but accepted the crucial role played by them in rebuilding their city. Bhachau at that time did not have an elected urban local body (ULB). The local body had been dissolved just before the earthquake in December 2000, anticipating fresh elections in January 2001. Unfortunately, in the interim period disaster struck the town. The council members of the old elected body played a key role in providing relief. They were also part of the citizens' group that had initiated the process of rebuilding the town. Although their understanding on rehabilitation and reconstruction was very limited, they were willing to play a major role in the process of rebuilding the town.

With the support of these individuals, a committee for rehabilitation was formed. It was not possible to have one single committee to take up the responsibility of various stakeholders and their interest in the process of rebuilding the towns. Several *falia* (a small cluster around a few streets within a larger area) level committees were formed. Around 15-16 such committees were formed with 6 to 7 members in each committee. These *falia* committees initiated discussions through formal and informal meetings on issues pertaining to the local area. In many instances, the officials from the local authority were invited to attend these meetings and to help find quick solutions to the problems.

As part of the social watch initiative, citizens also monitored the status of vulnerable groups in the community. The focus was on the most vulnerable families in each area. The *falia* committees started identifying the vulnerable families and acted as community grievance cells. Eight community centres were functioning in the town as part of the 'Sneha Samuday'. The committees started using these centres as contact points where community members discussed issues and shared their grievances on the process. They monitored the material provided to the vulnerable families by various agencies and reported any mismanagement to the relevant authorities. In this way, they acted as a link between the community, the government and other agencies, which helped in preventing corruption.

Committee members formed groups and supported the process of equitable distribution of compensation. They disseminated timely and correct information like which were the helping agencies, the nature of compensation, criteria for getting compensation etc. Citizen leaders were instrumental in identifying families who had been left out from the relief and rehabilitation process. In many cases, committee members accompanied the affected families to relevant officers to help fill the forms and initiate the process. In many areas, officials were disbursing relief money without proper assessment of houses and hence a number of cases of underestimation were reported by the citizen leaders. It was then that the officials decided to visit houses to assess them and then pay compensation according to the extent of damage. They also made some recommendations; one of which was to allow people who had lost their ration cards avail compensation on producing a letter from their public distribution scheme (PDS) shops.

The committees also assessed the infrastructure needs of the community, by analysing what was available and identifying the gaps. These gaps were then communicated to the BhADA for action. In this way, they ensured that the vulnerable families got access to basic services. Along with the issue of infrastructure there were also issues related to land entitlement. An informal group was formed in each *falia* that maintained a register, which listed all the families that did not have land titles. The data was also verified at the field level through a number of visits to meet the families.

As part of the implementation of the draft plan the citizens' group suggested the following: (i) people should be relocated in the same area, (ii) they should be provided *patta* (ownership) for the land and compensation for construction. The women's group suggested improvements in water supply and sanitation. They also asked for the inclusion of the social needs of women and their security and protection in the plan. Every stakeholder believed that the planning was being done for her/him and were hence, positive towards it. It was a common sentiment that if the town had been planned earlier and building regulations followed strictly, many lives could have been saved on the fateful day. The efforts made by the community based organisations and citizen leaders are illustrated in the following paragraphs.

Junavada Punarvasan Evam Vikas Samiti (JPEVS)

Junavada was a cluster of 700 households in Bhachau town. This area was shown as a Wild Ass Sanctuary in the new development plan. Later it was shown as a residential area when the plan was revised as per the demands of the citizens. The citizens from this area formed the Junavada Punarvasan Evam Vikas Samiti (JPEVS) for rebuilding the area. The key issue identified by them was that of land entitlement. When the first instalment of compensation (Rs. 20,000) was given, many of them used the money for other purposes and therefore could not start the construction of their houses. They were eligible for a total amount of Rs. 55,000. Around 400 families could not access the second and final instalment of compensation amounting to Rs. 35,000. In 2005, BhADA announced that it was the last opportunity for all affected families to claim their compensation since it would be dissolved in 2006. JPEVS realised that many families could not complete the construction as they had either not started it or did not have a land title. They contacted other funding agencies, government departments and NGOs working on housing in the town and negotiated with the municipality so that the amount they were entitled to was released to them. In addition, they contributed Rs. 15,000 per household from the community and made a list of households who required this support the most.

At this point, there was some dissatisfaction among the families that everyone was being given Rs.15,000 irrespective of the way the previous instalment had been utilised by them. To deal with this confusion, the members of the Samiti held meetings with the community groups and convinced them of the importance of the opportunity. The community came to an agreement and civil society organisations along with other civic agencies initiated the process. The Samiti took charge of purchasing the material, identifying masons from within the community, training them and supervising the construction work. In this way, they were able to effectively utilise both materials and human resources. This effort enabled 400 families to get land titles and a house for themselves.

Navagam Vikas Samiti

The citizens' groups continued to work on issues that were not addressed during the rebuilding process like land entitlement, basic services to areas that were not covered in the initial plan and safe housing for all. They had also started working on the issue of community based disaster preparedness.

One such case was the work done by the Navagam Vikas Samiti, which was a group of citizens from the area. Navagam is a cluster of 200-250 households located about 3 to 4 kilometres from the centre of Bhachau town. Although it was part of BhADA, the ULB did not consider it a part of the town and the infrastructure plan also ignored the area. The total budget for infrastructure development in the plan for the town was Rs.100 crore. As per the plan, roads, water supply, sewerage, streetlights, schools and health centres were to be provided in each area/ward. Navagam's share would have been Rs. 8 to Rs. 10 crore, which the municipality was not willing to spend on this area. In fact, they tried to integrate the area with an adjoining village, which would have changed its status from urban to rural.

The residents of the area would not accept this change as it was actually a part of Ward no. 6 of the municipal council and the people were listed in the municipality's voters list. On the other hand, because of vested interests and the benefits of an additional vote bank and revenue, the municipality wanted to include the area under its domain. The citizens of the area were paying approximately Rs.140 per annum to the ULB and if the area had been included under the ULB, they would have to pay Rs.600 per annum. The households were economically better placed and ready to pay for the services. The municipality did not have the money to invest in infrastructure and could not charge the people without providing them basic services for which it had to get clearance from BhADA. In the meantime BhADA had been dissolved. The Samiti continued to make representations on behalf of the community at various levels and to the government authorities to get clearances so that they could access the services.

Citizen leaders organised awareness programmes with the support of civil society organisations for providing technical and material support to the affected families. They organised *padyatras* (marches) and training programmes to generate awareness and set up a citizen support cell in response to the advocacy issues. Video shows were screened, booklets and pamphlets were distributed and exhibitions were held in local *melas* (fairs). Citizen leaders were also involved in developing designs for the houses, working out cost estimates and material planning. They organised community meetings in which they invited technical persons from different agencies. Their direct and collective involvement in the reconstruction of houses created a sense of satisfaction and ownership in the process and the final product. Citizen leaders were convinced that promoting technology for affordable and seismically safe houses with the support of local institutions was important for the safe future of the town.

Citizen's engagements helped in bringing the people together on a common platform and participate collectively. People showed a willingness to actively contribute to the reconstruction and rehabilitation of their town. During the construction and rehabilitation period, the role of the community and citizen leaders was crucial, because the GoG and other agencies were providing financial and technical support and the resources had to be utilised in a way that benefited all. The collective effort helped in ensuring equal opportunities and a space and role for various stakeholders of the town including the poor, vulnerable and minority groups. Given below is an example of how one of the citizen leaders helped the communities in accessing government schemes and services.

Active Participation and Leadership by Ismail Bhai

Ismail *bhai* is the owner of a tea stall who has been involved in community development activities since 1979. After the earthquake, he decided to dedicate his time to helping the affected families in the community. He started by mobilising a group of people and encouraged them to participate in relief work. There were a number of relief agencies and he contacted them, which enabled the community to access food, medicines and shelter. After the requirements for relief were met, he started working on accessing the compensation as per the package announced by the GoG. He provided support in conducting damage assessment, disseminated information on the compensation package and identified the vulnerable families who were left out of the compensation process. He was able to facilitate a fair and equitable distribution of resources.

Many families had lost their ration cards and the government regulations barred them from receiving compensation. Widows, slum dwellers and other vulnerable groups who did not have any proof were the worst victims of this guideline; in fact, people who had ration cards were also not able to access the grants. This issue was discussed in the community and it was brought to the notice of the concerned authorities. After three months of negotiations and discussions with the government, the guidelines were changed. As per the new guidelines, people who had lost their cards could produce a letter given by the PDS shop and those who did not have cards were required to take written permission from the government. Finally, all the families were able to benefit and access government grants.

Ismail *bhai* also realised that people were facing major problems while reconstructing their houses. He got in touch with various agencies and started working as an information provider to the community, particularly to the vulnerable groups like widows, single women and the elderly and provided them guidance on how to contact the relevant officers. People visited his tea stall with various issues related to water pipelines, electricity connections; issuing disability certificates etc. He also acted as a link between organisations working on livelihood issues and the people from the community who were seeking livelihood opportunities. He was able to set up 40 small businesses in the area.

He explored opportunities linked with other agencies and institutions and dialogued with them for the equitable distribution of resources and an inclusive reconstruction plan for rebuilding the city. Today his teashop is popular with officials, elected representatives and the community. It is also a platform for discussing emerging issues of the community.

Thus, it can be seen from the above examples that both 'invited' and 'open' spaces have been used by citizens, CBOs and intermediary organisations (UNNATI) in rebuilding Bhachau after the devastating earthquake. Citizens not only participated through invited spaces provided by the government like development planning of the town and public consultations etc. but also monitored the relief and rehabilitation work of the government through open spaces like *falia* committees and community centres in different localities. The initiatives made by citizen leaders like distributing pamphlets, conducting trainings, organising *padyatras* and holding exhibitions in local *melas* are all examples of the effective use of open spaces to mobilise participation at the local level.

Nature of Engagement with Government

Throughout the process of participatory planning and development of Bhachau, the relations between the community, citizen leaders, CBOs, intermediary organisations and the government officials were cordial. As the earthquake had brought about massive destruction in terms of material, financial and human loss to the state of Gujarat and specifically the four towns of Bhuj, the local community as well as the government were working in unison to handle the situation. The instant announcement of the rehabilitation package by the GoG, the spontaneous reaction of intermediary organisations in addressing post disaster psychosocial issues as well as the proactive participation of local citizens geared the process of planning and rehabilitation in the town.

In situations where the communities were not satisfied with the process of relief, rehabilitation and implementation of government schemes and policies, the role of the intermediary organisation (UNNATI) and citizen leaders was crucial in bridging the gap between the two. Local citizen leaders helped the authorities to identify and trace affected families to receive relief material and benefits from other government schemes as well as generated awareness among the communities regarding the same. Government officials on the other hand participated in *falia* committee meetings to discuss emerging issues. The setting up of the NSK (Citizen Support Cell) by UNNATI with the support of GSDMA and BhADA at the BhADA office was another example of mutual collaboration between the intermediary organisation and the government for the common good of citizens in the town.

Results of the Participatory Planning Process

The process of participatory planning in the development of Bhachau after the earthquake, not only led to the planned development of the town but also facilitated people's participation and engagement in the process. The community-driven approach as compared to planner driven development resulted in increased ownership of the local community and hence made the initiative more sustainable and the local community more empowered.

The intense process of mobilisation and creating awareness among the community by intermediary organisations provided citizens with a platform to articulate their concerns and put forward their ideas and views in the planning of their area. Interventions in terms of supporting communities to be better informed about the various government schemes and programmes like the setting up of the NSK with the support of

GSDMA as well as BhADA, reflect increased accountability on the part of the government towards the citizens.

Multistakeholder dialogues and the community's interface with the government and private consultants led to crucial changes in the draft plan, which had earlier overlooked the interests of certain weak and vulnerable sections of society. Citizens of the neglected areas raised their voices against the draft plan and demanded their concerns be incorporated in the final plan as well. Modifications in the plan like demarcation of a residential zone for Junavada settlements, Vadinagar being brought back to its original location, reduction in the size of the institutional area and accommodation of Rabarivas at its existing location are all examples of how enhanced civic engagement and participation by local communities in planning processes can create models of people-driven development.

Conclusion

The case study thus helps in understanding the significant impact of participatory models in the planning of cities and towns. It presents a solution for the emerging issue of imposed and discriminatory planning processes being adopted by government authorities and private consultants, which have a tendency to focus only on the middle and upper class citizenry.

The rehabilitation and planning process undertaken in the town of Bhachau is a true example of the potential role of communities in changing their course of development. It reflects that active participation and engagement of citizens can help them translate their aspirations into reality. The facilitation of external agencies like intermediary organisations, government bodies etc., in stirring the process of participation is also illustrated in the case study, which play a crucial role in capacitating citizens to exercise their citizenship rights.

References

Ford Foundation and UNNATI (2002). *Rebuilding Bhachau: An Initiative for Participatory Urban Planning*, April.

Government of Gujarat (2001a). *Gujarat Earthquake Reconstruction and Rehabilitation Policy*, Gujarat State Disaster Management Authority, Gandhinagar.

———. (2001b). *Rehabilitation and Reconstruction Package for Earthquake Victim*, February.

Rawal, V. and D. Prajapati (n.d.). "Rebuilding Bhachau: An Agenda for Urban Planning", *(http://www.peopleincentre.org/documents/bhachau_agenda.pdf)*, accessed on 28th April 2010.

Shrey, S., S. Kondoi and S. Srivastava. "Urban Planning in India", *http://home.iitk.ac.in/~skandoi/Urban%20Planning%20in%20India(2).pdf*, accessed on 28th April 2010.

Thomas. K and R. Bendapudi (n.d.). "Participatory Planning", Centre for Good Governance *http://www.sasanet.org/documents/Tools/Participatory%20Planning.pdf*, accessed on 28th April 2010.

UNDP and Ministry of Housing and Urban Poverty Alleviation (2009). *India Urban Poverty Report 2009*, New Delhi: Oxford University Press. *(http://www.corecentre.co.in/Database/Docs/DocFiles/urban_report.pdf)*, accessed on 28th April 2010.

UNNATI (2001a). *Rehabilitation Package for the Towns: Some Frequently Asked Questions*.

———. (2001b). *Participatory Town Planning in Bhachau: A Note on Public Consultation*, held in June.

———. (2001c). *Gujarat Earthquake Rehabilitation: A Report*. August.

World Bank and Asian Development Bank (2001). *Gujarat Earthquake Recovery Program: An Assessment Report*, submitted to Governments of India and Gujarat, (March).

Annexure A-7.1

Urban Planning in India includes (but is not confined to) the following:

- Town planning.
- Regulation of land use for residential and commercial purposes.
- Construction of buildings.
- Planning for economic development.
- Planning for social development.
- Construction of roads.
- Construction of bridges.
- Water supply for domestic use, industrial and commercial purposes.
- Public health care management.
- Sewerage, sanitation and solid waste management.
- Proper fire services.
- Urban forestation and maintenance.
- Protection of environment through sustainable development.
- Promotion of ecological balance and maintenance.
- Safeguarding the interests of weaker sections of society.
- Offering proper infrastructural help to the handicapped and mentally retarded.
- Population of the society
- Organised slum improvement
- Phased removal or alleviation of urban poverty
- Increased provision of basic urban facilities like public urinals, subways, footpaths, parks, gardens and playgrounds
- Increased public amenities including streetlighting, parking lots, bus-stop and public conveyances
- Continual promotion of cultural, educational and aesthetic aspects of the environment
- Increased number of burials, burial grounds, cremation grounds and electric crematoria
- Proper regulation of slaughter houses and tanneries
- Absolute prevention of/zero tolerance of cruelty to animals
- Proper maintenance of population statistics, including registration of births and deaths records.

Source: Shrey, S., S. Kondoi, S. Srivastava (n.d.). "Urban Planning in India", *http://home.iitk.ac.in/~skandoi/Urban%20Planning%20in%20India(2).pdf*, accessed on 28th April 2010.

8 Reclaiming Participatory Spaces in Health

A Study of Health Movement, São Paulo, Brazil

Lizandra Serafim and
Viviane Nebó Carlos Oliveira

Introduction

After long years of dictatorship, Brazil was democratised in 1985 which heralded the creation of participative institutions, enabling participation of citizens in policymaking, management, implementation and monitoring of social policies. The legal foundation for the establishment of new participatory institutions was provided by the 1988 Constitution. Institutions like management councils, conferences, participatory budgeting etc., were built in the interactions between social movements and governments and created spaces for the participation of citizens who had been denied these opportunities for a long time. Yet, these hard-won spaces often suffered threats from governments wary of providing such spaces and sharing power with citizens. The Health Council in São Paulo had to face resistance from the municipal government who wanted to deprive it of its powers, going as far as to derecognise it.

The health movement's struggle in São Paulo highlights the point that participatory spaces exist but are not entirely functional. This paper analyses the dynamics of the relationship between the health movement and municipal executive power during a specific period by showing the roadblocks created by the state to subvert participatory spaces and actions of the movement to protect these spaces. The underlying belief behind these actions was that only participatory spaces can ensure democratisation of the state and improve health conditions.

This paper explores the health movement and its relations with other actors and the government from the perspective of citizen leaders who played a critical role in reclaiming these spaces. The experiences and visions of these leaders are essential for comprehending the movement's reality. For the purpose, interviews were conducted with leaders of the movement, members of NGOs and members of the sanitarian movement who were responsible for strengthening the movement and dialogue with governments.

The Context

The east zone of São Paulo at the end of the 1970s was inhabited by nearly one-third of the city's population. This zone was characterised by poor sanitation, which was due to the lack of resources and non-existent public institutions. As a result, epidemics of meningitis, typhoid and a high rate of infant mortality were quite common. The public health system's facilities were maintained in distant downtown São Paulo by the Ministry of Health. As a result, health care remained largely inaccessible to the inhabitants of the east zone. The Ministry of Health's programmes focussed on urban and formal sector employees and completely neglected the urban and rural poor.

These conditions engendered the Popular Health Movement, a loose coalition of social and political groups, which included health professionals and occupational groups (sanitary doctors), intellectuals, trade unions, *Comunidades Eclesiais de Base* (basic ecclesial communities or CEBs), clubs of mothers, Societies of Neighbourhood's Friends (SABs), the workers' movement, *Pastoral da Saúde* (health pastorals or social movements related to the Catholic Church). The role of women and the mothers of Jardim Noroeste in the east zone was important as they organised meetings at their homes, in the church and also worked for community awareness.[1] The Church played a crucial role in the mobilisation process as it provided spaces for community meetings; while the sanitarians were able to provide a technical base for the demands as they worked closely with the state apparatus.

These were specific actors of the health movement in east zone of São Paulo; however, a similar set of actors was active in other parts of Brazil.

1. Bógus (1998).

This loose coalition of social and political forces in the 1980s made demands for reforming the public health system, so that adequate health facilities were available to all sections of society. Another important characteristic of the movement was its 'explicitly political character'[2] as it was fighting against the military dictatorship. The active participation of people in health issues was a strategy to provide spaces of participation to the people within the state thereby starting the process of democratisation of the nation. The movement had considerable influence in the shaping of democratic reforms in the coming period.

Legal and Institutional Framework of Health Management

After a prolonged struggle of popular movements, Brazil was declared a democracy in 1985, which paved the way for the establishment of several participative institutions in the country. 'The 1988 Brazilian Constitution formally sanctioned the decentralisation of policy making and established mechanisms for citizens to participate in the formulation, management and monitoring of social policies. It provided a legal foundation for establishing an extensive institutional framework for participation by citizens including participatory budgeting, conferences, management councils and deliberative mechanisms within regulatory bodies in the field of health, social assistance, environment and urban organisation.'[3] These participative mechanisms were adopted across Brazil as is evident from the establishment of 28,000 management councils in health, education, environment and others and practicing of the participatory budget process by 250 municipalities.[4] The management councils provided spaces for citizen participation in policymaking and monitoring of programmes. Participatory budgeting created the space for deliberation on budget issues, through which citizens could monitor government expenditure and performance and prioritise public investment in their municipalities.

The 1988 Constitution also recognised health as a right for all citizens and established the Unified Health System (SUS). SUS was based on the

---

2. Collins *et al.* (2000): 115.
3. Coelho *et al.* (2005): *174*.
4. Ibid.

principles of universality, equity, public financing, decentralisation and popular participation. SUS was established at all the three tiers of the government i.e., the Federal government, state government and municipal government. Popular participation in the health system was to be facilitated through health councils.

Brazil's decentralised health system delegates the power of health planning and the provision of health services to the municipal governments. The participation of people in planning and monitoring health services is to be facilitated through health councils. The health councils are collective bodies of members from different constituencies like citizens, health professionals, health service providers and government institutions. In the health council, 50 per cent of the people are elected directly by the people, 25 per cent are elected by health professionals and the remaining 25 per cent are nominated by health service providers and government institutions. The National Health Council has a strategic development role and controls national health care policy and implementation.[5] The Municipal Health Council assists the Municipal Health Secretariat (Executive) in planning and prioritising health programmes. It also has the power to veto the plans and accounts of the Secretariat; if it rejects the Secretariat's plan and budget, the Ministry of Health does not transfer funds to the municipal governments.[6]

Participatory budgeting is another instrument, which enables citizens to identify, discuss and prioritise public spending on the projects. Participatory budgeting derives its power from the 1988 Constitution, which defined states and municipalities as federal entities and stipulated their share of the national tax receipts. Participatory budgeting was introduced by the Mayors of municipalities to enable citizen participation in the budget making process. In the participatory budgeting process, citizens decide the budgetary allocations for different projects and elect the delegates for the area plenaries.

The demands of the citizens made through participatory budgeting are reconciled by the municipal council, which proposes the municipal budget, which is binding on city councils and can be vetoed only by the Mayor.

5. Collins *op.cit.*: 120.
6. Coelho (2007): 39.

Participatory budgeting has been adopted by nearly 250 municipalities in Brazil resulting in substantial improvement in sewer and water connections, health services and infrastructure development. Participatory budgeting assumes significance in view of the fact that nearly 18 per cent of the national budget is transferred to municipalities, so citizens can decisively influence the budget in favour of their priorities. For example, through participatory budgeting, the citizens of the east zone of São Paulo were able get a large hospital constructed in their locality. Thus, participatory budgeting was instrumental in carrying out health reforms in some municipalities of Brazil.

Another important aspect of the decentralised health system is the distribution of resources between Federal, state and municipal governments. The distribution system is guided by a basic operating rule (BOR), which regulates the transfer of resources from the Federal government to the state and municipal governments. BOR grades municipal governments into two categories: high grade municipalities and second grade municipalities, which determines the transfer of funds to the municipal governments.[7] The former is also referred to as a 'full management of the municipal system', where municipalities have greater autonomy and responsibility for health care, having control over both public and private service providers. The transfer of resources took place from the National Health Fund to the Municipal Health Fund. The latter referred to as 'full management of basic care' also received money from the National Health Fund but it did not have full control over public and private service providers who received resources directly from the National Health System.[8] Besides, getting its resources from the Federal government, municipalities raised their own local resources. Those having tax based sources of income are expected to allocate 10 per cent of the municipal budget to health. Similarly, states were also graded into 'advanced management of state system' and 'full management of state system'. For receiving resources from the Federal Health Fund, state and municipalities must get registered under BOR; otherwise, resources are directly provided to health service providers. It is important to mention here that until 1998, the requests of 2,032 *municipios* for registration in the two grades under

7. Collins *op.cit.*: 116-117.
8. Ibid.

BOR were approved by Ministry of Health. The registration under BOR enabled *municipios* to access funds from the National Health Fund.[9] The SUS thus had made available spaces for participation and the provision of funds for the health care system on an equitable basis.

With the creation of SUS, there was a great leap in the activities of the popular movement, which started more frequent dialogues with governments and government staff at the municipal level, transcending the local, neighbourhood level. The popular health movement focussed, in the beginning, on basic infrastructure and health services. Later it expanded its claim to the spaces for influencing the allocation of public resources and the choice of a model of health services. With the movement's development and organisation, the local population started comprehending their right to participate in politics through the continuous practice of citizenship.[10]

SUS, in fact, transformed the peoples' mode of interaction with the government. In the period prior to 1988, the interaction was either in meetings convened by the government or through confrontations, when marches were organised to pressure the State Secretariat of Health to improve health services. Popular councils *(Conselhos Populares)* and management councils (*Conselhos Gestores)* were spaces for the movements' interaction with the government on behalf of the people. Popular councils were elected bodies from the communities, acted as autonomous organisations within the health movement for representing demands of the people to the government. Management councils were elected bodies from the communities for monitoring the services at the decentralised health centres.

In the post-1988 period, the mode of interaction between people and the government happened more in institutional spaces like management councils, municipal councils, participatory budgets, conferences etc. However, from the point of view of popular movements, these institutional spaces still needed to be protected from the intrusive Executive and new participatory spaces had to be created. The participatory instruments of health management created by the 1988 Constitution still had to be implemented by municipal governments, which meant that municipal

9. Ibid.

10. Bógus (1998).

governments enjoyed the discretion of managing the health system. So the Popular Health Movement's struggle did not end after the approval and creation of these spaces, they still had an important role to play in making health reforms concrete and functional.

Interface with State

It makes it pertinent to examine the dynamics of the relationship between the Popular Health Movement and the executive in the city of São Paulo, which had a tremendous impact on the health reforms in Brazil. The discussion is limited to the period between 1989 to 2007 during which the elected government in São Paulo changed from the Worker's Party (PT) to the conservative parties (PSB, PSDB, DEM).[11]

The creation of the municipal council and participatory spaces happened during the mandate of Luiza Erundina (PT, 1989–1992), a historical ally of the sanitarian movement and other popular health movements. During this period, there was energy in the movement to implement the SUS and sustain dialogue with the government since the movement had positive relations with a mayor who gave importance to the participation of society in the public management of services and opened channels and tools for it to happen.

> Eundina started to implement SUS, which was only a seed. When her mandate was over, the full implementation of the programme was still very distant since it was a huge project and very difficult to put in practice. During her mandate, municipal conferences preceded by regional conferences were implemented. So, the communication, dialogue and relation with the government improved when everyone was participating. (Luiz José de Souza, UMPS member)

Besides, the allied sanitarians and members of the movements had become a part of the state as councillors, deputies and advisors and it helped in implementing SUS in São Paulo. Until today, the support and advice provided by those who shift from the movement to the state is very important for sustaining the popular movements in terms of ideas, dialogue and strategies.

---

11. Brazilian Social Democracy Party (PSDB), Brazilian Progressive Party (PPB), Democrats (DEM)

The whole picture changed during the term of the next mayors, Paulo Maluf and Celso Pitta (PPB, 1993–2000). During this period, the government questioned the legitimacy of the Municipal Health Council and its elected representatives. The government appointed a municipal council composed of its allies, thereby creating two parallel councils—one legitimately elected as per the Constitutional mandate and the other, only recognised by the municipal government.

The two mayors tried to curb the functioning of institutional spaces of participation like health councils and decentralised councils. Instead of consolidating the implementation of the SUS, they presented a model of managing the system called PAS (Plan of Health Attendance) which was contrary to the principles of SUS and was vigorously contested by the Popular Health Movement and considered a regression. According to members of the popular movement:

> During the term of Luiza Erundina (PT), the SUS had just been launched with the active participation of the Popular Health Movement supported by the government. Then, Pitta and Maluf arrived and unstructured the SUS but the movement still being highly organised protested. The health council organised a health conference on the stairs of the city hall as access to the hall was blocked by the government. It forced Pitta to recognise the recommendations of the conference and fought against the PAS (Plan of Health Attendance[12]) and against the decree of the council (created by Pitta), which was against Federal Law. (Luiz José de Souza, UMPS member)
>
> These anti-reform measures of Paulo Maluf and Celso Pitta delayed the SUS for eight years. Maluf implemented PAS (Plan of Health Attendance) blocking the whole process of pre-conferences, conferences and ignoring popular participation.[13]

---

12. PAS—Plan of Health Attendance was the health management model implemented by Paulo Maluf and Celso Pitta in São Paulo, not integrated to the Federal System (SUS), without channels for citizen participation and in which private cooperatives were subcontracted to provide health services.

13. Another mechanism of popular participation in *municipios* of Brazil are health conferences, which are convened every four years at the three levels of government. These conferences play a crucial role in the development of the decentralised health system in Brazil. The National Health Conference, for example, is attended by 4000-5000 delegates who are elected from the state and municipal health conferences. These conferences provide an important forum for deliberating health concerns and policy options.

> The SUS resources did not arrive because the municipal council could not make the budget in time. During the terms of Maluf and Pitta, the council worked hard to convene the municipal health conference but the Secretary of Health didn't turn up. When Pitta walked into the conference, everyone booed. Even though the conference came up with results and proposals to end PAS, etc. but these proposals were not accepted by the government. (Celina Maria José de Oliveira, UMPS member)

> Undeterred, Celso Pitta continued with PAS, which resulted in huge protests by people in the São Paulo City. People closed the Anhanguera highway demanding implementation of SUS. Everything was decided without the participation of people and the councils were composed without elections or participation. Dictatorship reigned. (Luiz José de Souza, UMPS member)

The fact that Paulo Maluf (1993–1996) and Celso Pitta (1997–2000) did not join the SUS and did not implement the reforms of the health system[14] contributed to the unification of many popular health movements in the city in 1997, generating the *União de Movimentos Populares de Saúde* (UMPS). The UMPS was created to 'contribute to the organisation, articulation and strengthening of the popular health movements in each region of the city in the struggle for public health and the right of citizenship.'[15]

UMPS was created through meetings, commissions, working groups, regional assemblies and executive coordination with representatives who were elected in annual meetings. The functioning of UMPS was regulated by well-defined rules, which were recognised by its members. These rules were written by coordinators of the movement and approved in assembly meetings held to elect representatives of the UMPS to the Municipal Council. They served to assure the recognition of the legitimacy of the movement's representation in the Council particularly in those moments when this legitimacy was being questioned, even by the municipal government. A leader of the Union says:

> In the process of creating UMPS, the City of São Paulo was divided into five regions and a statute was written. The UMPS is

14. Castro and Sacardo (2002).
15. Ibid.

> a popular movement, not an institutional one. They have created a legal entity to be able to receive donations, have a bank account and a cheque book...The entity, Cidadania e Saúde (Citizenship and Health), was created to serve as the movement's legal entity. There are 12 people working in the entity, a president, vice president, first secretary, second secretary, first treasurer and second treasurer, six members of the executive committee and three members of the fiscal council and three substitutes. These 12 people have to be members of the UMPS coordination committee. Every two years the coordination committee of UMPS is elected from each region, allowing re-elections without any restrictions (individuals can be re-elected as many times as they want). The rules of election to Citizenship and Health are different. Representatives to Citizenship and Health are not allowed more than two mandates. (Luiz José de Souza, UMPS member)

At the end of Pitta's mandate, the movement accomplished the government's recognition of the municipal council as a legitimate space and it got more impetus with the creation of UMPS, launching a wider articulation among the movements in different regions of the city. In the municipal elections of 2000, Marta Suplicy's (PT) campaign received strong support from UMPS leaders as she was known as an ally of the movement and popular participation.

> When Marta Suplicy began her mandate, the PAS had collapsed. She relaunched SUS in the city of São Paulo. There was already a proposal for manager councils being discussed in the municipal chamber (that Pitta and Maluf had blocked), and in February of her first year as Mayor, the Law of the manager council was approved. The implementation of manager councils in each basic health entity was a great step towards participation since the population was discussing health. (Maria do Carmo Albuquerque, Pólis' Researcher)

During Marta Suplicy's mandate (2001–2004), relations with the municipal government once again became positive. UMPS also contributed to the creation of the municipal PB and encouraged dialogue between PB and the municipal council in the health sector.

If new possibilities of dialogue with the state had been generated on the one hand, a feeling of euphoria among the popular health movements, the proximity to 'allied' governments on the other hand had brought new challenges to the UMPS's activities especially in the process of the consolidation of SUS.

> The Program Saúde da Família (Family Health Program –or PSF) was one of the main bases of the SUS. During the mandates of Maluf and Pitta, federal resources allocated to this programme did not come because the programme was never implemented. Therefore, the Federal Government created Qualis to serve as a PSF to send resources to homes and families. This has followed the SUS' guidelines of municipalising the management of health policies. The policy of municipalisation implemented by Erundina was still very new. When Marta arrived, the SUS was properly comprehended and it became clearer. (Luiz José de Souza, UMPS member)

> When members of the government were our friends, such as Eduardo Jorge who was Municipal Secretary for Health during the mandate of Marta, we found it difficult to maintain a critical position regarding him/her and his/her job. We still do. (Maria do Carmo Albuquerque, Pólis' Researcher)

Some leaders of UMPS have affirmed that this has revealed inequalities and lack of clarity in the movement's and government's proposals for the construction of a system of public health, which would really respond to the needs of the people and respect the SUS' principles.

In the following years, during the mandates of Serra/Kassab (PSDB/PFL-DEM, 2005–2008), the relationship of the movement with the government was again difficult because the movement fought against a model based on the acceleration of subcontracting of public services to private entities. The movement's leaders and studies based on the dynamics of the municipal council[16] agree that there was a process of emptying this space operated by the government, making the discussion of this issue in the municipal council even more difficult.

> The transition from Marta's mandate to Serra's was not as catastrophic as the transition of Erundina's to Maluf's but had many similarities. The main one is that Serra and Kassab say they are supporters of popular participation but it is not true.

16. Tatagiba and Teixeira (2007); Serafim (2008).

> This is proven by the confusion in the municipal council. The participatory decisions made here are not implemented. The council deliberates and the government ignores it. The government does not give any credit to popular participation. If the municipal council was disbanded, the same would happen with the manager councils in the neighbourhoods. Nowadays, they function only in name because the actual power to make decisions is very small. (Luiz José de Souza, UMPS member)

Some citizen leaders of UMPS point out that there were no consultations with the public by the municipal government in preparation of the strategic goals for health management. Most of the participatory decisions made with representatives of civil society in the municipal council were not approved and/or implemented by the government. Considering these challenges, the movement's representatives sought support at the Public Ministry, denouncing the lack of execution of the municipal council's decisions. This was a new form of action for the movement and it seems to have given some results and clearly became a tool of social control that could be used by the movement in cases when the government denies dialogue.

In 2007, in the process of the election of councillors to the Municipal Council of Health, the Municipal Secretary for Health did not approve of the election's results, questioning the legitimacy of the electoral process conducted by UMPS. As a way of defending itself, UMPS presented a public civil action in the Public Ministry (part of the judiciary power in Brazil) confirming in proceedings the suitableness of its internal regulation and the legitimacy of the electoral process. This result reinforced, to some leaders of the movement, the importance of having clear procedures and rules constructed by the movement to elect its representatives and also the possibility of using these control mechanisms and the judiciary to be able to exert social control and assure the movement's participation.

However, some citizen leaders felt that the excessive use of judicious tools weakened the chance of dialoguing with the government, aggravating the confrontation. If the channels of dialogue were closed due to unending conflict and polarisation, then not only would the existing participative spaces be affected but would also lead to the stringent imposition of control and sanctions by the municipal government. This problem was recognised by some of the citizen leaders, who said:

> The specific/partisan ideology constitutes a barrier to favourable responses and group work. This hinders relations and blocks the process of negotiation. The obstacles to acceptance and negotiation come from both sides. No one concedes anything. The political party is very important but they see us as the enemies. (Celina Maria José de Oliveira, UMPS member)

> At the municipal level, the movement was not able to learn from experiences on how to deal with the government and advance discussions. The movement is not able to understand that a government is a government, and a mandate has a specific timing, and the movement has its ideologies and wants to proceed until it gets something. The government believes the movement is a radical opposition and keeps some distance. There is no dialogue. Some leaders of the movement have already tried to negotiate with the secretariat's staff but it doesn't work, because they are not the ones who have the power to make decisions. The same happens in the municipal council. Some councillors talk to us, others don't. Some of them even wish they could dialogue but the government has cut the relationship. There is no more chance. (Celina Maria José de Oliveira, UMPS member)

Even the leaders in the movement realised that confrontation was hampering their cause, so they tried to negotiate with the municipal government but were unsuccessful.

However, the movement's interaction with the municipal government during Marta's term was much more positive. The municipal government in 2001-2004 was open to participation and negotiation but it did not mean that there were no conflicts over the implementation and management of public policies. Some of the decisions made by the municipal councils were never implemented.

> During the term of Marta, some partnerships were made with the Program Saúde da Família (Family Health Programme by social organisations which were philanthropic organisations). She opened new kinds of contracts and agreements, which were non-profit and of public interest in nature. (Luiz José de Souza, UMPS' member)

> Even though, Marta made new partnerships, opened the space of the council and the municipal government approved a number of resolutions it didn't mean they were executed. Moreover, there

> was not much transparency in the operations of the government. (Celina Maria José de Oliveira, UMPS member)

Thus, UMPS had tremendous responsibilities to fulfil, no matter which party (Left or Conservative party) was in power. Some citizen leaders felt:

> With the privatisation or sub-contracting of health services, the responsibilities of UMPS are going to increase as they need to monitor these services. The involvement of private actors has thrown up a new set of challenges and the movement should be prepared to handle it. (Celina Maria José de Oliveira, UMPS member)

> Sharing responsibilities of health with social and private organisations has impacted UMPS in a way it is not able to deal with. ... It is a new issue for the leftists in general, for the health movement and for SUS. Although the movement has grown a lot, there are still problems in finding ways of struggling to construct a public health system. (Celina Maria José de Oliveira, UMPS member)

> In addition, the movement should apply pressure for the execution of the resolutions of the health conferences at the state and Federal level. (Luiz José de Souza, UMPS member)

> Then there is the issue of non-transparency in the operations of the municipal government. Official information is only shared through newspapers. E.g. if there is going to be a bidding or contract, then it is published in newspapers. The movement cannot access documents through any other channel. Transparency simply has not improved in recent times. The transparency of government actions is always partial. The movement doesn't have access to the budget and finds it difficult to understand it. (Celina Maria José de Oliveira, UMPS member)

Some of the challenges faced by UMPS are new and it is continuously trying to adapt itself to new times. It is trying to expand the movement by involving other society actors. For example, recently, when facing problems in dialogue with the municipal government, UMPS decided to give more importance, along with the occupation of institutional spaces of interlocution, to articulation with other actors in society, especially the popular movements of other sectors such as housing. As a result, UMPS became a member of the *Central de Movimentos Populares* (Central Popular Movements or CMP) in 2008.

Although it clearly concentrates its action in institutional spaces of participation such as the councils, UMPS has started to focus on strategies of action such as campaigns and manifestations articulated with other movements to seek their goals and give more visibility to its struggle. This opening of varied articulations and actions was also a way of overcoming the problem of involving the new generation in the leadership of the movement, calling attention to the importance of the issue and the movement. UMPS, thus, had broadened the spaces of participation for demanding health rights despite facing constant resistance from the executive. UMPS's trajectory of struggle has varied from dialogues, construction of new spaces of participation for interface with the Executive to confrontation. Their relentless struggle resulted in certain tangible achievements in terms of protecting the power of health councils and better management of health services.

Role of Intermediaries

In the struggle for health rights in the city, along with UMPS, NGOs, CSOs and citizen leaders played a critical role of support in mobilising and preparing a knowledge base for the movement. Their role was similar to the role played by the sanitarians in the Popular Health Movement in the 1970s and 1980s who provided technical inputs, professional knowledge about health care and helped mobilise the movement. These intermediary organisations also collected information related to health management and disseminated it among the people.

The Polis Institute's School of Citizenship (*Escola da Cidadania*)'s survey, which interviewed representatives and leaders of UMPS pointed out that NGOs played a critical role in disseminating information, educating municipal councillors and employees of the basic health entities and the strategic planning of UMPS. In the 1980s, they were known as the centres of support, information and communitarian action. Delineating the role of NGOs in this period, Maria do Carmo Albuquerque, School of Citizenship coordinator at Polis Institute said:

> The NGOs took pictures, filmed, typed, used the mimeograph and lent their rooms for the movements' meetings. The NGOs monitored the movements, which became more and more independent from the Churches. The relation between the

> movements and the NGOs became more professional when planning, definition of goals, analysis of the scenario, etc., were realised but the work was still one of daily monitoring. The NGOs participated in the movements and helped to coordinate the meetings, mobilise participation in the neighbourhoods and communities and were, therefore very related to the movements. (Maria do Carmo Albuquerque, Pólis' Researcher)

However, the role of intermediaries changed substantially in 1990s, they also started giving technical inputs to the movement. Maria do Carmo Albuquerque, Pólis' researcher, says:

> These organisations started to play a technical role but also developed a quotidian relation with the movement, and were not restricted to only monitoring the daily routine. They were different but each one played its role...Polis started to separate the relation of friendship and quotidian monitoring as it developed a joint partnership with the movement. The movement's trust in Polis helped to qualify the movement's action since the relation was not of an institution that gave definition to the movement but one that elaborated a joint action programme. The relation got deeper and more mature: leaders built the School's activities with our team; they are getting more and more qualified, allowing the construction of a better and more collective action.

The role of intermediaries was not only restricted to advice and support with information dissemination, organisation and mobilisation but financing of the activities organised by the movement.[17] Some UMPS members believed that, 'UMPS should not be institutionalised or register itself as a legal entity, as it might affect the autonomy and mass based character of the movement.' However, 'the need to raise funds for the activities of education and organisation lead to the creation of a non-profit entity called *Cidadania e Saúde* (Citizenship and Health)' and the issues of institutionalisation of the movement continue to be debated by its coordinators.'[18]

Citizen leaders were also important intermediaries, who played a very important part in UMPS. They were torchbearers of the community who

17. Castro and Sacardo (2002).

18. Ibid.

had come forward to espouse the communities' health concerns. They were different from the big leaders of UMPS who led the movement, therefore were in the limelight. Yet, the contribution of these citizen leaders though very important at the grassroots was often invisible and went unrecognised. The story of Geralda Marfisa (see Box 8.1) may seem like the story of a single woman who struggled for the health rights of communities but in reality, is the story of hundreds of women and men in the east zone of São Paulo who mobilised and organised communities for years for access to health services.

Box 8.1

Citizen Leader Geralda Marfisa

Geralda Marfisa was born in Minas Gerais state and moved to the city of São Paulo at the age of 18 years. She took a nursing course, worked in public service for 19 years and then retired. Since 1984, Geralda is a resident of the Cidade Tiradentes neighbourhood. She worked at Heliópolis Hospital for several years doing the night shift and every morning when she returned home there were many people eagerly awaiting her arrival so that she could check their blood pressure. There was no hospital in her neighbourhood, just one emergency room (ER) that was not enough to serve the entire population.

Residents felt the need to fight for better health care in their neighbourhood. They began to meet in different houses and with help from the priests of the Catholic Church discussed what could be done to improve the health situation.

Over the years, the number of people living in the district increased considerably, so meetings moved to schools, churches and neighbourhood associations and they began to discuss health as a right to be claimed as a public policy. They had the support of social movements from other districts of São Paulo, such as Itaquera and Guaianases.

Due to an increase in the density of population, the residents of Cidade Tiradentes felt the need to fight for a hospital, since emergency rooms and health clinics were no longer enough. Their fight for the right to health was difficult and time consuming, because governments refused to invest public resources in that region. A lot of organised groups and social movements often protested in the streets with banners, posters, whistles and pots but they were never heard.

The demand for hospital construction was achieved during the Marta Suplicy government (PT, 2000-2003) through a participatory budget. The hospital was finally completed during the following government's term (Serra/Kassab, PSDB) and it was launched in August 2007.

Box 8.2

Establishing Cidade Tiradentes Municipal Hospital

Cidade Tiradentes municipal hospital was an old demand from UMPS. It became possible through the participatory budget during Marta Suplicy's tenure as Mayor (PT, 2000–2003). The hospital was launched in August 2007. Its emergency room is capable of attending to 800 patients per day in paediatrics, surgery, gynaecology, medical clinic, obstetrics and orthopaedics. There are 230 beds for hospitalisation and the hospital receives approximately 25,000 patients per month.

It is the first municipal hospital in São Paulo city to be managed by a social organisation called Casa de Saúde Santa Marcelina. The partnership between City Hall and Santa Marcelina was possible through a management contract, which includes service delivery, monitoring and evaluation, payment system, estimates end use, universality, integrity and gratuity. City Hall passes the resources to Santa Marcelina every month, which in turn is responsible for managing these resources in providing health services according to a target plan.

The management contract does not guarantee any kind of social control mechanism, i.e., the participation of civil society in monitoring the public services provided by the social organisation. This is quite contrary to the Federal law of the Unified Health System (SUS), which gives social control to a Health Manager Council. Its purposes are: 1) plan, evaluate and monitor health services delivery; 2) have access to technical, administrative, economic, financial and operational information and have access to budget execution (participation in development and accountability); and 3) discuss proposals, complaints and denunciations made by the general public.

The implementation of a Manager Council at Cidade Tiradentes hospital is a demand of civil society, mainly by the health movement in the region, since the resources managed by Santa Marcelina are public. There is an evaluation committee of the hospital composed of legislative and Executive representatives, Santa Marcelina managers, hospital technicians and users of the service but it does not work in practice. Therefore, UMPS and the municipal council are still fighting to implement a Health Manager Council at Cidade Tiradentes hospital.

Outcomes and Learning Experiences

The tangible outputs of years of struggle of UMPS, intermediaries and citizen leaders were not only the claiming and strengthening of participatory spaces in the face of stiff resistance from political executive but also the construction of a large hospital in the east zone of São Paulo, which fulfilled the long-felt demand of the communities. The residents no longer had to travel downtown for health problems, they could avail good health services in the Cidade Tiradentes municipal hospital. However, the participation of citizens (manager council, evaluation committees etc.) in managing the hospital, remains an issue.

Creation of participatory spaces by the construction of SUS was a landmark achievement by the Popular Health Movement in Brazil. In the words of Celina Maria José de Oliveira, member of UMPS:

> The construction of SUS was made possible by the Popular Health Movement and the community as a result of popular engagement. The members of the movement understood that we should includc health policies in the new Federal Constitution and that policies should be inclusive for all without discrimination (for those who can and cannot pay) and universal. The SUS came to defend the health system as a right of the citizen and a duty of the state: it should be for everyone, with no discrimination and complete, from regular vaccination shots to transplants, in an equal system, spending more on the cases when it was necessary to spend and spending less in the less needed areas. This process was based on the needs and struggles of the people and in the debates that lasted day and night to include a Chapter like that. From that moment, the movement confirmed its influence along with its users, the common population and the workers of different cultures, the intellectuals and the sanitarian movements that launched this process. If this engagement wasn't present, we would never have written the SUS Chapter which is inclusive and gives us rights. The rich and dominant society doesn't appreciate a project in which the population has more access to the health system. Economic power impedes the advancement of SUS; they invent autarchies, etc., to privilege themselves.

The creation of SUS ensured the recognition of the fundamental right of the citizens and the establishing of laws and systems for health management in Brazil. SUS was operationalised by the Organic Law of Health (LOS) in the Federal Constitution of 1988, containing guidelines that should be followed by those responsible for the management of the health services. It also includes the creation of the Municipal Council of Health of São Paulo and management councils in decentralised health units, hospitals and health coordinations in sub-municipal governments, favouring the presence of the movement in institutionalised spaces of decision-making and monitoring of health services and policies.

As could be seen from the unending contest between the UMPS and political executive in the earlier sections, the presence of participatory spaces was not enough for effectively managing the health system and guaranteeing social control over management. The urgent need was reclaiming and revitalising of participatory spaces, which was done by UMPS. It not only carried out a sustained battle for the implementation of SUS in the east zone of São Paulo but also participated in available participatory spaces. The leaders of the movement highlighted the confrontation of PAS, implemented during the mandates of Maluf and Pitta, in which the movement defended the principles of SUS. There were eight years of resistance to the Maluf and Pitta mandate, which was blocking SUS a non-participatory mandate, during which the movement was still organised, autonomous and strongly articulated in all regions of the city.

It also strengthened citizen's access to information and the comprehension of the processes of the management of health policies and services, ultimately leading to qualified participation of citizens in health management. These processes undoubtedly led to increased coverage of health services in the city. In addition, it led to the blocking of possible retrogressions in the health services and improvement in the quality of services due to the setting up of the decentralised health units' management councils for monitoring and accounting.

Another accomplishment in the fight against the retrogression of participation and social control exerted by the UMPS was the seizing of power in the municipal council by the elected councillors of civil society in 2007. The result came as a shock to the Municipal Secretariat for Health, which questioned the election's result. The exuberance of electoral victory was reflected in the words of a citizen leader:

> We have recently witnessed a historical fact when the population was able to reverse the situation of the municipal council in São Paulo. It was a great positive step. The government wanted to cancel the council, remove the participation of the community in decision making and the community fought back, defending the legitimacy of the council, affirming it was institutional and based on laws, etc. With these learning experiences of the movement, civil society moved forward. If we hadn't learned that much, the movement wouldn't be able to recover as it did and have

conditions to clearly mobilise. (Luiz José de Souza, UMPS member)

UMPS had important achievements, both tangible and intangible, to its credit. The tangible achievements have been the construction of hospitals, the effective use of participative spaces like the health council, expansion of decentralised councils in new territories in the city, the realisation of regional, municipal, state and national health conferences, negotiations with municipal governments; while the intangible achievements have been bringing people into the movement, citizen leaders acting on their own and demanding accountability, engagement with new actors like private players etc. UMPS recognises that the future is going to throw up new challenges for which it is trying to prepare by organising educational workshops and networking with other movements and organisations.

References

Bógus, Cláudia Maria (1998). *Participação Popular em Saúde*. São Paulo: AnnaBlume.

Castro, Iracema Ester do N e Gislaine A. Sacardo (2002). *Conselhos de Saúde*. São Paulo, Instituto Pólis/PUC SP. (Série Observatório dos Direitos do Cidadão: acompanhamento e análise das políticas públicas da cidade de São Paulo, No.8).

Coelho, Vera Schattan P., B. Pozzoni, M. Montoya and J. Bass (2005). *Participation and Public Policies in Brazil*.

Coelho, Vera S.P. (2007). Brazilian Health Councils : Including the Excluded, in Andrea Cornwall and Vera S.P. Coelho (eds.), *Spaces for Change: The Politics of Citizen Participation in New Democratic Arenas*. London: Zed Books. p. 39.

Collins, Charles, José Araújo and Jarbas Barbosa (2000). "Decentralising the Health Sector: Issues in Brazil", *Health Policy* 52 (2): 115, June.

Serafim, Lizandra (2008). "Controle Social nos Conselhos Municipais de Assistência Social e Saúde de São Paulo", in Relatório de pesquisa *Governança e ação coletiva: Fundamentos da responsividade. Comparações entre São Paulo, México e Delhi*. CEBRAP/IDS.

Tatagiba, Luciana e Ana Cláudia Chaves Teixeira (2007). *Saúde: Controle Social e Política Pública*. São Paulo: Instituto Pólis. (Série Observatório dos Direitos do Cidadão: acompanhamento e análise das políticas públicas da cidade de São Paulo, No.29).

9 Using Right to Information for Improving Public Distribution System and Basic Infrastructure in Delhi, India

Manish Sisodia

India's economic growth in the last decade has been quite good and the future is also expected to be bright with experts predicting that India's gross domestic product's (GDP) growth rate between 2015 and 2050 would exceed that of all the major countries of the world including China and that its total income would reach almost 80 per cent of that of the United States in 2050.[1] What is worrying is the significant percentage of people who still remain poor. The majority of Indians, i.e., 836 million, live on less than Rs. 20 per day (Arjun Sengupta Committee).[2] India is placed at 132 in the latest UN Human Development Index (HDI) and Transparency International relegates India to 85th place in the list of least corrupt countries in the world. The number of people living in slums in India has more than doubled in the past two decades and now exceeds the entire population of Britain. It is the latest illustration of how India's recent economic boom has left millions of the country's poorest people behind, raising fears that social unrest could undermine further growth.

Such conditions exist in spite of the fact that there has been a fifteen-fold increase in the Central government budget spending on anti-poverty programmes from around Rs. 7,5000 million in 1993-94 to well over Rs. 1,20,0000 million in 2008-09.[3] It clearly leads to the conclusion that inefficiency and corruption in the government welfare schemes continues

1. Panagariya (2008): xvii.
2. As cited by Aiyar (2009).
3. Ibid.

to be huge. The accountability mechanisms of the government are not effective in India. Civil society organisations have tried out various experiments like social audits and public hearings to ensure accountability of the government departments and this case study of Delhi being taken up for discussion is one such case. People in selected locations of Delhi used the legal instrument of the Right to Information (RTI) for demanding transparency and accountability of the government departments like the public distribution system (PDS), the Delhi Water Board and Engineering departments. This case study attempts to explore numerous dimensions of participation tried out by the citizens of Delhi to demand transparency and accountability from the governance system. How important was the peoples' based organisation's role in enhancing the participation of people and what were the dynamics of interface between citizens and the government are some crucial questions which would also be taken up for discussion. Before taking up these issues, a brief discussion about the background of Delhi would be quite relevant.

Context—Delhi and Its Population

Delhi: From a City of Hope to a City of Growing Population and Misgovernance

Delhi, the capital of India, is situated in northern India and stands on the west bank of the Yamuna River bound by the state of Uttar Pradesh to the east and north and by Haryana in the west and south. The city is historically important as it was the capital of the Mughal Empire. According to Mirza Ghalib, the famous poet, 'The world is the body and Delhi its soul.' Apart from its historical significance, Delhi also happens to be the political hub of India. The name 'Delhi' is said to originate either from the Persian word *dahleez* (threshold or frontier) or from the name of a Mauryan king, Raja Dhillu. Some people say the original name of the settlement was Dhillika.

Delhi is spread over an area of 1483 square kilometre, 216 metre above sea level and has a population of approximately 14 million. Along with the satellite towns of Faridabad, Ghaziabad, Gurgaon and Noida it is known as the National Capital Region. Delhi is the fifth most populated urban area in the world.

More than five million of its total population lives in slum colonies that are chronically overcrowded and lack even the most basic amenities.[4] Over the last 60 years, millions of people have migrated to Delhi in search of work and a better life. In 1947, there were two million people living in Delhi. Now there are more than seven times that number living in the city. Rapid and chaotic urbanisation places enormous strain on the city's infrastructure.

The Poor of Delhi

The slums of Delhi can be found next to railway lines, under bridges, on swampy ground or next to five-star hotels. They have one thing in common—the people who settle there never own the land. Slum dwellers live in the constant fear of eviction from their homes as the authorities can decide to reclaim the land at any time, with little or no notice.

As per the *Economic Survey of Delhi* (2007-08)[5], there are eight types of colonies in Delhi.

- *jhuggi-jhopri* clusters (JJ clusters),
- slum designated areas,
- unauthorised colonies,
- resettlement colonies,
- rural villages,
- regularised unauthorised colonies,
- urban villages, and
- planned colonies.

The first two categories account for the bulk of the slum population. Legally notified slums are those, which have been designated as slums under the Slum Areas (Improvement and Clearance) Act (1956). JJ clusters are illegal occupants or squatters on public or private land. Resettlement colonies, as the name suggests, comprise of JJ cluster households that have been resettled in new colonies. The total population in resettlement

4. *Economic Survey of Delhi* (2008-09). p.169, *http://www.delhi.gov.in/wps/wcm/connect/DoIT_Planning/planning/economic+survey+of+dehli/content+2008-09/poverty.*

5. Ibid.

colonies is estimated to be 20 lakh (2001).[6] The first resettlement programme was carried out in 1961 and subsequently many JJ clusters have been shifted to resettlement colonies. Many slums also fall under 'unauthorised' colonies and 'regularised unauthorised' colonies, though the exact proportion is not known. Urban villages are another category where due to the lack of basic amenities and rapid population growth the living conditions are like those in slums.

Schemes for Slums and Resettlement Colonies

A number of government schemes do exist that seek to provide better living conditions for the people living in slums. For instance, as per the *Economic Survey of Delhi*[7], the government made provisions for the following schemes in JJ clusters:

- Food security through public distribution system.
- Infrastructure development.
- Sanitation.
- Water supply.
- Electricity.
- Development of parks.
- Other welfare schemes, e.g., old age/widow pension.
- Social security schemes for widows and girls.
- Urban basic services.
- Dispensaries and health centres.
- Free health services for poor people in hospitals.
- Integrated Child Development Scheme.
- Education.

However, the success in achieving the desired objectives of the different schemes initiated by the government has been limited because of corruption and the lack of a holistic approach towards welfare.

---

6. Ibid: 171.
7. *Economic Survey of Delhi* (2008-09). *http://www.delhi.gov.in/wps/wcm/connect/DoIT_Planning/planning/economic+survey+of+dehli/content+2008-09/poverty.*

Legal Framework

Despite having a plethora of schemes with huge amounts of allocated funds, people are highly dissatisfied as these are marked by inefficiency and corruption. The Government of India's public grievance machinery is dysfunctional, as it is not mandated by law to solve the dispute within a stipulated time. In this situation, the RTI becomes a blessing in disguise, as it provides information about all the activities, expenditure details, the role and responsibilities etc., of the government departments. It helps in getting information about where things have gone wrong in the government departments. The exposure of such details sometimes improves service delivery or leads to an improvement in the delivery mechanisms of the government departments. Before discussing the case studies, it would be pertinent to discuss the provisions of the RTI Act 2005.

RTI has been classified as a fundamental right in India. The Right to Freedom of Speech and Expression is also one of the fundamental rights enumerated in Article 19(1) A of India's Constitution. As early as 1976, the Supreme Court declared RTI as part of our fundamental rights. In the case of Raj Narain *vs.* State of Uttar Pradesh, it declared that the RTI is inherent in Article 19(1) of the Constitution. The Supreme Court said that the Right to Freedom of Expression is incomplete without RTI as people cannot speak or express themselves unless they have information. The court further said that the people have this right because we live in a democracy, where people have a right to know how they are being governed and how their money, collected as taxes, is being spent. Since then the RTI has been interpreted as one of the fundamental rights a citizen enjoys in India.

The Right to Information Act, 2005 (RTI Act 2005) was passed to ensure that citizens get the information they desire. It also provides systematic machinery and lays down the rules and procedures for its effective implementation. This Act is applicable to all Indian states except Jammu and Kashmir and clearly specifies that any citizen of India can seek information from the government. Barring a few exceptions, it is mandatory for the government to provide the requested information according to the Act. If the government fails to do so in the stipulated time period, a penalty can be imposed on the concerned government official according to the provisions of the Act. Various citizen groups and the media have played an important role in the enactment of the RTI Act.

The RTI Act guarantees five basic rights to the citizens, namely:

- Right to question the government.
- Right to see government documents and make notes.
- Right to take certified photocopies of government documents.
- Right to inspect government works.
- Right to take samples of material used in government works.

The Act also provides for *suo moto* disclosures of information relevant to citizens by the government from time to time. The RTI Act was implemented by the province of Delhi in October 2001 much before the RTI Act, 2005 was legislated at the national level. So the examples in the case studies are from the year 2001 onwards as massive mobilisation campaigns were launched to promote its use, which enabled people to use the Act. There is not much difference between the two acts except for the appeal procedures and fee structures.

Methodology of the Study

The case study intends to test the assumption that legal instruments like RTI help in promoting transparency and accountability in governance. For this purpose, the people's experiences of using RTI in the public distribution system (PDS) and infrastructure projects like sewage lines, roads have been selected as a large number of RTI applications were filed during 2001-2004 in Delhi on these issues. People were aggrieved about malfunctioning and corruption on these issues and they filed RTI applications to bring transparency and accountability into the relevant government departments. This case study is based on secondary literature, focussed group discussions (FGDs) with the community and interviews with the activists and the citizen leaders.

The experiences of using RTI in the PDS are being taken up first, which will be followed by a discussion on the use of RTI in infrastructure and urban services.

Using RTI in the Public Distribution System

Before discussing the use of RTI in the PDS, it is necessary to describe the functioning of PDS in Delhi as it would help us in understanding the objectives of PDS, the role of PDS shopkeepers and the Department of Food and Supplies in the delivery of food grains and why the problems afflicting the PDS need to be corrected urgently. After that, the active role played by the people based organisation, Parivartan which launched a people's campaign for transparency and accountability has been described. This campaign raised a cadre of citizen leaders who not only used RTI but were also a part of the social audit process of PDS in selected localities of Delhi. This movement for transparency and accountability led to a confrontation between government officials and PDS shopkeepers, which was ultimately resolved in the favour of people through the intervention of the Chief Minister of Delhi. This case study shows that it is quite difficult but not impossible to establish transparency and accountability in a governance system, where the system is highly corrupt and inefficient.

Public Distribution System: An overview

The government provides food (selected cereals such as rice and wheat) and other essentials (such as sugar and kerosene oil) at highly subsidised rates to the poor through the PDS. The commodities are distributed through a chain of shops called ration shops or fair price shops. The government issues licences to private parties to run these shops. The shopkeepers get a commission from the government for the service they provide.

There were 2,772 PDS outlets in Delhi at the end of March 2007. On an average, each fair price shop handles about 1,000 ration cards.[8] The government issues cards for three types of beneficiaries, above poverty line (APL), below poverty line (BPL) and Antyodaya cards.[9] There is little

---

8. *Economic Survey of Delhi* (2007-08). p.227, *http://www.delhi.gov.in/wps/wcm/connect/DoIT_Planning/planning/economic+survey+of+dehli/content+2007-08/poverty.*

9. The Task Force of Planning Commission of India had defined the poverty line (BPL) as the cost of an all-India average consumption basket at which calorie norms were met. The norms were 2,400 calories per capita per day for rural areas and 2,100 calories for urban areas. These calorie norms have been expressed in monetary terms. The Planning Commission recently released State Specific Poverty Line and their number on the basis of NSS 61st round (July 2004-June 2005). Accordingly, the poverty line for rural Delhi was estimated as Rs. 410.38 as against All-India estimates for same sector at Rs. 356.30. Like-wise in case of urban Delhi, the poverty line has worked out to Rs. 612.91 as against Rs. 538.60 at the All-India level. The total number of people below poverty line in Delhi comes to 22.93 lakh which amount to 14.7 per cent of the total population. *Economic Survey of Delhi* 2008-09, Government of Delhi, pp.238-239 *http://www.delhi.gov.in/wps/wcm/connect/DoIT_Planning/planning/economic+survey+of+dehli/content+2008-09/poverty*

subsidy on rations for APL cards. Antyodaya cards are issued to the poorest of the poor and rations are issued to them at highly subsidised rates. People living below poverty line are offered food grains at moderately subsidised rates.

The PDS in India is extremely inefficient and supplies are always being siphoned off. People face tremendous difficulties in getting food grains from the ration shops as is evident from the facts mentioned below:

- The shop does not open regularly.
- Even if it opens, the usual plea of the shopkeeper is that there is no stock.
- Even if there is stock, the ration provided is so adulterated or of such poor quality that it is unfit for human consumption.
- Ration issued to a person is less than the entitled quota for that person.
- The rates charged are much more than the official prescribed rates.

In a nutshell, a shopkeeper tries his best to prevent people from taking rations from his shop, so that he can sell the maximum amount in the black market. This is perhaps one of the most heinous types of corruption wherein the poorest of the poor are deprived of their due share of food by greedy individuals. Falsifying of the records in the PDS, also leads to further corruption. The shopkeepers siphon off food grains by making false entries in the stock registers. Fake thumb impressions or signatures of beneficiaries are used to show that the food grains are being regularly sold to the intended beneficiaries when actually they are not.

The extent of losses in the PDS is astonishing. The government spends more than Rs. 3,000 billion on food subsidies every year to procure food grains for distribution to the poor and economically weaker sections of society. Yet, as is evident from past experience, these funds are filling the coffers of the rich instead. It is often assumed that more than 95 per cent of the funds are misappropriated. There have been some noteworthy improvements in the system due to a few honest government officials and some initiatives by self-help groups but these positive changes are not enough and much more needs to be done to curb widespread corruption in the system.

Parivartan's Movement for Transparency and Accountability in the Public Distribution System in Delhi

The people based organisation, Parivartan in Delhi felt that the movement for transparency and accountability in governance should be started with the PDS in Delhi. The organisation believed that hunger is an issue, which touches the lives of the poor and deprives the most and any effort for stopping the large scale leakage in the PDS system in Delhi would be appropriate at that time. The activists of Parivartan started mobilising people in Sundarnagari Colony on the RTI. They conducted house-to-house campaigns, meetings at public places and provided handholding support in filing RTI applications. Encouraged by the campaign, people filed RTI applications in large numbers asking for information related to the PDS, scholarships for poor students, infrastructure projects etc. In most of the instances, they found that the services were delivered even before the information requested for was provided. Slowly word spread among the community that RTI was working and people started filing RTI applications in large numbers. Given below are two examples of common people from the poor and disadvantaged community who used RTI to get a regular supply of food grains from PDS shops. These instances inspired several people in the colony to use RTI.

Confrontation and Negotiation with the State

Encouraged by the results in Triveni's case (Box 9.2), Parivartan decided to access all the records related to 17 PDS shops in Sundarnagari. For this purpose, it applied for information under RTI in March 2003. Parivartan planned to conduct a social audit of the PDS system by collecting and collating all the information in the locality, so that the nature and modus operandi of corruption indulged in by the PDS shop dealers could be exposed. In the social audit process, all the records related to the PDS system would be shared with people, so that they could see for themselves how much ration had been siphoned off in their names.

Box 9.1

Wage Worker Gets Entitlements through RTI

Nannu's story is the most popular and perhaps one of the first success stories of the use of the RTI Act. Nannu is a daily wage worker who resides in Welcome Colony, an East Delhi slum. The government had issued him a BPL ration card. In accordance with the rules, he was to receive subsidised rations for e.g. rice at Rs.2 per kg. Nannu lost his ration card in March 2002 and applied for a duplicate with the department. He made many futile visits to the Department of Food and Supplies for three months. The clerks and the officials of the department refused to attend to him. Sometimes he was not even permitted to enter the department. He was asked for bribes but he did not have money to pay them.

Nannu met a few RTI activists working for Parivartan. The activists helped him in drafting a RTI application. He filed the application with the Department of Food and Supplies. Within two days an inspector from the department came to his house and informed him that his ration card was ready, which he could come and collect. When Nannu went to the department to collect his ration card, the area head not only received him well but also offered him tea and snacks before handing over his ration card. Moreover, the official also requested Nannu to take back his application since his work had been done. Nannu, who was *persona non grata* till a few days ago, had suddenly become a VIP in the eyes of the very same officers. How had this magic happened? What had he asked for in his application?

- The daily progress report of his application for a duplicate card—who was responsible for processing that request, how long had the official taken to process the request and what action had the official taken during that period?
- The names and designations of the officials who were supposed to have taken action and had not done so.
- According to the rules, a duplicate ration card should have been made in 10 days. The officials had not adhered to the time limit. Nannu's RTI application asked what action would be taken against these officials for violating all the rules and for causing mental agony to the public and by when this action would be taken.
- The RTI application had also asked when his ration card would finally be ready.

These requests for information are not easy for officials to answer. After all, what do they answer when no progress has been made? How do officials admit that they take no action for months?

Nannu's success in getting his duplicate ration card on the basis of his RTI application raised the others' hopes. His experience proved that exercising the RTI not only opens government files but also helps in the completion of pending tasks.

Box 9.2

Poor Women Gets Food Grains at Prescribed Rates

Triveni is a very poor woman who lives in Sundarnagari, a slum colony in East Delhi. She holds an Antyodaya card. Antodaya card holders are supposed to get wheat at Rs. 2 per kg and rice at Rs. 3 per kg. The ration shop owner in Triveni's area used to give her wheat at Rs. 5 per kg and rice at Rs. 10 per kg. This was almost equivalent to the market price. So, she did not collect her ration from September 2002 to February 2003. Triveni was unaware of the subsidised rates at which she should be getting grain from the ration shop.

It was through Parivartan that Triveni became awarc of the rates at which she should have been getting grain. She was shocked because she had never received grain at such cheap rates and no one had told her what her rights and entitlements were. Guided by Parivartan, she filed an application under the RTI Act. On 17 February 2003, she filed an application asking for the details of ration issued to her as per the records and also copies of cash memos (receipts for every transaction) purported to have been issued to her. The shopkeeper is supposed to take the customer's signature on the cash memo.

She received a reply on 11 March 2003. As per the reply, she had been issued 25 kg of wheat @ Rs. 2 per kg and 10 kg of rice @ Rs. 3 per kg every month for the last three months. The cash memos in her name had thumb impressions. Triveni is a literate woman and can sign her name. It was obvious the thumb impressions were not hers and the shopkeeper had been drawing rations in her name for the past few months.

Triveni was appalled by this duplicity. Now she had foolproof evidence to take the next step to ensure action was taken against the shopkeeper. However, the shopkeeper came to her house and pleaded with her not to proceed with her complaint. He promised to mend his ways. Triveni started receiving the right quantity of ration and at the right price.

This case is an eye opener about how the tool of RTI places enormous powers in the hands of the common people. It redefines relationships between the people and the government in real terms. In the ordinary course, no one would have listened to a poor person like Triveni but equipped with the information that she received under the RTI Act, she could get the ration shopkeeper to deliver as per her entitlements.

Before discussing the efforts made by Parivartan to conduct the social audit, it is necessary to explain the meaning of social audit. Social audit is emerging as the method for ensuring accountability at the grassroots level in contemporary India as other accountability mechanisms i.e., government audits have failed to yield results. It is also referred to as 'peoples' audit' as people or end-users are closely associated with the audit process. Social audit can be defined as the process by which, the details of resources, both financial and non-financial, used by public agencies for development programmes are shared with people, often through a public platform.[10] People are part of the process right from the beginning i.e., collection of government records, testimonials by the beneficiaries, till the end i.e., data collating, preparation of reports and sharing of the report. Social audit allows people to enforce transparency and accountability, providing the end-users an opportunity to scrutinise development programmes. It not only creates downward accountability but also strengthens the voice of the poor and marginalised sections of society.[11]

Social audit was initiated by some voluntary organisations like Mazdoor Kisan Shakti Sangathan (MKSS) in Rajasthan in 1996. The organisation with the help of the village people conducted a social audit of the employment guarantee programmes. The social audit results were shared with the villagers, local elected representatives and media. Sometimes, the meetings were also attended by government officials. The social audits exposed large scale corruption in these schemes in Rajasthan. The audit process played a crucial role in educating people and created pressure on the government to take corrective measures. These audits remained largely a voluntary exercise without any legal sanction. This tool's success in ensuring accountability in development programmes has built pressure on the government to provide it legal sanction. As a result, since the year 2000, many Central government programmes like the National Rural Health Mission (NRHM), Education for All, National Rural Employment Guarantee Scheme (NREGS) have inbuilt components of community monitoring, which if presented before the people for discussion can be called social audits. The social audits mandated by the law are taken up by locally elected representatives with the involvement of people.

The exercise of social audit in PDS was taken up voluntarily by Parivaratan in the year 2003. In order to collect data for the social audit, Parivataran applied for information related to PDS records from the Department of Food and Supplies. Replying to the application, the department said that the asked information could not be provided, as the

10. PRIA (2009).

11. Ibid.

records were the private property of the PDS shopkeepers. How could records maintained by shopkeepers for disbursing government supplies be private records was beyond the comprehension of the Parivartan activists. Aggrieved by the attitude of the government department, Parivartan filed an appeal before the Public Grievance Commission (PGC). On 6 June 2003, the PGC ordered that the records be made available to Parivartan within 15 days. However, the Department of Food and Supplies did not provide the information despite several requests by Parivartan.

Fearing similar requests for disclosure in other areas, the PDS shopkeepers got together and a large contingent of them met the PGC chairman. They made false allegations against Parivartan and tried to persuade the chairman to withdraw his earlier order. The chairman refused to do so. After a few days, the delegation of shopkeepers again approached the PGC chairman along with a member of the Delhi assembly, Veer Singh Dhingan. The chairman again refused to change his order. The shopkeepers then approached the Minister for Food, the Commissioner and several other authorities.

On 14 July, Parivartan received a letter from the Assistant Commissioner (AC), Department of Food and Supplies that the records asked for by Parivaratan had been submitted by all the PDS shopkeepers and that the relevant information had been sent to the Deputy Commissioner (DC) . The letter advised Parivartan to collect the records from the DC after making the necessary payment. However, the DC denied having received any records. This continued for the next five days. Every day, the AC would say that records had been sent to the DC and the DC would say that the records had not been received. In the meanwhile, the PDS shopkeepers moved the Delhi High Court for a stay. On 22 July, the date of hearing, the Department of Food and Supplies did not send its advocate to the court. The judge granted an *exparte* stay till the next date of hearing.

The anxiety of the PDS shopkeepers was understandable since their corrupt practices would have been exposed if the records had become public. The Department of Food and Supplies officials' eagerness to help the PDS shopkeepers is inexplicable. The PGC had ordered that the records be provided within 15 days. However, these orders were ignored. Further, the Department of Food and Supplies was in possession of the records for a full one week but the records were not provided to Parivartan. Clearly, the AC and DC were helping the PDS shopkeepers by giving them sufficient time to approach the Delhi High Court to get a stay. The collusion between the PDS shopkeepers and the government officials was apparent in the whole episode.

The people of Delhi led by Parivartan decided to force the issue. On 29 August 2003, about 400 people from different parts of Delhi met at the Gandhi Peace Foundation. They marched to the Commissioner's office at ITO. There, 109 applications seeking copies of the PDS shopkeepers' records for different areas of Delhi were filed under the RTI Act.

The Commissioner took the stand that since the Delhi High Court had granted a stay against Parivartan in another case, the records could not be provided to anyone. However, that stay was an *exparte* stay for records of certain shopkeepers only. It was not a blanket stay. Hence, the Commissioner was not bound by the earlier stay order. Within a fortnight, the applicants started receiving letters from the government intimating them about the date, time and venue when they could come and inspect the records. This was a major victory for the people of Delhi who had put up a long and patient fight to access the records of the food department.

The first inspection was to be done by a few women of Nand Nagari in the area office of the Food and Supplies Officer (FSO) on 23 September 2003. However, on the afternoon of 23 September, Panini Anand and Rajiv Kumar, Parivartan volunteers who had gone to assist these women, were abused and attacked in the premises of the Assistant Commissioner's office by a group of about 40 PDS shopkeepers led by a local leader and ration shop owner Jagatpal Singh.

The volunteers were severely beaten up and Anand was hit by a brick, while he was on his way to Nand Nagari police station to file a complaint. He nonetheless filed a FIR (No. 548/2003). Subsequently, more than 250 PDS shopkeepers surrounded the Nand Nagari police station for over four hours and prevented Parivartan volunteers from leaving the station. The police, including the SHO, remained mute spectators. It was only on the intervention of the Deputy Commissioner of Police (north east zone) that the volunteers, including four women, were evacuated in a police vehicle to safety.

For the next few days, a reign of terror was unleashed by the PDS shopkeepers all over Delhi. Almost all those people who had filed applications seeking inspection of records were approached and were offered bribes in the form of money, free food grains, etc. These were attempts to pressurise them into withdrawing their applications. Even government officers tried to convince the people to withdraw their application.

Numerous cases of coercion and monetary benefits were reported from many colonies of Delhi. Lata Sharma, who stays in Yamuna Vihar, had sought to inspect records of all the shopkeepers in her area. PDS shopkeepers offered her mother Rs. 80,000 in return for her withdrawing her application. They even threatened her. Ankur and Bhalswa Lok Shakti Manch, local community based organisations reported similar incidents from Bhalswa resettlement colony. Two women in Welcome Colony were offered sacks of grains if they withdrew their applications. Some people in a few areas yielded to the threats and pressures. However, many others stood firm and united, ready to fight against vested interests.

Overwhelmed by the spate of such attempts of coercion, Parivartan activists met the Chief Minister of Delhi in the first week of October and informed her of the threats and physical abuse of people who were asking for information from the Department of Food and Supplies. Parivartan demanded that the records of the ration dealers be made available to the public in the Commissioner's office as the people were scared of inspecting the records in field offices after the recent incidents of violence. The Chief Minister directed the Chief Secretary to take necessary steps. The incidents of violence stopped after Parivartan's meeting with the Chief Minister. In the next few days, the Commissioner was transferred.

The new Commissioner ordered that all the requested records be submitted to his office, from where they were made available to the applicants on 29 October 2003. As soon as the records were inspected, some PDS shopkeepers in Welcome Colony approached the applicants and publicly apologised before a gathering of about 40 women for all their misdemeanours. They further requested the women not to use the records obtained. The women agreed to give them another chance.

However, food grains under the PDS were still not being given to the people who had not filed RTI applications. In December 2003, a public meeting was held in which most of the people of the locality said that the women who had applied for the records were getting the food grains but others who had not were still not receiving the rations due to them. This led to a strong demand that a social audit of the records be done.

Social Audit of Public Distribution System

The process of verification of records of the PDS shopkeepers began on 15 December. Teams of Parivartan workers and local residents were formed to inspect the records related to distribution of wheat, rice and kerosene during June 2003 by four PDS shopkeepers in Welcome Colony in East Delhi. The social audit process involved verification of records like sales registers and stock registers available with the PDS shopkeepers and cross-checking it with food grains issued to the people. The team went from house-to-house informing people about the amount of food grains that had been issued to them as per the records obtained and asked people how much they had actually received and their feedback was recorded. Entries made in PDS cards issued to people were also checked. People were aghast to see the quantity of supplies that had been siphoned off in their names while the PDS shopkeepers had been telling them that the government had stopped sending supplies.

During the process of verification of records on 27 December, at around 12.30 p.m., one of the survey teams was attacked by some of the PDS shopkeepers and their supporters. The team members, including women, were physically beaten up and their records snatched and burnt in the marketplace. Immediately a complaint was lodged with the local police station. The police arrested two people, who were released on bail the next day. These attacks created a lot of furore among the local residents. Two days later, a meeting was organised which was attended by local residents, some respected senior citizens of the locality, office bearers of PDS shopkeepers of Circle 48 (administrative zone of food department) and Parivartan workers.

In that meeting, the president of the PDS shopkeepers association, Mr. Rashid, apologised for the incident and acknowledged that people have had to face a lot of difficulties in obtaining supplies. He promised that the dealers would take all possible steps to improve the situation. He also offered that he would come and resolve the grievance if anybody faced any difficulty in obtaining rations in the future. They requested Parivartan to stop the social audit and defer plans for a *jan sunwai* (people's hearing) for some time to check if the system worked correctly. Parivartan agreed to the wishes of the people and decided to suspend the social audit for a few weeks.

Surveys Expose Corruption in PDS System

Parivaratan decided to continue probing into the malfunctioning of the PDS system through surveys. It started a survey to cross-check the food grains distributed through the PDS based on the records provided by the food department. The door-to-door survey revealed that out of a total of 182 families in Welcome Colony, 142 families had not received a single grain of wheat and 167 families had not received a single grain of rice during the month of June 2003. As per the daily sales registers, out of a total of 4,650 kg of wheat and 1,820 kg of rice, which was supposed to have been distributed to the people, only 595 kg wheat and 110 kg rice respectively had actually been received by the beneficiaries. The balance wheat (87 per cent) and rice (94 per cent) had found its way to the black market.

There was enough data to prove that in the name of ensuring food security for the poor, the PDS shopkeepers were actually lining their own pockets. These details were shared with the media which covered it extensively. In 2003 and 2004, the *Indian Express* (a leading national daily) published a number of articles and stories related to corruption in the PDS system in Delhi and how the poor people has used RTI to get a regular supply of food grains under the PDS system. The media coverage built tremendous pressure on the Department of Food and Supplies to take action against those who were involved in the siphoning off of food grains meant for the poor.

The media coverage about corruption in the PDS system angered the PDS shopkeepers and the attacks on activists and people started again. Despite continued attacks, the people remained determined; in fact, each attack seemed to increase their courage rather than scaring them away. PDS cardholders in Welcome Colony announced they would not take food grains unless the government took serious action against those who were siphoning off food grains and the attacks against social workers stopped. This public outrage sent a strong message and the Chief Minister of Delhi personally instructed senior officials to be more vigilant. Almost 90 per cent of PDS cardholders did not pick up food grains in February 2004 in protest. The absence of sales threatened the existence of the government department and hurt the shopkeepers. Under pressure, PDS shopkeepers started asking for negotiations with the people. A series of public meetings took place during January and February 2004, some of which were also attended by the Ration Dealers Association. The discussions during these meetings resulted in a change in the behaviour of a number of shopkeepers.

Parivartan decided to check the results of change in attitude through another survey in March 2004. About 82 families were interviewed for the purpose. All the families said that they were getting their full entitlement of food grains at the government prescribed prices. The survey also revealed that two shopkeepers had not mended their ways and still refused to give food grains as per the prescribed quality and price. Armed with evidence against them in the form of survey findings and records obtained under the RTI Act, Parivartan filed a complaint against these two shopkeepers to the Department of Food and Supplies in the last week of March 2001. An enquiry was ordered against them by the department, after which their licences were cancelled.

After much criticism from the public and media, the Delhi government decided to take significant steps to make the PDS more transparent and accountable to the beneficiaries. Instructions were issued to the Department of Food and Supplies to make all the PDS records public. Orders were also passed that any PDS card holder could inspect his/her records on every Saturday at the District Food and Supply office. Complaints could be made directly to the senior officials in the department. The officers were directed to take immediate action on the complaints and in case the charges against the PDS shopkeepers were proved, their licence was to be suspended immediately.

The transparency and accountability drive also found support among a few government officers who favoured the implementation of the RTI Act in the PDS in Delhi. Vijay Dev, the Food and Supply Commissioner of

Delhi, initiated the self-disclosure provisions of the RTI Act in his department. This initiative also exposed discrepancies in the issue of PDS cards. Several fake PDS cards were found. For instance, 901 cards were issued in the name of a woman in Badarpur Colony, who did not exist. This reveals the modus operandi of PDS shopkeepers who registered fake names for siphoning off food grains and demonstrates the scale of corruption in PDS in Delhi, which could be checked by building transparency and accountability into the system.

The Government of Delhi tried to make the PDS transparent and accountable by passing a series of orders and instructions but poor awareness of the people, the PDS mafia and the apathetic attitude of the Food and Supply officers hampered the effective implementation of the government's orders. Many people still face opposition from officers when they request an inspection of PDS records in their areas and the records are made available only after a lot of hesitation and arguments.

On the whole, though, one can infer from the above mentioned examples that the people of Delhi have been successful in at least highlighting the malpractices in the PDS and ensuring quality of food grains at prescribed prices. A lot more is still to be done to curb corruption in the PDS. One can say for sure that the effective use of RTI has brought about a significant increase in the disbursement of food grains to the intended beneficiaries. If people are willing to come forward and demand accountability, then improvements can be seen not only in PDS but also in the government's welfare programmes.

Using RTI for Improving Infrastructure and Urban Services

The exercise of RTI through the collective efforts of citizens for the betterment of Delhi's infrastructure and urban services has been quite successful. An example of these efforts can be seen in East Delhi's Sundarnagari and Seemapuri colony in 2002, where the activists, Parivartan started the campaign for transparency and accountability. Using RTI, they obtained records of all infrastructure work done in the locality by the Engineering Department, Municipal Corporation of Delhi (MCD). Activity reports, expenditure reports and samples of materials used in the construction accessed through RTI revealed large scale corruption in the construction of the infrastructure projects in the area.

After collecting documentary proof of corruption, the activists tried to ascertain from the people whether a particular job was done in the manner described in the bid documents. Parivartan activists went to every single lane in an area, assembled people and informed them of the development that was due there and documented their testimonials about infrastructure projects like roads, sewage lines, toilets etc., People said that the projects were either incomplete or of very poor quality.

When the data was collected and testimonials by the people were collated, the scale of corruption became clearer. As per government records, at least 185 infrastructure projects had been completed in Sundarnagari in the past two years. Local people, however, said that 68 of the said 185 works had not even been started. In other words, these 68 works were only on paper. The total budget for these 68 works was approximately Rs. 1.3 crore. It means that this amount had been embezzled by the government officials and contractors. If this was the scale of corruption in a small locality of Delhi, then the amount of corruption in the capital of India could well be imagined. What was more appalling was that it was happening under the noses of top political leaders and bureaucrats of India. People were enraged at this revelation. They decided that there should be a public hearing on the issue and the public servants should be held accountable for the incorrect entries and embezzlement.

Public hearing is a new term in India where all the stakeholders are called to discuss any issue that concerns the common people. In the past, meetings convened to discuss any public issue were referred to as public consultations, multistakeholder dialogues etc. The crucial distinction between public hearing and public consultations or multistakeholder dialogues is that the former is more of an accountability seeking exercise where the role of a particular actor is probed into or questioned, while the latter is more of an opinion seeking exercise or developing a common understanding on an issue. Public hearing has gained currency in the last decade in India and civil society organisations have convened it for discussing issues like working of employment guarantee schemes, educational programmes, development projects etc., at various levels namely village, block, district, state or national. Inviting the media to these meetings builds pressure on the government agencies to check malpractices or corruption in the development schemes.

Parivartan convened a public hearing on the corruption in infrastructure projects in Delhi on 14 December 2003. Several journalists, judges, common people, elected representatives, government officials and social workers were invited to discuss the issue. The public hearing was attended by nearly 2,000 people. The information obtained through the RTI Act was presented at the hearing. The difference between work to be done and the evidence collected to show the actual work done was revealed to the assembled people. The fallacious entries in the registers were made public and the corruption in the engineering department was exposed. A report of this hearing was sent to the government and Parivartan filed a public interest litigation. The court instructed the Delhi police to file FIRs against the implicated officers.

The main impact of this hearing was an increasing belief in the efficacy of RTI checking poor performance and corruption in government departments. Today, whenever there is a new road being constructed or any development work being undertaken in Delhi, people ask for relevant details, information and inspections under the Act. People also obtain information on the local councillor's activities. In one instance, it was found that the local council member had spent Rs. 60 lakh from the development funds earmarked for his area on a musical fountain in Sundarnagari. It is significant that the people of this area wanted amenities such as public toilets, drinking water and schools while the local councillor had built a musical fountain. These exposes through public hearing published widely in the media mobilised people across the city to use RTI. It helped in converting the cynics who believe that an inefficient and corrupt governance system cannot be changed and increased the momentum for transparency and accountability in the city.

Resident Welfare Associations and Citizen Collective's Actions for Transparency and Accountability

In the last two decades the actions of the Resident Welfare Associations (RWAs) in the urban landscape especially in large and medium cities has often been considered a new form of civic activism and 'new face of urban civil society in India.'[12] RWAs are the registered organisations of

---

12. Coelho and Venkat (2009): 358.

neighbourhood colonies, which have regular elections and are being increasingly recognised by the government in monitoring development programmes and managing law and order. For example, in the city of Delhi, the Government of Delhi has been sponsoring the Bhagidari Scheme (citizen-government partnership programme) since 2000. Under this scheme, nearly 1600 'citizen groups' representing some three million of Delhi's population meet government officials in government organised workshops on the issues of water, electricity and policing.[13] Though questions have been raised about the representation of the poor and deprived in this partnership RWAs have gone out of the workshop or event based mode of partnership and taken up the people's demands related to poor service delivery or non-performance of government institutions. While putting up the peoples' demands, as can be seen in Delhi, RWAs adopted a non-political route, which means that they deliberately avoided any linkages with political parties. Aided by peoples' organisations and NGOs like Parivartan and Kabir, they relied on mass mobilisations, media campaigns and individual actions like filing of RTI applications. The method of action for transparency and accountability was different in the poorer areas of Delhi as these were irregular colonies not recognised by the government. As a result, the RWAs of these colonies could not be registered and people had to rely on collectives to put forward their demands. So, the pattern of struggle of the rich areas and poor areas differed but the common medium was RTI.

In Rajendra Nagar, Model Town and Defence Colony, three prominent rich colonies of Delhi, RWAs had waged a crusade for transparency and accountability since 2004. The Rajendra Nagar Residents Welfare Association asked for information under RTI, which was related to the roads constructed by the MCD. To their surprise, they found out that the roads had been re-laid thrice in the same year. The issue obviously was the poor quality of materials being used by the government departments.

It is important to point out here that roads are one of the most important requirements of Delhi residents. Road construction and maintenance is one of those government jobs, which have immense potential for large scale corruption. When awarding a contract, it is a well

---

13. Srivastava (2009): 343.

known fact that the amount of bribes to be given to officers is pre-determined, related to the amount of the contract for constructing the road.

The RWA decided to probe deeper into the issue. The Secretary of the Rajendra Nagar Welfare Association, S.P. Gupta, enquired under RTI whether the government had ascertained the quality of the road repair prior to paying the contractor and he also asked for the quality content of materials used in building roads. It is important to point out that any citizen can ask for a sample of materials used by the government for construction work under the RTI Act. The citizen can also get the quality of the material tested by an independent agency or laboratory. Similarly, any citizen can survey any work done by the government. It is the responsibility of the concerned government department to provide the necessary documents and arrange for survey of the work being done.

He was informed that the payment had been made only after the quality of the work was found to be adequate. A photocopy of the inspection report was made available to Gupta. According to the report, prepared by Sunil Tyagi of the Quality Control Department, the ratio of cement to sand mixture to pebbles in the inspection was found to be 1:1.8:5. Thereafter, Gupta got the sample of materials used for the construction tested at the Sri Ram Laboratory. It was found that the quality of material was far below the prescribed standards. The report found that the contractor had kept the cement ratio very low. The ratio in the sample was 1:1.5:7 while the government standard was 1:2:4.

This was a clear case of fraud. The contractor had used far less cement than the prescribed standards. However, the fault did not lie with the contractors alone; the engineers of the MCD tasked with judging the construction quality were also clearly involved. Thus, the Rajendra Nagar Resident's Welfare Association filed a complaint with the police against the MCD engineers in this case. However, four years after this complaint, the only response from the police was that the enquiry was still being conducted. This incident of deliberate procrastination was made public in the *Times of India*, a leading national newspaper. The published report mocked the Delhi Police for having failed to take action for such a long time. In the meantime, a new and honest officer, Dilip Kumar, was posted in the Vigilance Department of the Delhi Police. Kumar read the piece in the newspaper and immediately took action by arresting an Executive

Engineer and two Assistant Engineers of the MCD. The cases against the three accused are sub-judice and the matter is being investigated in depth to teach a lesson to corrupt officers.

Similarly, Mohit Goyal of Model Town waged a campaign to improve the deteriorating condition of roads in his area. He raised the issue with the help of Parivartan and Kabir and used the RTI Act. While Gupta is 78 years old and Secretary of a very active RWA, Goyal, a young person decided to take up the issue individually as the Model Town RWA was not very active. Goyal started his campaign on his own and obtained noteworthy success.

In April 2008, Goyal found that the conditions of the roads in his area had deteriorated despite repairs. He obtained information about the road repairs in front of his house, including a sample of the material being used. He sent the sample for testing to the Sri Ram Laboratory. The standard ratio of cement to sand mixture to pebbles was 1:2:4 whereas the Model Town sample had a ratio of 1:3.5:7. The ratio of sand mixture to pebbles *vis-à-vis* cement was very high. This was the reason the roads were damaged despite being repaired so often. The road in front of Goyal's house is 96 metres long and according to the construction records, cost Rs. 6 lakh to repair. As soon as Goyal asked for the information, the MCD repaired the said road as well as other roads in the neighbouring areas. However, Goyal filed a complaint about this fraud with the Delhi Police.

In a similar case, a software engineer, Uday Gosain, noticed that the road (Outer Ring Road in front of the Indian Institute of Delhi), which he travelled daily when going to work had been repaired in February 2003 but had developed cracks within a month. This was surprising. Aware of his RTI, he asked for a photocopy of all construction related documents as well as certified samples of the material used for construction.

For some days after the filing of the application, the officers of the Public Works Department (PWD) avoided Gosain but then fixed a time and date for him to come and collect the samples. However, prior to the said date, the street was repaired. The PWD officers informed Gosain that the same contractor had re-laid the road within the original budget. The officers then took Gosain for an inspection of the construction site and asked him to point out any flaws, indicating that the contractor would be paid in full only after the work was deemed satisfactory by Gosain.

Residents of Patparganj colony (Navkala apartments) of Delhi used their RTI for installing streetslights. Here also, there was no RWA but a collective of citizens who started the action. The public area of this colony was plunged into darkness as soon evening fell, as there were no streetlights in the area since 2001. The residents had made several complaints but no action was taken. A resident, Kailash Goduka, asked for information under the RTI Act. He wanted to know what action had been taken on the complaints. Within five days, an Assistant Engineer surveyed the area and within a week, all the streetlights were installed and working. Work that had not been undertaken for 7 years was completed within 7 days.

While people relied on RWAs and individual action for solving their problems in the richer areas of Delhi, people in poorer areas (Sundarnagari) of Delhi depended on citizen collectives for putting up their demands. These collectives were led by civic leaders and provided support by local level intermediaries.

The residents of East Delhi's Sundarnagari were forced to use dirty toilets or the road side for their daily ablutions till 2003. Sewer lines had been laid in the area as far back as 1983 by the DDA but due to coordination problems between the Delhi Development Authority (DDA) and Delhi Jal Board (DJB)[14], the sewer lines were not functional. In 1989, as per the government's orders, this work was handed over to the DJB on an 'as is where is' basis. As per the engineers of DJB, since they had not received a copy of the plan, the existing lines were useless and they were not responsible for the lines not being used.

For 20 years, the people of the colony had been requesting their local leaders and officers to get the sewer lines connected. This issue was raised in every election but leaders would make empty promises in order to garner votes and on being elected, would promptly forget all about it.

In March 2002, with the help of Parivartan, the residents of Sundarnagari asked DJB when the sewer lines would start functioning. In reply, the Board repeated the story about not receiving the plans from DDA and said that the sewer lines which had been laid would be operational by

---

14. DDA is the government department, which looks after planning in the city; while DJB manages the water and sewage of the city.

June 2003. A year later, it was found that the sewer lines had been laid in three blocks but no work had been done in the remaining eight blocks.

In March 2003, Naushe Ali, assisted by Parivartan, using the RTI Act asked the DJB for photocopies of all sewer related documents and the activities undertaken periodically. Ali was astonished to find that there was no government file on the matter while in the previous years the residents had been told that the file was moving, or was being dealt with by some officer, or had been submitted for the minister's perusal, etc. This meant that the information provided by the DJB in 2002 was wrong. It was the use of RTI that made the Sundarnagari residents aware of the reality of the situation.

The residents of the locality again asked for the status of the sewer lines through a RTI application. The officers were nervous about the application this time, as they had previously provided false information and there was great resentment among the public. The officers hastily conducted a survey and prepared an estimate. The proposed expenditure was approximately Rs. 80 lakh.

In order to keep up the pressure, citizen collectives and organisations like Parivartan initiated a signature campaign and prepared a petition to be presented to the Chief Minister. The petition was signed by 4,000 residents. The signature campaign was also used as a platform to make all residents aware of the issue and prepare them for the fight ahead. A representation of 30 residents met with the Chief Minister and apprised her of the problem and the simmering resentment among the people. The Chief Minister understood the gravity of the situation and immediately assigned the task to S.P. Marwah, the Administrative Member of the DJB. The work on the proposal was completed during the Board meeting of 31 July 2003.

The RTI has been used by many of Delhi's residents to pressurise government departments and officials to improve the conditions of roads and obtain information on construction activities of development related projects. While awareness and use of the RTI Act is increasing, there is still a long way to go before the government learns to provide welfare and development to its citizens honestly and efficiently.

The most successful and noteworthy application of RTI in Delhi has been in the implementation of development of citizen welfare programmes and highlighting instances of corruption in these programmes. There are plenty of examples where the people of Delhi, by playing the role of active citizens, have forced government departments to transform the way the government functions, setting the way for government departments to do their work properly and honestly.

Conclusions

The battle for transparency and accountability using the legal instrument, RTI was led by a people based organisation, Parivartan in selected localities of Delhi. A small number of the organisation's activists started mobilising and organising people around the issue of malpractices and corruption in the government programmes. People were encouraged to use RTI to get the records of the PDS, infrastructure projects like roads, sewage, streetlights etc. However, the pattern and method of struggle in different localities of Delhi assumed different dimensions.

In Sundarnagari and Seemapuri, poorer areas of Delhi, mobilisation by Parivartan generated a huge response. People filed RTI applications in large numbers, thereby creating panic among the PDS shopkeepers and government officials who feared that their misdemeanours would be exposed due to peoples' pressure. They reacted viciously filing false police complaints, physical attacks and threats against people and activists. However, the people were able to withstand these tactics in order to eradicate corruption and get access to better service delivery. The social audit process, public hearings and surveys not only enhanced peoples' participation but also built credible evidence against corruption in the welfare schemes of the government. These processes helped in raising a cadre of citizen leaders who 'learnt by doing'. These leaders formed the backbone of struggle in these locations of Delhi. They helped other people in filing RTI applications and were in the forefront of protests against the police and the Department of Food and Supplies.

However, the movement reached a deadlock with PDS shopkeepers, government officials and police on one side and people on the other. The battle for transparency and accountability was being increasingly caught in the web of red-tapism and court cases. People also dithered and decided to suspend the social audit process on the assurance of PDS shopkeepers that they would mend their ways. The people were perhaps tired of the long struggle and needed a respite. Being poor, they were also losing daily wages as most of them were employed in the informal sector, which does not fall under the ambit of labour laws.

Parivartan as per the peoples' wishes decided to suspend the social audit process but kept the movement alive by starting a survey of PDS and regularly updating the media on corruption in development programmes in Delhi. Parivaratan also made representations to the Chief Minister of Delhi and senior officers of the Department of Food and Supplies to intervene in the matter. Regular press briefings and coverage of the stories by the media also built pressure on the government to resolve the issue quickly. The Government of Delhi ultimately passed directions and orders to the concerned departments to take measures for transparency in all its activities. However, the mechanisms for 'downward accountability' or accountability to the people in the development programmes for the government were not established, which could perhaps be achieved by another movement in the future. This movement amply demonstrates that close interaction between institutional spaces (RTI Act) and open spaces (campaigns, protests, representations, negotiations etc.), if used strategically can deliver quick results. However, it was not a deliberate strategy of the movement's leadership to use both the spaces together; rather it happened spontaneously as the movement progressed. The movement was caught in various procedural complexities and was stalled at times but people were able to ensure significant improvements in the functioning of PDS and infrastructure projects like sewage in their localities.

In contrast to the movement of Seemapuri and Sundarnagari, the movement in the middle class and rich colonies of Delhi was more through RWAs, small citizen collectives and individual actions. RWAs have emerged as a new phenomenon in India's urban landscape and are playing a crucial role in the mobilisation of urban citizenry. It is often seen that RWAs are more a phenomenon of the rich and middle class areas in the city as poor people mostly reside in informal settlements where RWAs are difficult to form as they can not be registered. In such situations, poor people mostly rely on citizen collectives to put forward their demands, mostly through open spaces. However, it would be a broad generalisation to say that RWAs are a feature of rich areas and not poor areas alone, as different cities have different demographic compositions, master plans and legal arrangements for the registering of RWAs. For example, in the cities of Bengaluru and Chennai, several RWAs are registered in poor areas and have raised voices of citizens from time to time. In this case study, we found that RWAs were a forum for action in rich and middle class colonies. Parivaratan was also closely involved with RWAs in mobilising people for transparency and accountability in governance. Members of these RWAs filed RTI applications asking for information about roads, sewage, infrastructure and streetlights. In the place where, RWAs were not active, individuals filed RTI applications. In all these instances, RWAs and individuals were mostly using legal instruments like RTI to solve service delivery problems and expose corruption in the concerned departments. They hardly used open spaces or confronted the government on any issue. Surprisingly, there were some minor threats or physical attacks[15] even though they were challenging powerful vested interests like contractors and government officers. This brings us to the conclusion, that the processes of struggle for service delivery and transparency in governance systems are difficult and very long drawn out for the poor in Delhi.

The two case studies from Delhi located in different areas demonstrate that RTI has been successful in promoting transparency and accountability in governance systems in Delhi. However, various methods of participation for effectively using democratic spaces need to be combined innovatively and strategically with RTI to get results.

---

15. Rajendra Nagar RWA faced minor problems when they were exposing wrong doings of MCD. There was one instance where MCD officials told the illegal shop owners that, 'their shops would be closed due to RTI applications by RWA.' The shopkeepers under pressure from MCD protested before RWA.

References

Aiyar, Mani Shankar (2009). "Politics of Poverty", *India Today*, August 24.

Centre for Good Governance (2006). *A Manual for Public Authorities*, Hyderabad: Information Officers and Appellate Authorities.

Coelho, Karen and T. Venkat (2009). "The Politics of Civil Society: Neighbourhood Associationism in Chennai", *Economic and Political Weekly* XLIV (26 & 27): 358, June 27.

Government of Delhi. *Economic Survey of Delhi* 2008-09. *Website-http://www.delhi.gov.in/wps/wcm/connect/DoIT_Planning/planning/economic +survey*

———. *Economic Survey of Delhi* 2007-08. *Website-http://www.delhi.gov.in/wps/wcm/connect/DoIT_Planning/planning/economic +survey*

Panagariya, Arvind (2008). *The Emerging Giant*, as quoted in Goldman Sachs' paper, "Dreaming with BRICs (Brazil, Russia, India and China): The Path to 2050", New Delhi: Oxford University Press, p.xvii.

PRIA (2009). "Social Audit: A Resource Kit", Handout 1, Meaning of Social Audit, New Delhi: PRIA.

Srivastava, Sanjay (2009). "Urban Spaces, Disney-Divinity and Moral Middle Classes in Delhi", *Economic and Political Weekly* XLIV (26 & 27): 343, June 27.

The Right to Information Act 2005. (*The Gazette of India*, dated 21, June 2005).